Reading

WOMEN

Writing

a series edited by Shari Benstock and Celeste Schenck

Woman and Modernity: The (Life)Styles of Lou Andreas-Salomé
by Biddy Martin

The Unspeakable Mother: Forbidden Discourse in Jean Rhys and H.D.
by Deborah Kelly Kloepfer

Women and Romance: The Consolations of Gender in the English Novel
by Laurie Langbauer

Autobiographical Voices: Race, Gender, Self-Portraiture
by Françoise Lionnet

Reading Gertrude Stein: Body, Text, Gnosis
by Lisa Ruddick

WOMAN AND MODERNITY

The (Life)Styles of Lou Andreas-Salomé

Biddy Martin

Cornell University Press

First published 1991 by Cornell University Press.

International Standard Book Number 0-8014-2591-3 (cloth)
International Standard Book Number 0-8014-9907-0 (paper)
Library of Congress Catalog Card Number 90-55718

Printed in the United States of America

Librarians: Library of Congress cataloging information
appears on the last page of the book.

♾ The paper in this book meets the minimum requirements of the
American National Standard for Information Sciences—
Permanence of Paper for Printed Library Materials, ANSI Z39.48-1984.

For Gabi

Contents

Foreword

As the editors of *Reading Women Writing*, we are committed to furthering international feminist debate. To that end, we seek books that rigorously explore how differences of class, race, ethnic background, nationality, religious preference, and sexual choice inform women's writing. Books sensitive to the ways women's writings are classified, evaluated, read, and taught are central to the series. Of particular interest to us are feminist criticism of noncanonical texts (including film, popular culture, and new and as yet unnamed genres); confrontations of first-world theory with beyond-the-first-world texts; and books on colonial and postcolonial writing that generate their own theoretical positions. Dedicated primarily, although not exclusively, to the examination of literature by women, *Reading Women Writing* highlights differing, even contradictory, theoretical positions on texts read in cultural context.

Biddy Martin's *Woman and Modernity* is not simply a reading of Lou Andreas-Salomé's writing, or a biography, or even a critical biography; this book attempts to read Salomé the "writer, thinker, and lay analyst" institutionally, that is to read her life and work *in* as well as *against* its historical, political, and intellectual context. As a result, it evolves its own particular form, beyond biography, to demonstrate how a specific individual's life and work interpenetrate, and to show how that individual's negotiations with her immediate and wider culture may tell us important things about German feminism, about fin-de-siècle intellectual relationships, about the place of woman and the construction of femininity in late-nineteenth-century Germany. Salomé becomes, for Martin, a "concrete historical site and a set of texts" that emphasize the constraints and conventions within which Salomé's life and writing have been received.

By focusing on the methodological issues raised by her work on Salomé, Martin questions the pretensions to legitimacy and/or inclusiveness in conventional generic divisions such as biography, autobiography, literary criticism, and she notes the distortions that arise when the subject is a woman, especially such a woman as the near-mythic Salomé. While analyzing the mixed genres of Salomé's writing, the book itself mixes genres or moves beyond genre: Martin's portrait of Salomé is thus as much a chapter in German intellectual history and European feminism as it is a radically new interpretation of this remarkable subject. As Martin herself would have it, however, this interpretation is just one of any possible readings or versions of Salomé's life—especially given that Salomé's own life/writing was a compilation of literary styles, poses, possibilities of agency, self-presentations, lifestyles, discipleships, relationships of power, relationships of love.

The terrain Martin covers is vast: turn-of-the-century Europe; the psychoanalytic circles of Vienna; Salomé's ambiguous liaisons with men, especially those "master stylists of the feminine," Nietzsche, Rilke, Freud; Salomé's own figurations of woman, of female homosexuality, of sexual identity; the tantalizing ellipses of her relationships with women; the cult and literary historiography of Salomé's "personality"; her purposive alternation between discipleship and autonomy, and her equally fluid "negotiations among available definitions of femininity"; her extraordinary, complex oeuvre: more than a hundred essays, fifteen novels, at least four critical studies, psychoanalytic papers, memoirs; finally, the range of ways in which biographers and literary critics have written differently distorted Salomés into history.

It is Martin's goal to thaw the fixed images of Salomé as femme fatale (antifeminist biographers) or victim (feminist apologists) and to replace them with a moving image of Salomé drawn from her own works: "Woman," Salomé once wrote, "runs a zigzag path between the feminine and the human." Martin uses this notion of deliberate oscillation between positions to give us a Salomé who lives "a different passage between the old and the new, the traditional and the modern, the world of fantasy and the world of reality, dependence and independence." Her book thus aims in no way at a validation of the myth of Salomé, but rather at an exploration of her strategies, stances, positions, dilemmas, paradoxes. Salomé "excavate[s] and refigure[s]" for Martin "the discursive terms in which sexual difference was defined" in a specific place, at a specific moment.

The particular poignancy of nineteenth-century woman as Salomé embodied her, as of Martin's reading of her as she reflects upon it in the conclusion, has to do with the specific cost of a bind that allowed women intellectuals in Germany to pursue a life of the mind only at the expense of their femininity. Salaomé's constructions of femininity aim to overcome this disjunction, but for all their free play still "had to avoid masculine appearances and 'mannish behavior' and to disavow feminism as the manifestation of just such 'distortions.'" In her closing lines, Martin wonders provocatively whether "a repressed or invisible homosexuality necessarily underlay Salomé's construction of femininity and her production of herself as its purest type." But even if Martin ends with no latter-day canonization of Salomé as a knowing critic of feminism, given that the historically specific ground she occupied is far too distant from our own, she does take up the important question of Salomé our contemporary. In Salomé's strategies, *Woman and Modernity* finally implies, we may read the struggles, the positionings, and the self-censorship of contemporary academic women. For "the lure and dread of the 'masculine' woman," concludes Martin, "worked, and works now even within oppositional discourses on sexuality, to exclude positions other than man and woman and the heterosexuality that requires and reproduces them."

SHARI BENSTOCK
CELESTE SCHENCK

Acknowledgments

The College of Arts and Sciences at Cornell University provided support for this project in the form of two summer research grants. A faculty fellowship at the Society for the Humanities at Cornell in 1988–1989 gave me time and intellectual stimulation in the final stages of my work. I am grateful to Rudolph Binion, who generously made his copies of some of Salomé's unpublished letters and diaries available to me. And I owe a great deal to David Bathrick, Evelyn T. Beck, Jost Hermand, Elaine Marks, and Sander Gilman for their critical advice at an early stage of this project and for their continued support.

For their particular interest in my work on Lou Andreas-Salomé, and for their invitations to share that work, I thank Joan Scott, Andreas Huyssen, and Kathleen Woodward. William Warner provided a valuable and enjoyable exchange at a time when I felt a particular need to discuss my work with someone knowledgeable about Lou Andreas-Salomé who shared some of my theoretical concerns.

The comments of the anonymous readers for Cornell University Press helped me revise the manuscript and make this a better book, as did the excellent, painstaking work of my editor, Judith Bailey, to whom I am particularly grateful. For his help in checking the manuscript, my thanks to Jeffrey Schneider.

A number of friends and colleagues have contributed to this book. Dorothea von Mücke, who read the entire manuscript at a crucial point in the revision, gave me generous and invaluable criticism, suggestions, and encouragement. I thank David Bathrick, Nelly Furman, Isabel Hull, and Sharon Willis for offering their superb editorial advice, for sharing their ideas, for maintaining their humor as they listened and responded to my ruminations, and above all for their friendship. I am deeply grateful to Susan Savishinsky, whose valuable stylistic criticism helped me change my presentation of the material and who contributed so much in the form of support and teaching.

I owe a special debt of thanks to Gabriele Strauch for her critical responses to all my work on Salomé and for excellent editorial advice and, more important, for her support, encouragement, and friendship through all the stages of this project. For friendship and intellectual community over many years, I also thank Evelyn Beck, Nancy Bereano, Julie D'Acci, Laura Engelstein, Katie King, Elaine Marks, Tamar Mayer, Chandra Talpade Mohanty, Ellen Mortensen, Sandra Pollack, and Ba Stopha. Finally, I am especially grateful to Pat Floyd; her interest in this work and her help, encouragement, and presence saw me through the last stages of the project.

Parts of the Introduction appeared first in "Feminism, Criticism, and Foucault" and "Representing Lou Andreas-Salomé," *New German Critique* 27 (Fall 1982): 3–30, and "Zur Politik persönlichen Erinnerns: Lou Andreas-Salomé," *Vom Andern und vom selbst*, ed. Reinhold Grimm and Jost Hermand (Königstein im Taunus: Athenäum, 1982), pp. 94–104. Parts of the Introduction and "Salomé, Freud, and Narcissus" also appeared in "Woman and Modernity: The (Life)Styles of Lou Andreas-Salomé," Center for Twentieth-Century Studies, University of Wisconsin–Milwaukee, Working Paper Series 5, ed. Kathleen Woodward (Fall 1986), reprinted in *Modernity and the Text: Revisions of German Modernism*, ed. Andreas Huyssen and David Bathrick (New York: Columbia University Press, 1989), pp. 183–99.

Excerpts from Lou Andreas-Salomé, *Lebensrückblick: Grundriß einiger Lebenserinnerungen*, edited by Ernst Pfeiffer, copyright © 1968 by Insel Verlag, Frankfurt am Main, and from *Friedrich Nietzsche, Paul Rée, Lou von Salomé: Die Dokumente ihrer Begegnung*, copyright © 1970 by Insel Verlag, quoted by permission of the publisher.

BIDDY MARTIN

Ithaca, New York

WOMAN AND
MODERNITY

Lou Andreas-Salomé, 1897. Photograph by Sophia Goudstikker

Introduction

Lou Andreas-Salomé was a writer, thinker, and lay analyst who spent the greater part of her life among the cultural and intellectual elites of turn-of-the-century Europe. She has survived the exclusionary practices of conventional literary historiography on the basis of her liaisons with famous men, her appeal for, alleged inspiration of, and ultimate infidelity to such master stylists of the feminine as Nietzsche, Rilke, and Freud—in short, on the basis of what is fetishized, glamorized, and trivialized as her "lifestyle" or "personality." Salomé's contemporaries noted her avid intellectual curiosity and talent, her brilliance in conversation, her remarkable gift for drawing others out, her courageous indifference to moral convention, and her beauty. There have also been those who have diminished or denied those qualities by subordinating them to what they take to be her seductiveness, false self-representations, dilettantism, and opportunism, which some derive from her supposedly unresolved incestuous desires for her father and her ultimately pathological wish to usurp his position.

Salomé continues to fascinate, partly because of her failure, as the biographers and critics see it, to have left a clear record of her relationships and herself, to have demarcated precise boundaries among friendship, intellectual exchange, and sexual liaison. She creates difficulties for those who attempt to separate out the intellectual from the erotic, scenes of pedagogy from scenes of seduction, knowledge from its basis in what Salomé called love. She also creates difficulties for those intent on establishing the pattern of intellectual debt in her relationships with men, that is, her debt to them. Certainly Salomé drew no clear line between their work and hers. Though she expressed what sometimes seemed excessive gratitude to Freud, she avoided the language of debt and defined femininity as a freedom from anxiety over intellectual property and products.

One response to the tendency to base her fame in personality might be to suppress the fascination with what is called lifestyle and isolate her texts from biographical contingencies. But the suppression of biographical and social contingency in favor of an exclusive study of texts has not undone the traditional biographical monumentalization of modern male literary giants. Nor has it ended the marginalization of women writers and intellectuals such as Salomé. What interests me about Salomé is how she figures "woman" and herself as woman in the effort to open up the conceptual, and, for her, social possibility of intellectual exchanges that were irreducible to the false alternatives of submission to men or imitation of them. In Salomé I find a concrete historical site and a set of texts that allow for the exploration of sexual difference, intellectual debt, and self-representation from within the specific biographical and intellectual constellations in which Salomé's work was located. This book focuses on her appropriations and inflections of the terms in which sexual difference and modernity were constructed in late nineteenth-century Germany.

Salomé was born and grew up in St. Petersburg. When she arrived in Zurich in 1880 at the age of nineteen, she entered a Europe in which the so-called woman question was a discursive arena of enormous importance for aesthetic, philosophical, psychiatric, medical, legal, economic, and political debates. In Germany, where Salomé ultimately settled, the "woman question" emerged along with the "sexual question" and "the social question" partly in response to the economic, social, and cultural changes brought about by the rapid industrialization of Germany in the second half of the nineteenth century.[1] Debates over sexuality and sexual difference were

[1] For an important historical discussion of the situation of women in late nineteenth-century Germany and of the meanings of the "woman question," see Ute Frevert, *Frauen-Geschichte zwischen bürgerlicher Verbesserung und neuer Weiblichkeit* (Frankfurt am Main: Suhrkamp, 1986), or its translation, *Women in German History:*

at the heart of the development and legitimation of a range of knowl-edge and social practices in Wilhelminian Germany. Definitions of sexual difference were central to racist and imperialist national pol-itics, as well as to the various forms of opposition to official Wil-helminian culture.[2]

Salomé entered a discursive and social universe in which gender polarity was essential to what George Mosse has shown to be the increasingly enmeshed development of nationalism and bourgeois respectability.[3] The desire for sharp delineation of the sexes was not new, as Karin Hausen's influential work on gender polarization in the early nineteenth century makes clear.[4] Nevertheless, Mosse doc-uments increasing intolerance of gender ambiguity despite, or per-haps because of, the economic and social challenges to conventional sexual division. The Romantics had idealized the androgyne, but by the end of the century, according to Mosse,

> the androgyne as utopian ideal was replaced by a quite different, fright-eningly real image. The new fear of androgyny was projected onto woman, and by mid-nineteenth century the androgyne as an aggressive and almost masculine *femme fatale* had become a familiar figure in popular literature. . . .
> By the *fin de siècle* the androgyne was perceived as a monster of sexual

From *Bourgeois Emancipation to Sexual Liberation*, trans. Stuart McKinnon-Evans in association with Terry Bond and Barbara Norden (New York: Berg, 1989).

[2] Marie-Louise Janssen-Jurreit provides an important discussion of the relationship between bourgeois feminism and racist demographic politics in Germany in "Na-tionalbiologie, Sexualreform, und Geburtenrückgang—über die Zusammenhänge von Bevölkerungspolitik und Frauenbewegung um die Jahrhundertwende," in *Die Überwindung der Sprachlosigkeit: Texte aus der neuen Frauenbewegung*, ed. Gabriele Dietze (Darmstadt: Luchterhand, 1979). For an excellent discussion of the configurations of femininity and modernity in turn-of-the-century Vienna, see Nike Wagner's study of Karl Kraus, *Geist und Geschlecht: Karl Kraus und die Erotik der Wiener Moderne* (Frank-furt am Main: Suhrkamp, 1982).

[3] George L. Mosse, *Nationalism and Sexuality: Middle-Class Morality and Sexual Norms in Modern Europe* (Madison: University of Wisconsin Press, 1985).

[4] Karin Hausen, "Die Polarisierung der 'Geschlechtscharaktere'—eine Spiegelung der Dissoziation von Erwerbs- und Familienleben," in *Sozialgeschichte der Familie in der Neuzeit Europas*, ed. Werner Conze (Stuttgart: 1976), pp. 367–93; translated by Cathleen Catt as "Family and Role-Division: The Polarisation of Sexual Stereotypes in the Nineteenth Century—an Aspect of the Dissociation of Work and Family Life," in *The German Family*, ed. Richard J. Evans and W. R. Lee (London: Croom Helm, 1981), pp. 51–83.

and moral ambiguity, often identified with other "outsiders" such as masochists, sadists, homosexuals, and lesbians.[5]

Salomé was drawn to "avant-garde" intellectual and aesthetic circles for their critiques of bourgeois culture, their celebrations of "life," their spirit of renewal and transformation, and their experiments with (life)style. What would now be identified as a Nietzschean *Freigeisterei* was part of Salomé's credo before she met or read Nietzsche, evidence of her liberal upbringing and her idiosyncratic education and also of the social upheavals and the spirit of revolt and renewal in Russia during the 1860s and 1870s, as she herself would later acknowledge. The turbulent atmosphere in the Russia of her childhood, together with early religious experience, family history, and studies, helped produce her particular understanding and unquestioned pursuit of the freedom to "become herself." In the context of largely "bourgeois, antibourgeois" male cultural and intellectual circles, Salomé not only explored but often seemed to represent the power of the feminine and the possibilities of modernity. There is no question that Salomé's work draws on the fantasies of male avant-garde explorations of the repressed, as well as the discursive terms in which these explorations were conducted. The interesting and critical difference is that Salomé, in the words of Gisela Ecker, "made woman the subject, rather than the mere object, of once-repressed and now utopian wishes.'"[6] But Salomé's feminine subject was not the self-identical subject of consciousness.

Salomé figured femininity and feminine subjectivity as the fluid interaction of conflictual drives—the impulse toward self-assertion or individuation on the one hand and toward erotic submission and dissolution on the other. The coexistence in "woman" of these "doubly directional" drives grounded what Salomé called woman's self-sufficiency, or in later psychoanalytic terms, her narcissism.[7] It also exempted her from man's transgressions and negativity. The inter-

[5] Mosse, *Nationalism and Sexuality*, pp. 103–4.

[6] Gisela Ecker, " 'Die glückselige Einheitlichkeit des Weibes' und 'Woman is Perfect'—Lou Andreas Salomé und H.D. 'in der Schule bei Freud,' " paper delivered at the meeting of the Modern Language Association, New York, 1987.

[7] Salomé developed her conception of the "double directionality" of the drives most clearly in her psychoanalytic essay "Narzissmus als Doppelrichtung," *Imago* 7.4 (1921): 361–86.

penetration of contradictory drives in woman accounted for what was dangerous about femininity, the potential loss of self in the other, which would forestall the development of thought and sociality. How to negotiate conflictual drives without sacrificing the boundlessness of desire or the drive toward self-definition—that is the question posed by Salomé's constructions of sexual difference.

In Salomé's work, the figure "woman" contains masculine and feminine in a reciprocal relation within herself. She wrote explicitly against the idealist and romanticist views of woman's complementarity to man, which she took to be a fundamental misapprehension of woman's actual self-sufficiency. Moreover, her constructions worked against the assumption of woman's lack and her need for or envy of man. They also challenged the assumption that men and women had to become heterosexual in order to be whole. Salomé's "woman" was the affirmative woman, neither castrated nor castrating—beyond castration.

Salomé's construction of femininity did not challenge the ultimate fact of sexual difference or the presumption of heterosexuality head on. What Salomé did do, however, was figure woman's masculine will and strength as the mark of her completeness in herself. The double directionality of "masculinity" and "femininity" within woman only made her more woman; it differentiated her from modern man, who had renounced his own basis in what Salomé called the primal ground of life or, later, narcissism. In him Salomé located lack, envy, and need (for woman), but in what she called femininity, Salomé included all possible forms of expression and endeavor, even those that outsiders perceived as "unfeminine distortions," as long as they avoided the appearance of direct competition with men, as long as they could be interpreted as primarily about woman's self-seeking. Affirmative femininity, free of competitiveness and *ressentiment*, exposed man's lack and his need, but it also reassured him, protected him from the threat of direct challenge, and protected her from the threat of rejection or reprisal. It accounted for Salomé's ambivalent positions on feminism.

Salomé's figure "woman" resisted the renunciations required of masculinity and the consequent sacrificial choices demanded of a woman intent on participating in a male-dominated social and intellectual world, even as it challenged the containment of women in masochistic "feminine" desires. "Woman," she once wrote, "runs a zigzag path between the feminine and the human." For her, the relationship of feminine and masculine was a conflict at the heart of culture and subjectivity, not a problem to be solved once and for all. In her view, both of the strategies put forward by German bourgeois feminism were equally misguided. In the rationalists' campaign for equal rights with men, she perceived an attempt to eradicate difference, but the romantics' efforts to elevate femininity by equating it with motherhood and (hetero)sexuality were no better. In a double-edged polemic she argued that both conceptual schemes externalized women's subjectivity by locating it in imitation of man or in dependence on man or child. What is significant about women's lives, in all their seeming banality, according to Salomé, is the way they negotiate, not resolve, the double directionality at the heart of subjectivity from case to case, "Fall zu Fall."[8]

Despite its often tenuous and always slippery association with women, "woman" also operates in Salomé's work as a diagnosis of masculinity. Salomé occupied the position of analyst-observer of her male interlocutors long before her introduction to psychoanalysis. More than one of her male friends was convinced that she actually inhabited his psyche and spoke his deepest truths. Her offense, in the eyes of her detractors, was her apparent gift for understanding, even anticipating, their desires without satisfying them, for provoking their desire to possess and define her without being faithful to the desire she provoked. Her even greater offense, it would seem, was her insistent exposure of the basis of their knowledge, their disciplines, and their authority in what she called narcissism. Male artists, philosophers, and scholars such as Rilke, Nietzsche, and Freud retained access to the "unconscious roots of life," which were activated in their work by way of fantasy. Salomé was careful, however, to protect the appearance of their heterosexuality; she argued

---

[8] Salomé develops this conception of oscillation from case to case both stylistically and thematically in "Der Mensch als Weib," Neue Deutsche Rundschau 10 (1899): 225–43, reprinted in Lou Andreas-Salomé, Die Erotik: Vier Aufsätze, ed. Ernst Pfeiffer (Frankfurt am Main: Ullstein Materialien, 1985), pp. 7–44, and as "Die in sich ruhende Frau," in Zur Psychologie der Frau, ed. Gisela Brinker-Gabler (Frankfurt am Main: Fischer Taschenbuch, 1978), pp. 285–311. The strategy and thematics characterize her fiction as well.

that their access to the unconscious and their fundamental bisexuality never threatened them with effeminacy.

Salomé's memoirs construct her relationships, first with God and then with "great men"—including, most notably, her deified teacher Hendrik Gillot; her husband, F. C. Andreas; and Sigmund Freud—as struggles to demystify "god-men," to recognize the extent to which they were the objects of her idealizations and hence merely occasions for the discovery of her own desires and strengths.[9] She told the daughters' stories in her early fiction as well as her memoirs through encounters in which daughters narrowly escape the death of either consciousness or desire. She developed those encounters as sites of intra- and intersubjective struggle, of seduction and resistance. It is no surprise that her early fiction, which several commentators described as teeming with desire and youthful passion, employs the figure of incest for her expositions of the confrontation of daughter figures with fathers and pedagogues.[10]

Long before she began her study of psychoanalysis, Salomé had written of the importance of recognizing a gap between love or desire and its investment in objects. The recognition of that gap required a concept of unconscious mental life. The figure of "woman" served as the symbol of that which is no longer and not yet conscious, of the gap between love and its containment in only apparently inevitable or natural (social) object investments. "Woman," as the symbol of a narcissistic desire that could not be contained by an object, opened up the possibility of self-sufficiency, of woman's being first and foremost for herself, apart from man, child, or career.

By stressing the figurative, as opposed to literal, meanings of Salomé's "woman," I work against the tendency among feminists to reduce her work completely to the biological essentialisms and antifeminisms that dominated late nineteenth-century constructions of sexual difference. I will not argue, however, that Salomé's negotiations completely escape the problems of essential gender polarity or antifeminism. Despite her even prepsychoanalytic claims

[9] Lou Andreas-Salomé, *Lebensrückblick: Grundriß einiger Lebenserinnerungen,* ed. Ernst Pfeiffer (Frankfurt am Main: Insel, 1968).
[10] See, for example, Angela Livingstone's assessment of Salomé's early fiction in *Lou Andreas-Salomé: Her Life and Work* (Mount Kisco, N.Y.: Moyer Bell, 1984), pp. 204–8.

to the relative autonomy of psychic life from biology, her "woman" inevitably draws on prevailing constructions of biologically based distinctions between the sexes. And despite the distinction in her writing between the figurative operations of "woman" and literal women, "the feminine" often bears a prescriptive and dismissive relation to what Salomé and her compatriots considered distortions in the feminist struggles of actual women. Nevertheless, Salomé's constructions and negotiations of sexual difference open up interesting conceptual possibilities and tell us a great deal about the significance of sexuality and sexual difference in late nineteenth-century Germany.

Salomé was born on February 13, 1861, into the German-speaking colony at the heart of St. Petersburg, the daughter of a Russian general of Huguenot-German descent, whom she is said to have idolized.[11] She grew up with five brothers, with whom she reputedly had good relationships that she tried to reproduce with the men in her adult life. Indulged by her father, she left formal schooling early, and one of her biographers suggests that she may have failed out of school. She was then educated, or perhaps inspired, throughout her life by some of the most prominent male thinkers of her time. In 1878 she met and studied with the Dutch Reform preacher Hendrik Gillot, who introduced her to philosophy, literature, and religious history in an attempt to bring her out of what he considered to be the enclosed world of fantasy, out of the East and into the world of Western culture and civilization. Salomé would later reconstruct her life as a series of idealizations modeled on her idealization of, and love for, Gillot.

In 1880, after rejecting Gillot's marriage proposal, Salomé left St. Petersburg for Europe in poor health, accompanied by her mother. In Zurich she continued her study of the history and psychology of religion by auditing classes with Gottfried Kinkel, among others. In 1882 her health forced Salomé and her mother to leave Zurich for Rome, where they met the circle of post-48ers, the intellectuals and artists who gathered around the idealist Malwida von Meysenbug.

---

[11] The major outlines for this sketch are taken from Leonie Müller-Loreck's biographical sketch in her study *Die erzählende Dichtung Lou Andreas-Salomé: Ihr Zusammenhang mit der Literatur um 1900* (Stuttgart: Hans Dieter Heinz, 1976).

Through Meysenbug, Salomé met the positivist philosopher Paul Rée, who introduced her to Nietzsche. Salomé made plans to live and work with these two like-minded intellectuals in Paris, Vienna, or Munich, despite familial, religious, and moral outrage over the sexual liaisons this plan seemed to entail. Salomé spent part of the summer of 1882 with Rée's family in Stibbe and part with Nietzsche in Tautenburg. Both men proposed to her, and Nietzsche openly expressed his desire to make her his disciple and heir. The plans to live and work together fell through sometime between the summer and the fall of 1882, and Salomé then moved with Rée to Berlin, where they lived together in the midst of a prominent group of scholars for nearly four years. In 1887 Salomé married the orientalist Friedrich Carl Andreas. Although she never consummated the marriage, it lasted until his death in 1930. In Friedrichshagen, where she lived with Andreas, Salomé developed close ties with the major figures associated with Naturalism in Berlin, Gerhart Hauptmann, Bruno Wille, the Hart brothers, Max Halbe, John H. Mackay, and Richard Dehmel.

During the 1890s, Salomé wrote and published over fifty essays and reviews on the psychology of religion, philosophy, Russian art, theater, woman, and eroticism. In 1894, on the basis of her acquaintance and work with Nietzsche, she published *Friedrich Nietzsche in seinen Werken*, the first book-length study of the development of his thought. The same year, during one of her stays in Paris, Salomé met Frank Wedekind, with whom she maintained contact in spite of his legendary misunderstanding of the nature of her interest in him. She spent time in Vienna in 1895, establishing relationships with Arthur Schnitzler, Hugo von Hofmannsthal, Richard Beer-Hofmann, and Peter Altenberg. Then in Munich in the spring of 1897, Salomé met Rainer Maria Rilke; the two were intimately involved for several years and remained friends until the end of his life, in 1926. Salomé moved in 1903 to Göttingen, where Andreas had received a professorship. During the next three years she traveled extensively and published two novels and several important essays. In the summer of 1911 she met Sigmund Freud at the International Psychoanalytic Congress in Weimar, and she spent the following year studying with him in Vienna. Soon after she left Vienna, Salomé began her practice as a lay analyst. Freud referred patients to her, corresponded extensively with her about significant developments in his work, and respected her enormously as an ally and colleague. Between 1912 and 1920, Salomé published extensively in the psychoanalytic journal *Imago*. In the 1920s she continued her work as a lay analyst, began her friendship and collaboration with Anna Freud, and published a play, two novels, and her book on Rilke. And in the 1930s, she worked on her memoirs, titled *Lebensrückblick*. She died in 1937, several days before the Nazis came to confiscate and destroy her library, ostensibly because of her involvement with Jews and subversives.

These facts are, of course, no more truthful than the fact that Salomé was the daughter of Louise Salomé, with whom she traveled and who helped her maintain her precarious health, even as she struggled against becoming her mother's daughter. They are no more truthful than the fact that her memoirs, her fiction, and her theoretical essays deal centrally with "femininity," with relations between women, with ambivalent separations from "the mother." Nor do they belie that she was as much an autodidact as a student of famous men. It was her own insatiable intellectual curiosity that brought her to study with Gillot, and she continued to educate herself all her life.

Salomé characterized her childhood, during which she was surrounded by father and brothers, as a regressive containment in her own fantasy world. During her adolescent years in St. Petersburg, dominated as they appear to have been by her experience of Gillot, Salomé nevertheless kept a photograph of a notorious Russian woman terrorist in her drawer. Russian feminism, the push for women's education, and women's participation in radical politics in St. Petersburg did not leave her untouched. She compared her move to Zurich at the age of nineteen to the choice made by many young Russian women to study there in preparation for revolutionary work with the Russian peasantry.

Salomé idolized Malwida von Meysenbug and identified with her accounts of her struggles as a woman and idealist. She was particularly close to Frieda von Bülow and Helene Klingenberg, whose names appear frequently in her diaries and memoirs. Indeed, we seldom see photographs of Rilke and Salomé together in or around Munich without Frieda von Bülow. During her stays in Munich, which present-day commentators so strongly associate with Rilke,

Salomé was a frequent presence in the Hof Atelier Elvira, the photography atelier designed by August Endell, a gathering place for gay men and lesbians. Salomé's diaries for 1897 document frequent evenings with "Puck," the self-declared lesbian photographer Sophia Goudstikker, who took what became the most famous photograph of Salomé.[12]

Salomé knew and addressed herself in her writing to the important feminists of her time, among them her friend Ellen Key, a leading Swedish feminist, and the German feminists Helene Stöcker, Hedwig Dohm, Helene Lange, and Anita Augspurg, through whom Salomé met Puck. Her theories of femininity and eroticism were widely discussed among German feminists, and many of the reviews she published in literary journals dealt with women's writings now lost to us. According to her accounts, she went to Vienna during the first decade of this century to visit the sister of Friedrich Pinneles, who is assumed to have been her lover during that period. When in Vienna, she never failed to see Marie von Ebner-Eschenbach, whose work she admired tremendously. Her repeated stays in Berlin included visits to Käthe Kollwitz as well as to prominent male figures and analysts. Her companion, Ellen Delp, traveled with her often and stayed with her in Vienna in 1912. And her relationship with Freud never involved the kind of contact that she had with Freud's daughter Anna. In addition, Salomé developed close connections with a number of younger women who sought her counsel after reading her books.

In relation to figures such as Nietzsche, Rilke, and Freud, Salomé has been variously construed as murderous seductress, phallic mother, narcissistic parasite, and total disciple or, more positively, as muse, inspiration, support, and interpreter. What is striking, of course, is the structural similarity of those positions, always the guarantee of "his" identity, "his" significance, and the critic's "truths." But Salomé poses a challenge to the terms in which great thinkers are monumentalized. Her significance to Nietzsche, Rilke, or Freud is undeniable, but it is not easily contained by conventional

[12] For information on this relationship, I am indebted to Ursula Welsch and Michaela Wiesner's biography *Lou Andreas-Salomé: Vom "Lebensurgrund" zur Psychoanalyse* (Munich: Internationale Psychoanalyse, 1988). Goudstikker's photograph faces page 1 of this book.

stereotypes of the adoring daughter, the domesticated wife, or the femme fatale. She has thus provoked convoluted arguments on the part of her critics, who continue to mythologize her power even as they set out to undermine her significance in the lives of those men whose reputations depend on the erasure of their all-too-human desires and failings.

"Patriarchy," according to Jane Gallop, "is grounded in the up-rightness of the father. If he were devious and unreliable, he could not have the power to legislate. The law is supposed to be just— that is, impartial, indifferent, free from desire. . . . The father's law is a counterphobic mechanism."[13] The scholars and protectors of great men have taken it upon themselves to veil the fathers' desires, given the actual fathers' apparent lapses. What disturbs them about Salomé is not only the extent of her apparent self-sufficiency and autonomy but also her desire for exchange, for a position other than that of the daughter before the law. Jane Gallop shows the signifi-cance of that desire in her discussions of the renegade once-Lacanian analyst Luce Irigaray, who

> impertinently asks a few questions, as if the student, the women, the reader were not merely a lack waiting to be filled with Freud's knowledge, but a real interlocutor, a second viewpoint. And in her questions a certain desire comes through, not a desire for a "simple answer," but for an encounter, a hetero-sexual dialogue. Not in the customary way we think heterosexual—the dream of symmetry, two opposite sexes comple-menting each other. In that dream, the woman/student/reader ends up functioning as mirror, giving back a coherent, framed representation to the appropriately masculine subject. There is no real sexuality of the *heteros*. "Will there ever be any relation between the sexes?"—asks Irigaray.[14]

In biographical accounts and in her own self-accounts, Salomé's connections to other women are relegated to the margins and emerge

---

[13] Jane Gallop, *The Daughter's Seduction* (Ithaca: Cornell University Press, 1980), pp. 75–76.
[14] Ibid., p. 66.

in fragments from the recesses of memories.[15] In a very real sense, the forgetting of these relations constitutes the contours of those accounts of her which have survived, constitutes the condition for her entry into literary and cultural history in any form. Literature, art, and theory have been institutionalized and canonized on the heterosexual, oedipal-familial model of legacy and debt. The structure of Salomé's own representations of self inevitably marginalizes her relations to women as well. I am not interested in offering a counterbiography that would locate the "real" Salomé in a maternal lineage, a tradition and a world of women. To replace a story of intellectual debt through the fathers with a narrative of debt to the mothers would simply repeat conventional gender divisions and absolute conceptions of identity and difference. The two biographical stories I have offered differ in content but not in structure, and to privilege one or the other would reduce the challenge the figure of Salomé poses.

Michel Foucault's *History of Sexuality* offers a productive approach to late nineteenth-century studies of sexuality and sexual difference.[16] It is not really a history of sexuality in the conventional sense but a history of the discourses on sexuality and the various ways in which those discourses, and the pleasures and powers they have produced, have been deployed in the service of hierarchical relations in Western culture over the past three hundred years. His work challenges the traditional notion of sex as an instinctual drive or force, intrinsically liberating for the individual when expressed. Foucault works against the "repressive hypothesis"—the argument that the past two to three hundred years have been characterized by sexual repression. Western culture, far from having repressed sexuality, has actually produced it, multiplied it, spread it out as a particularly privileged means of "policing" society through normalization rather than prohibition. Foucault shows that rigid definitions of sexual difference and heterosexuality are the effects of a

---

[15] Welsch and Wiesner provide the most focused and thorough discussion of Salomé's relations with women in *Lou Andreas-Salomé*.

[16] Michel Foucault, *The History of Sexuality* (New York: Pantheon, 1979), vol. 1.

diffuse regulatory economy, what he calls the "apparatus of sexuality." As Judith Butler notes,

> Foucault suggests that the category of sex, prior to any categorization of sexual difference, is itself constructed through a historically specific mode of *sexuality*. The tactical production of the discrete and binary categorization of sex conceals the strategic aims of that very apparatus of production by postulating "sex" as a "cause" of sexual experience, behavior, and desire. Foucault's genealogical inquiry exposes this ostensible "cause" as "an effect," the production of a given regime of sexuality that seeks to regulate sexual experience by instating the discrete categories of sex as foundational and causal functions within any discursive account of sexuality.[17]

Foucault's work has been essential in the historiography of homosexuality, and several of his claims have made their way into discussions of the politics of coming out. First, Foucault maintains that the idea of homosexual identity, the "homosexual" as a particular type of personality, came to a head in the late nineteenth century, as part, Jeffrey Minson notes, of "the efforts in the human sciences to regulate and control by way of the construction of definite categories of personality."[18] At the same time that "deviance" and "perversion" were located and confined in marginal types and communities, sexual pathologies of all kinds were discovered to be potential in "the normal family," justifying the intervention of pedagogical, medical, psychiatric, and social-welfare experts. At stake in late nineteenth-century Europe was the health of the "family" and its role in securing the health of the "race." Foucault locates the deployment of sexuality at the center of a racist eugenics.[19]

In contrast, then, to conventional assumptions that the Victorian age was characterized exclusively by the repression of sexuality, Foucault argues that sexualities and discourse on sexuality proliferated in the late nineteenth century in Europe. Moreover, he asserts that the deployment of sexuality as an apparatus of normalization

---

[17] Judith Butler, *Gender Trouble: Feminism and the Subversion of Identity* (New York: Routledge and Kegan Paul, 1990), p. 23.

[18] Jeffrey Minson, "The Assertion of Homosexuality," *m/f* 5 (1981):22.

[19] See especially the final section of Foucault's *History of Sexuality*, vol. 1.

and control involved the inducement to speak the truth of one's sexuality, to locate the truth of one's self in a buried sexual essence, and to confuse autobiographical gestures with liberation. The "repressive hypothesis" itself served to mask the actual workings of power, which established sexual difference and heterosexuality as "natural."

Foucault and others see the emergence of "sexual science" in the second half of the nineteenth century as strong evidence for his line of argument. This emergence is closely linked, of course, to a certain hegemony established by the relatively new field of biology. In the lengthy history of scientific interest in women's nature, "the sexual science that arose in the late nineteenth century was something more than simply another chapter," according to Cynthia Eagle Russett. "It attempted to be far more precise and empirical than anything that had gone before. In addition, it was able to draw on new developments in the life sciences as well as on the new social sciences of anthropology, psychology, and sociology. And, finally, it spoke with the imperious tone of a discipline newly claiming, and in large measure being granted, decisive authority in matters social as well as strictly scientific." As Russett suggests, biology in the late nineteenth century "was steeped in an atmosphere of evolution."[20]

In the face of an increasingly organized women's movement, much of the work done in the fields of biology and medicine was directly antifeminist, insisting not only on the fundamental difference between the sexes but on the superiority, developmentally speaking, of the male. Men such as the Italian criminologist-anthropologist Cesare Lombroso, the German sexologist Richard von Krafft-Ebing, the physician Paul Möbius, and the Darwinian Ernst Haeckel declared that woman was less evolved and, like the savage and the child, more undifferentiated, suited for her reproductive function and for maternity. Education and work outside the home would use up energy required for reproduction, and women who pursued equality in education and employment were deviant *Mannweiber*, viragoes or manly women. As one of Russett's chapter titles suggests, "Women of genius are men."

[20] Cynthia Eagle Russett, *Sexual Science* (Cambridge: Harvard University Press, 1989), pp. 3–4.

I am interested in how Salomé read and inflected these biological-sexological definitions of sexual difference in the service of what she called woman's self-sufficiency, for what it can tell us about the possibilities and limits of certain discursive and social relations. Women understood then as now that they were faced with the challenge of refusing either to be the other of male discourse or, equally important, to be integrated as the same. In this book I trace the ways in which Salomé negotiated this challenge, how her difference(s) figures most specifically in her intellectual and personal relations with those masters of the modern, Nietzsche and Freud, and those active German feminists for whom Salomé's work was both a thorn and a seduction.

To understand Salomé's positions, it is essential to recognize that the question of "woman" was central not only in Europe but in the intellectual, aesthetic, and political debates of the St. Petersburg in which she grew up. According to Barbara Alpern Engel, as educational opportunities began to open up for women in Russia and as women themselves became increasingly active in political opposition and intellectual life during the 1860s and 1870s, the "woman question became one of the burning issues of the day."[21] While Salomé was still a child, the edict that freed the Russian serfs was finally published. In the wake of "emancipation" and its unfulfilled promises, political opposition to the czar's regime mounted, and tensions between dissidents and the government grew in St. Petersburg, where an oppositional intelligentsia had begun to emerge. Engel shows that at that time, progressives who wanted to mitigate women's subordination to despotic familial and state authority fell into three rough groupings: those in favor of liberalizing the family and granting women some prerogatives in the public sphere; the nihilists, who advocated the abolition of the family and women's liberation from it; and those who emphasized social and political change over "personal stance" and tended to subordinate the woman ques-

---

[21] Barbara Alpern Engel, *Mothers and Daughters: Women of the Intelligentsia in Nineteenth-Century Russia* (Cambridge: Cambridge University Press, 1983), p. 46, hereafter cited in the text.

tion to what were conceived to be larger political questions. Moderates as well as more radical nihilists often justified the escape from traditional familial roles in terms derived from religious definitions that lauded woman for her "humility and the capacity for suffering and for self-sacrifice" (4). Thus rebellious daughters who left home in favor of self-development were portrayed as having "fulfilled an ethical vision by devoting themselves to society as a whole" (5).

As a privileged daughter within the German-speaking colony in St. Petersburg, Salomé was insulated against the political struggles that surrounded her and prevented from participation in the emerging antiauthoritarian intelligentsia. Nonetheless, she was not immune to what she herself called the spirit of revolt in the city in which she grew up. For her, this spirit of renewal and the notoriety of rebellious and politically active women supported her own commitment to knowledge and to self, her own interest in intellectual and aesthetic movements.

Her views on sexual difference and sexual relations with men, which appeared idiosyncratic to the Europeans she encountered, were nevertheless often consistent with the demands and strategies of nihilist women in Russia. These women imagined and lived companionate, often unconsummated marriages as one antidote to the dangers of coming under the sway and power of men and of their own emotions by falling in love. In her discussions of literary representations of the "new people" of St. Petersburg, Engel highlights the centrality of discussions of alternative social relations between the sexes. One such depiction, Nikolai Chernyshevskii's novel *Chto de lat'* (What is to be done? tales of the new people), "proved extraordinarily influential." Chernyshevskii portrays these people "with unflagging sympathy," always calling them the new people, "never us[ing] the word *nihilist*."

The central character is Vera Pavlovna, a deeply moral young woman who escapes an unwanted marriage and her mother's persecution by marrying her brother's tutor, a young medical student by the name of Dmitrii Lopukhov. The newlyweds set themselves up in a suite, where they have separate rooms, and they exercise great care to treat each other respectfully and to avoid trespassing on each other's privacy. It is never quite clear whether or not they engage in sexual relations. . . .

Respect from her husband, a room of her own, personal happiness, and even sexual freedom are not enough for Vera Pavlovna. She requires economic independence, too. (73)

Many other new or nihilist women were committed to waiting until their thirties before getting involved in sexual relations with men, and they openly discussed the dangers of sexuality as imprisonment. Salomé's own dream of living together with a like-minded male intellectual in two rooms separated by a common living area filled with books and flowers sounds very much like Vera Pavlovna's ménage.

When Salomé left St. Petersburg for Zurich, she followed the path of Russian women who went there to study medicine. In one of the largest colonies of Russian emigrés in Europe, these women were among the most radical members. Many ran into trouble with the Swiss, Engel notes, "by being openly contemptuous of Swiss values, by smoking in public, by perpetually attending meetings, and by going about the streets unescorted" (136).

It was inevitable that they should encounter such difficulties, because having defied convention at home, Russian women students were scarcely likely to conform to convention in another and even more restrictive form elsewhere. For although it is true that Russian radicals rather indiscriminately used the word *bourgeois* to condemn values and behaviors of which they disapproved, these women nevertheless had good reason to perceive that, in some ways, Swiss bourgeois expectations of behavior, feminine behavior especially, were even more limiting than the restrictions imposed on them by authoritarian Russia. (136)

In fact, as James Albisetti has shown, the Russian students' infamous political radicalism and supposed sexual immorality were used to some advantage by Germans who opposed women's education on the grounds that it would lead to just such behavior.[22] The alarm over the Russian women's political engagement was sounded at home when the czar ordered them all to return to Russia in 1873.

Salomé had come to Zurich with her mother; she had little to do with the Russian emigré colony and nothing at all to do with political

[22] James C. Albisetti, *Schooling German Girls and Women: Secondary and Higher Education in the Nineteenth Century* (Princeton: Princeton University Press, 1988), p. 126.

radicalism. Nevertheless, she, too, was to encounter difficulties in her failure to conform to convention, and she took on some of the dimensions of the Russian woman student in the fantasy lives of at least some Germans. Elisabeth Förster-Nietzsche, for example, seems to have shared with others the notion that most of these women were Jewish. As Albisetti shows, German anxiety over political radicalism and foreign influence often coalesced in anti-Semitism.[23] Nietzsche's sister, disturbed by Salomé's unconventional choices and her association with Jewish men, went so far as to attempt to have Salomé deported. Neither completely Russian nor German and hence less bound by convention than other women of her class, Salomé entered a Europe in which the woman question and the perils and promises of modernity constituted a virtual obsession and in which the name of Salomé, that murderous seductress of old, Herod's daughter, inspired the creative imaginations and the fears of male artists and thinkers.

Salomé was a prolific writer and a significant participant in the intellectual and cultural debates of her era, who took enormous pleasure in the exchange of ideas with both women and men. She published fifteen novels and collections of short prose, as well as book-length studies of Nietzsche, Ibsen, Rilke, and Freud. She wrote and published over a hundred essays and reviews on the psychology of religion, the woman question, the erotic, and literature, as well as several psychoanalytic essays. She kept extensive diaries and journals that attest to the seriousness with which she took her intellectual work, its importance to her sense of well-being, and her constant preoccupation with contemporary epistemological questions. Though she was well known at the turn of the century and for the first decade thereafter as a psychological novelist and essayist, her literary and critical work had been all but forgotten by the time of her death, and little of her substantial corpus has been reprinted.[24]

[23] Ibid., p. 245.
[24] It comes as no surprise that her correspondence with Nietzsche, Rilke, and Freud and her *Freud Journal* were the most readily available until very recently, and the only texts in translation prior to the 1980s. Her memoirs, published in the fifties, have still not been translated into English. Her book on Nietzsche was not reprinted until 1983. Siegfried Mandel published his translation of Salomé's Ibsen study, which

Salomé's work has usually been assessed as derivative of her male mentors by critics who reproduce the nineteenth-century view that women are incapable of creating, that at best they can only imitate men in matters of the intellect. Or her work has been reduced to the impact of her personality, particularly in the earlier biographies.[25] For H. F. Peters, Salomé is a female Faust whose desire "to detect the inmost force that binds the world and guides its course,' . . . to know it, to experience it, to live it," was the key to the riddle she represented to her contemporaries. "Like the great hetaerae of old, she knew that there is far more to the art of love than the physical act. An intimate rapport has to be established between mind and spirit before the body can come into play. Only then, only after reaching the most intense spiritual affinity, can two people enter into the fullness of love."[26]

Rudolph Binion's formidably documented psycho-history takes a different tack. The secret of Salomé, we learn at the outset, was her inability to be a woman. Binion uses a rather punitive psychoanalytic model to make Salomé the object and substantiation of oedipal inevitabilities. The biography attempts to expose Salomé's accounts of her life as lies and fables and to document her failure to represent the actual significance of the men in her life. His text is deeply involved in the now one-hundred-year-old debate over Nietzsche's relationship with Salomé, and in the foreword Walter Kaufmann congratulates Binion for having proved that it was Nietzsche who rejected Salomé and Salomé who fabulated her importance to him. The truth for Binion is castration; Salomé's refusal to accept her father's no, or her own castration, led to her repeated pattern of desiring, then usurping and destroying various father figures.

In *Lou Salomé, génie de la vie*, François Guery reads Salomé as the object of male fantasmatic production, as the embodiment for the men who desired her of the culturally produced image of woman

he titled *Ibsen's Heroines*, in 1985, and his translation of Salomé's book on Nietzsche, *Nietzsche*, in 1988.

[25] See Ilonka Schmidt Mackey, *Lou Salomé: Inspiratrice et interprète de Nietzsche, Rilke, et Freud* (Paris: A. G. Nizet, 1956); H. F. Peters, *My Sister, My Spouse* (New York: Norton, 1962); Rudolph Binion, *Frau Lou: Nietzsche's Wayward Disciple* (Princeton: Princeton University Press, 1968).

[26] Peters, *My Sister*, pp. 12–13.

which characterized the period.[27] Guery suggests that Salomé was victimized by that image, that she feigned its meanings and exceeded its grasp. His work is very suggestive, but Guery, too, succumbs to the obsession with diagnosis and suggests that Salomé's detachment can be explained as a "Don Juanistic" fixation in the anal stage, which he reads, again, as partly an effect of unresolved penis envy characterized by an utter disregard for anything other than the pleasures of the process of production. Salomé and Don Juan refuse to give themselves, and that refusal accounts for their magnetism and appeal.

Salomé's work has been reduced by those who set out to show that it is typical of her period—typical of *Jugendstil* in its imagery, of post-Darwinist vitalism and biologism in its thinking, and of neo-romanticism and *Lebensphilosophie* in its stylistic excesses. Such reductions follow from an exclusive focus on content, on what the texts contain, rather than what they do. More recent biographies by women have taken the route of sobriety and "objectivity" in their efforts to separate Salomé's status as writer and thinker from her reputation as femme fatale. These biographies attempt to avoid the subordination of work to personality, usually by presenting them as an exceptional unity.[28]

Some feminist critics have joined Salomé's contemporary Hedwig Dohm in labeling Salomé an antifeminist, both because of her liaisons with notorious male misogynists and because her representations of herself and her work appear to draw on and repeat essentialist and romantic conceptions of femininity and sexuality.[29] She has been read not only as the proponent but also as the literal personification of misogynist turn-of-the-century stereotypes, the living reflection of the Lulus and Salomés, the femmes fatales who dominated the imaginations of turn-of-the-century male artists.

There is no question that Salomé worked from within the terms

---

[27] François Guery, *Lou Salomé: Génie de la vie* (Paris: Colmann-Lévy, 1978).

[28] See Angela Livingstone, *Lou Andreas-Salomé*; Cordula Koepcke, *Lou Andreas-Salomé: Ein eigenwilliger Lebensweg: Ihre Begegnung mit Nietzsche, Rilke, und Freud* (Freiburg im Breisgau: Herder, 1982); Koepcke, *Lou Andreas-Salomé: Leben, Persönlichkeit, Werk* (Frankfurt am Main: Insel, 1986); Welsch and Wiesner, *Lou Andreas-Salomé*.

[29] See *Beyond the Eternal Feminine: Critical Essays on Women and German Literature*, ed. Susan Cocalis and Kay Goodman (Stuttgart: Hans Dieter Heinz, 1982).

of what have at various points been considered to be incorrigibly antifeminist discourses. It is equally true that there is no real Salomé apart from her own fantasmatic production of herself and that of her contemporaries and subsequent biographers and critics. Until recently, virtually every biography set out either explicitly or implicitly to substantiate Salomé's autobiographical claims and performances as true or to expose them as lies. Ursula Welsch and Michaela Wiesner's *Lou Andreas-Salomé: Vom "Lebensurgrund" zur Psychoanalyse* manages to avoid both aggressive and defensive postures, and it does the greatest justice to Salomé's work and to her relationships with women. My purpose is to trace the critical potential, the effects, and the limits of Salomé's efforts to conceive and to enact positions other than oedipal ones, her efforts to imagine and to perform the oxymoron of feminine individuality, to imagine and to live a different passage between the old and the new, the traditional and the modern, the world of fantasy and the world of reality, dependence and independence, the irrational and the rational.

Salomé disavowed and studiously avoided competition or conflict with her male counterparts and any hint of envy of them. Avoiding what would be perceived as challenge was integral to her project. It was also essential to the privileged place she enjoyed among her male colleagues and associates, and it constituted implicit, if not explicit, resistance to her identification with contemporary feminism. Her particular negotiations did not fully insulate her against the charges of deviance or unnatural manliness brought against women who chose public lives and careers, but they did protect her, to some extent, from misogynist and homophobic disavowals by male colleagues who would have felt threatened by direct competition. Those compromises reinscribe heterosexuality as norm and gender polarity, though unstable and open to multiple enactments, as nonetheless inevitable, particularly in the realm of the symbolic, where intellectual debt continues to conform to the oedipal model. In focusing on her negotiations of self in the context of predominantly male intellectual and artistic circles, I am constantly reminded of the limits of their shared aesthetics of autonomy and their celebrations of style, which then banish the social all over again by disavowing positionality, political conflict, and *ressentiment*.

This study of Salomé's approach to modernity, subjectivity, and sexual difference begins with questions of self-representation and debt by exploring the terms in which Salomé represented herself in her memoirs. It then uses the stories generated about her friendships with Paul Rée and Friedrich Nietzsche, her published work on Nietzsche, and her essays on the psychology of religion to discuss her relation to questions of sexual difference and modernity. Next, it seeks through Salomé's reading of Ibsen's female figures, her work on femininity and eroticism, and her prose fiction to draw out the particular relations between fiction and femininity in her work. The final section of the book explores Salomé's relation to Freud and psychoanalysis, with particular attention to the strategies by which she established both her unity with and differences from Freud on the grounds of narcissism.

1.

Questions of Self-Representation

Salomé claimed over and over that all her writing was autobiographical but irreducible to representation. The autobiographical quality and appeal of her work arise not from self-representation per se but from the continual repetition and recasting of certain themes and questions that invite, but also frustrate, attempts to get at the "real" Lou Andreas-Salomé. Even Salomé's explicitly autobiographical writings have a strangely anonymous and universal quality. Salomé revised and rewrote not only manuscripts meant for immediate publication, but her diaries and journals as well. This constant remaking of herself in writing, which she and Nietzsche celebrated as the importance of style and the aesthetics of personality, has confounded biographers trying to get at the "the truth" behind what have come to be seen as deceptive masks or masquerades. Salomé refused to subject herself to the kinds of truth in representation required of the confessor. It would seem that she saw the relation between her life and her writing as an attempt to invent social as well as literary forms, not for the sake of transgression but in the service of (life)style.

The most explicitly autobiographical piece of her published writing, *Lebensrückblick: Grundriβ einiger Lebenserinnerungen* (Looking back: an outline of some life memories), was written in sections in the 1930s and later organized by Ernst Pfeiffer, executor of her estate. Though Rudolph Binion suggests that Salomé made some effort to have the memoirs published during her lifetime, Pfeiffer published them for the first time in 1951.[1] The memoirs are divided into two sections, whose titles might be translated "Contents" and "Supplement." "Contents" includes "The Experience of God," "The Experience of Love (Hendrik Gillot)," "Experience in the Family," "The Experience of Russia," "The Experience of Friendship (Paul Rée)," "Among People," and "With Rainer." "Supplement" includes "April, Our Month, Rainer—," "The Experience of Freud," "Remembrances of Freud (1936)," "Before and Since the World War," "F. C. Andreas," and "What's Missing from the Outline (1933)."

As the chapter titles indicate, the memoirs are concerned with what Salomé conceived to be fundamental or typical experiences (*Erlebnisse*). Experience for her referred less to occurrences and external detail than to the psychological dynamic through which outer impressions were assimilated and made significant. She and Nietzsche agreed that all great personalities were organized through typical psychological experiences. It is significant, in this context, that her most explicitly autobiographical text is conceived as memoirs, not autobiography. Salomé explores her own life by way of her experience of others, with whom she is implicitly identified and from whom she is often more explicitly differentiated. Her particular deployment of "experience" shapes the accounts in such a way that they are neither exclusively *about* them, her male others, nor *about* her. I limit my focus in this chapter to how Salomé constructs what is "typical" about her experiences of the men whose names figure so centrally, yet parenthetically, in the chapter headings. In every case, Salomé assumes the detachment of the interpreter or analyst of their psyches and her own. "Experience" thus clearly comes to mean knowledge of psychic dynamics. Her detachment and lack of moral judgment have disturbed those critics who deny her the authority to analyze the men she was supposed to have merely ad-

[1] Pfeiffer subsequently discovered a later manuscript, which he used to revise and update the memoirs, choosing it in part because it appeared to be the more recently corrected version. The fifth and all subsequent editions are based on this later manuscript, but the differences from the earlier editions are not significant. In this book I use the fifth edition of Lou Andreas-Salomé, *Lebensrückblick: Grundriß einiger Lebenserinnerungen*, ed. Ernst Pfeiffer (Frankfurt am Main: Insel, 1968), citing it parenthetically in the text. Translations are my own.

mired. Yet in a journal entry about Nietzsche's psychological complexity, which she wrote while staying with him in Tautenburg in 1882, Salomé notes that she would like to have been "inside the skin of every human being." What Nietzsche considered to be her brilliance in turning experience into speculative analysis is on full display in her memoirs.

Salomé's particular view of authorship was crucial to her conception of (her)self as site, rather than author or object, of experience and knowledge. Salomé disavowed pretenses to authority and originality: "There is a similar, unavoidable confusion bound up in all our activity when we sign our names to what was actually dictated to us and take one for the other in the most obvious way when we see what we call a creative act in any field" (36). In her *Freud Journal* of 1912, Salomé suggests that the decision to avoid the autobiographical form, with its demand for detail and coherence, was deliberate:

> So, too, we could imagine a *literary* technique (that old dream of mine) which would be true to that very unity of formation. It would concentrate its poetic creativity on just this, instead of on spatiotemporal representation. . . . Freud once remarked that it would take an artist to reconstruct a completed analysis in reverse, from the end to the beginning. The supremely individual stays back of itself, away from the typical, in which we recognize everything once more in its particular form, and so the great elemental themes that children love and legends create recur. Yes, even the fairy tale, the descendant of the legend, would become genuine and possible again, rather than mere "imitation." (translation modified)[2]

Lebensrückblick makes Salomé's life an instance of the "great elemental themes" and a site for the universal struggles of the human subject. To the extent that the "individual stays back of itself," the memoirs, like other autobiographical accounts, have an anonymous quality and operate from a textual, rather than a referential model of biography and representation. By that I mean that Salomé makes no attempt to legitimate her reflections as an exhaustive and, in that sense, accurate representation of the details of her life. She conceived of her memoirs as an attempt to unravel the intersubjective dynamics

---

[2] *The Freud Journal of Lou Andreas-Salomé*, trans. Stanley Leavy (New York: Basic Books, 1964), pp. 49–50.

at work in her relation to her world, with less attention to the facts of her life than to what she called its architectural outline. For that reason, we discover few details of her relationships and almost nothing about her alleged sexual liaisons. For Salomé, sex was never just particular.

To begin the memoirs, Pfeiffer chose a sort of Salomé credo about authorship:

Human life—yes!
Life itself—is poetry. Unconscious of it, we live it day by day
Piece by piece—In its inviolable wholeness, however, it lives, it writes us.
Far, far from that empty phrase about
Making one's life a work of art—
We are not *our* own work of art.[3]

According to Salomé, the memoirs "narrated themselves to her," presented her with the "incalculable life memories of all those human repetitions of the mortal which do not catch up with us until old age, as if they needed to be under way for a long time before they could show us what is immortal about them" (80).

Salomé's interest in religious experience was at the center of her particular model of reading and interpretation, and religious affect served as the foundation for her conception of modernity as renewal, growth, and transformation. The text moves from her account of the psychic dynamics at work in god-creations to her assessment of psychoanalysis as the analysis of precisely that dynamic. I highlight her figuration of her relation to the significant men in her life in order to illuminate the rhetorical and interpersonal strategies introduced in her account of her God, of setting herself apart, but only from within what she first establishes to be an underlying unity. In the process of such differentiation out of undifferentiation, Salomé implicitly challenges conventional boundaries even as she attends to the importance of imagining new ones. Sexual difference figures centrally, though often only implicitly, in her strategic negotiations of identification and differentiation.

[3] Pfeiffer took this credo from a passage in Salomé's *Mein Dank an Freud: Offener Brief an Professor Sigmund Freud zu seinem 75. Geburtstag* (Vienna: Internationaler Psychoanalytischer, 1931), p. 14.

Salomé begins the narrative of her fundamental experiences with her own production of God, which she understands to be part of the unconscious mental life of all human beings. The first chapter, "My Experience of God," begins with her conception of her own birth. "Our first experience," she writes, "is, strangely enough, a disappearance . . . as we were forced into being born" (9). If anything is primary or originary it is this disappearance, this coercion into *human* being. Life begins with loss and a desire for return which can never be satisfied. Because human life originates in loss, there is no origin to which we might return and no adequate substitute for "preworld unity." There is no bridge for the gap between faith and thought: "Our first experience is of something that is already part of the past and a resistance to the present; the first 'memory'—as we would call it just a little later—is also a shock, a disappointment at the loss of that which no longer is, and it has something of an after-effect in the certainty that it should have been" (9).

In her memories of God and "his" loss, Salomé concentrates on the difficult sacrifices demanded of human subjects, the need for subjectivity and sexual identity. Her reaction to the price exacted from her is the fantasmatic production of a God of infinite generosity who authorizes her wildest fantasies and her desires to live in a world of her own creation, to be and to have all. She writes of this grandfatherly God as the grandparent of her primary narcissism, located on the threshold of her entry into a sacrificial order:

One could picture it in something like the following image: as if one had moved from the parents' lap, from which we sometimes have to slide, onto the midst of the lap of God, as if onto the lap of a grandfather who spoils us much more and allows everything, who is so generous with gifts that it is as if he had all his pockets full and as if one could become almost as all-powerful as he, even if not nearly as "good"; he signifies, in fact, both parents combined into one: maternal warmth/nurturance and paternal omnipotence. (To have to separate and distinguish them from each other, into the spheres of power and love, is already a violent break in what we might call a wishless [desireless] preworld well-being). (11)

Salomé characterized her production of this grandparent as a *Zurückrutsch*, a sliding back or regression, which inhibited her "normal development out of childhood." For she remained caught up in a world of fantasy that allowed no limits on her omnipotence wishes and denied the limits and (sexual) divisions that reality imposed. She offers two anecdotes to explain how she sustained her denials by refusing to *see* a lack or an absence. In the first, having been seriously traumatized by seeing herself in the mirror, in which she appeared discrete, bounded, and cut off, she subsequently avoids all mirrors. Her second story concerns a Christmas cracker, which she imagined to contain clothing made of silk paper and trimmed in gold. When she was told that it held no such thing, she simply decided not to crack it. In general, she writes, she preferred the gifts hidden away in the grandparent's pockets, and she needed no visible evidence of them.

Her insular world of fantasy came to a sudden and painful end. Salomé explains the impact of her loss of God with the story of how she came to accept transience and death. A servant came in one day and reported to her that he had seen a couple standing in the snow outside her miniature house in the garden and had ordered them to leave. When the servant returned the next day, the child asked him whether the couple was still there. When he said no, she suggested that they must have followed his orders and left. The servant replied that they had simply become thinner and smaller until finally they no longer existed. Unable to understand or to deny this story and unable to get any help from her fantasized God, the child was shocked into disbelief and into the loss of God.

Salomé contrasts the child's disappointment to the usual disappointed expectations of childhood, which force children to revise or adjust their expectations as they find a balance between wishes and realities. Because the child Salomé had so disavowed reality, her disappointment introduced a difference between wish and reality not simply of degree but of kind. Her early religious feelings were never integrated with and, hence, never diminished or replaced by her adaptation to reality. "Perhaps [her faith] could never be repaired, covered up, or replaced by any later formulations because the god-creation that preceded the disappearance had something all too childlike about it" (23). In making this argument, Salomé anticipates questions about the effects of her childhood faith then and now. She answers that the disappearance of God and the undeniable fact of a godless universe were what remained operative for her; they left her unable to subscribe to, believe in, and be loyal to any particular intellectual system, but also with a profound sense of her shared fate with other people and with everything that is.

> Nothing intellectual ever touched that old, former faith—as if it could not have trusted the intrusion of mature thinking. As a consequence, all areas of thought, even the theological, remained on the same level for me, mere curiosities, interesting thoughts. . . . Of course, I recognized and often even admired the way that others operated when they came by way of rational avenues to a kind of substitute—a very clear, intellectualized substitute—for their religious past and found a way to combine it with their mature thinking.
>
> What attracted me most powerfully to people—dead or alive—who devoted themselves to that kind of thought material were the people themselves. No matter how they guarded against it in their philosophical expressions, it remained legible in them that in some driving sense, *God* was the first and last experience for them in everything that they experienced. (22–23)

Her inability to believe had compensations, however: "Something positive remained from the childlike quality of this loss of God: it turned me equally irrevocably toward the life of the real around me. I know for sure that for me—autobiographically speaking, and according to my best knowledge and faculties—any formation of a god-substitute which had made its way into this realm of feeling would only have diminished it" (23–24). In place of faith, she had an openness to life in all its unansweredness.

By the time Salomé wrote this passage in her memoirs, she had stressed the importance for women of a turn from the world of fantasy to the world outside them in a range of genres and texts. The memoirs emphasize Salomé's affirmation of life as it is, "as if there were nothing that needed to be justified, elevated, or devalued next to the circumstance of its presence as existence" (24). The death of God and the confrontation with the incommensurability of life and its forms, of fantasy and reality, demystified a moral and social order that had been robbed of self-evidence. It then also produced a profound reverence for the life that lived through but was not encompassed or mastered by the conscious self. The intervention of reason and external reality ultimately made faith in God impossible, but it left her with a sense of security, freed her from fear of falling out of the world. That sense of security distinguished her, in her eyes, from her male colleagues, who mourned the death of God differently, and for whom fantasy and reason, which were more unified in woman, came apart more irreparably.

Salomé argues that the religious appeal to a preordained moral order died along with God for her, and for Nietzsche too, with the important difference that for Nietzsche that death required constant murder.[4] Salomé ultimately described their difference in terms of Nietzsche's desire for a god-substitute, even in the form of the self-overcoming Übermensch within himself, and she implicitly and explicitly opposes his self-overcoming to her lack of panic over loss and the absence for her of barriers to be overcome: "At the same time, because of his disposition, his intellectual goal took on what I would call a Christian-religious character, in that he grasped it out of a painful state from which he needed to be freed, as a kind of salvation. My equivalent intellectual aims took hold of me in a complete state of happiness: it is this difference that is the most apparent between us and can be seen in all our developmental struggles."[5]

Salomé, too, saw the confrontation with "the death of God" as the challenge of her age, but she confronted it without falling into an asocial nihilism, on the one hand, or into the aridity of positivism, on the other. As we will see, her work on religious belief makes a less virulent critique than either Nietzsche's or Freud's, for she insisted upon the continued importance of those emotions and needs out of which religious belief emerges. To lose sight of what God symbolized by either embracing the substitute "science" or abandoning the feelings altogether would, she believed, spell the death of sociality and passion. Salomé continued to be interested not in the truth value but in the symbolic value of religious feeling and

---

[4] Salomé embedded her account of her similarities with and differences from Nietzsche in her chapter on the experience of friendship, subordinating it to her discussion of their shared friend Paul Rée. Although Salomé maintained throughout her life that Rée was the one who mattered to her personally, some critics have balked at what they perceive as her willful and perhaps defensive effort to diminish Nietzsche's actual importance to her. For Rudolph Binion, Salomé *was* "Nietzsche's wayward disciple."

[5] Ernst Pfeiffer, ed., *Friedrich Nietzsche, Paul Rée, Lou von Salomé: Die Dokumente ihrer Begegnung* (Frankfurt am Main: Insel, 1970), p. 188.

myth. "What does it matter," she asked, "whether generations that come long after us look back again as if on collapsed rubble and see in it the same thing that we still see in the loftiest dreams of past epochs: of our own loftiest dream merely a symbol?"[6]

Religiosity, according to Salomé, involves a particularly paradoxical form of egoism, the production of a god to which we then kneel in devotion. That egoism expresses for Salomé, as it did for Nietzsche, the founding paradox of human subjectivity, that we are most ourselves in our determination by an other, most free when we recognize that determination as our own inner necessity and embrace what only appears to us to be external coercion. In her 1896 essay "Jesus der Jude" (Jesus the Jew), Salomé had written that "for the person who is utterly absorbed in his love for God, God can only reflect himself as love, and this only if no alien representations or trimmings blur or tarnish the image" (344).[7] Worshiping that which is most intimate and personal as that which is outside and above us is a necessary contradiction, according to Salomé, one which we experience as a unity in moments of the most genuine and childlike simplicity and naïveté. "The person who feels one with his God, who feels completely like his child, can only grasp or conceive of this God as father," according to Salomé in "Jesus der Jude." "The great achievement of all religious leaders is the invention not of new gods but of a new relation to them, the restoration of intimacy between God and world and of the desired feeling of unity which is revealed once again to be the basis of all religion" (345). Judaism, she thought, restored that intimacy most successfully, and Jesus was, for her, an exemplary Jew who had been misapprehended by Christianity. In "Der Egoismus in der Religion" (Egoism in religion), she makes it clear that a religiosity that imagines God to be the unconditionally loving father can also dispense with a Christian afterlife and with moral convention, with any one particular set of representations, and with any one specific political system.[8] Religion, for Salomé, always involved relations of love without content or object.

[6] Lou Andreas-Salomé, "Vom religiösen Affekt," *Die Zukunft*, April 23, 1898, p. 154.

[7] Lou Andreas-Salomé, "Jesus der Jude," *Neue Deutsche Rundschau* (1896): 342–51.

[8] Lou Andreas-Salomé, "Der Egoismus in der Religion," in *Der Egoismus*, ed. Arthur Dix (Leipzig, 1899).

Salomé generalized the religious experience of a loss of self at the point of the most powerful self-expression to all creative activity and to eroticism, and she argued that the religious person was always the most powerful intellectually. She implicitly offered her own religious experience and Nietzsche's as examples of the personal achievement of what all religious leaders achieve for others.

Like Nietzsche, to whom Salomé brought her considerable preparation in the history and psychology of religion and with whom she felt a deep affinity over the importance of religious feeling, Salomé resisted both metaphysical claims to the truth of God and positivist pretenses to having killed "him" off completely. Both attitudes obscure what for Salomé is the most interesting and complex aspect of religious devotion, its underlying psychic dynamic. In a critique that anticipated her enthusiasm for psychoanalysis, Salomé suggested in 1896 that the methods employed by rationalist scholars of religion stop at precisely the point at which the material becomes the most interesting, "where the secrets of what have become highly individualized and concentrated forms of religiosity" in the modern world are most inaccessible to conventional scientific analysis. "In their focus on the *human* production of gods," she writes in "Jesus der Jude," "modern scholars underestimate the psychological significance of the other side of the story. When they begin with the human being, instead of with gods, as they once did, they almost arbitrarily overlook the fact that the actual religious phenomenon really only emerges in the back-effect [*Rückwirkung*] of a god on the human beings who believe in it, no matter how that god originated" (342–43). What interested her was the process of idealization, which, in her view, was currently most evident in religious geniuses such as Nietzsche and in artists such as Rilke.

Salomé nevertheless makes it quite clear in the memoirs that the most significant of all her encounters with pedagogical father figures was her relationship with the Dutch Reform preacher Hendrik Gillot, whose teachings and preachings of German idealism she claimed to have chosen over religious orthodoxy, on the one hand, and arid rationalism, on the other—a choice she made years before reading or meeting Nietzsche. According to the Salomé of the memoirs, Gillot was "the decisive person through whom the door to life first really opened for me, and then left behind more of a boyish preparedness than a feminine dependence" (39). Salomé remembers having approached Gillot in 1879, the year her father died, in order to escape confirmation in her family's church. She recalls presenting herself and her goals as a devotion to knowledge and a passion for freedom from the constraints imposed by her family's and their society's expectations. She represented her plea as a longing and a passion for something "higher." On the basis of the relationship she developed with Gillot, Salomé made the convergence of erotic and intellectual idealizations a theoretical preoccuption and stressed the dangers for woman of being contained in either the narrowness of the domestic or the boundlessness of desire and fantasy.

The adolescent Salomé began her intensive study of the history of Western thought and the history and psychology of religion with Gillot. She explains that Gillot saw his project as an effort to bring her out of the world of fantasy, childhood, romance, the East, and orthodoxy, and into the world of rationality, logic, and the West. She attributes her deification of Gillot, the erotics of that deification, and the necessity of overcoming it to her inhibited development and consequent inability to accept him as an actual other:

> A living human being took the place [of childlike fantasies and day-dreams]: he did not take a place next to them, but embodied them—he became the incarnation, then, of all reality. But in addition, this god-man appeared as an opponent of all the fantasizing. Pedagogically, he advocated an unswerving orientation toward the development of clear understanding, and I obeyed him all the more passionately, the harder it was for me to make that shift: the change was hastened by an over-whelming passion. (28)

Gillot intended to "cure" her of feminine containment in a world of fantasy and give her the possibility of reason and understanding. He was her "god-man" precisely because he made possible what her fictionalized God could not: he authorized and facilitated her "self-expression." The accounts of Gillot's relation to her read like the account of an analysis. Gillot, it is said, agreed to take her as a student only if she agreed to tell him everything, especially that which was hardest to tell, and to count on him and his knowledge to bring her out of the world of fantasy.

The countertransference must have been particularly strong, given

Gillot's investment in his student. In one of her early novels, *Ruth*, Salomé turns the young woman's dilemma into a study of the desire of the male mentor, into a sort of Pygmalion story in which the master's desire and the student's needs conflict.[9] The novel contrasts the young woman's naïve confusion of erotic and intellectual passions with the teacher's less innocent desires. When he presents his student with his decision to leave his sick wife and marry her, she is shocked into a choice between love and self and chooses to pursue her education and growth apart from her mentor. In the memoirs, Salomé offers a critique of what she calls the novel's overly romantic approach. It lacked an analysis of what the inhibitions in her own development contributed to the "abnormal" course of her relationship with Gillot. Salomé explains that at the moment in her life when her passion for him emerged, she had achieved neither the emotional nor the physical maturity that would have allowed her passion to become a "real" relationship.

Gillot possessed very little reality for her as a separate human being; he served as the site for the projection and emergence of her needs and desires. Salomé acknowledges and explains her difficulty accepting his separateness when he actually proposed marriage:

All of a sudden, that which I had worshiped dropped from my heart and feelings and became something foreign—something that made its own demands, something that no longer brought my own fulfillment but, on the contrary, threatened it, something that wanted to divert my efforts to become myself, efforts that it had once guaranteed, and make them useful to another's existence. Like a flash of lightning the other himself arose before me. In reality, then, an actual other stood there: someone I could not have recognized under the veil of idealization. Still, my deification of him had been right for me, because up to that point he had been the one whose effect I required in order better to come to terms with myself. (29)

Salomé acknowledges what she considered to be the particularly childlike and "abnormal" transformation of an actual human being into a mere symbol and occasion for her own desires. Still, she affirms what that idealization of a pedagogical or authoritative father

[9] Lou Andreas-Salomé, *Ruth: Eine Erzählung* (Stuttgart: J. G. Cotta, 1897).

figure contributed to her development toward a world of knowledge and reality outside the conventional bounds of femininity. She "diagnosed" her tendency toward idealization as the product of a preoedipal narcissism. She celebrated the feminine desire and capacity for self-dissolution over masculine oedipal renunciations only if the "feminine" tendency to remain locked in a childhood misperception of the other as the locus of the self and the consequent lack of ego boundaries were countered by an equally strong passion for knowledge and for being *in* the world.

Though Salomé calls her relationship with Gillot abnormal and attributes it to "inhibitions in her development," she contends that it was "abnormal only in comparison to the kind of relationship that ends in bourgeois marriage, with all its consequences," that it was "abnormal as a result of the religious background of my childhood." "Because of that, the love affair, from the beginning, was never directed to the usual end, but merely used the personal experience to go beyond the loved person to his almost religious symbolism" (33). She also suggests that her experience was merely a heightened form of "normal" experiences of love: "Because the most powerful fantasmatic eruptions are combined with the most powerful real demands on the other person, the lover is little more than the piece of reality that inspires writers to a poetry that cannot take account of any other purpose for their object in the practical world" (34). Her memoirs suggest that the experience of love in the person of Gillot convinced her that a final or perfect resolution of the double directionality of self-assertion and self-dissolution was not possible, at least not for her. She emphasized the dangers of the desire for Gillot: "If I had ever loved another man the way I loved Gillot, I would have fled him, because I would have believed in the possibility of a passion but not in the possibility of a marriage and a life" (289–90).

She repeats her experience of the loss of God by giving up the object, here Gillot, without losing the feelings of security and love, without falling out of love. She managed to have Gillot confirm her in a Dutch church so she could get the necessary permission to leave Russia, and him. She would later have Gillot marry her to Andreas, and she continued to think of him as the one who gave her her "boyish readiness," her freedom, and her more masculine name,

Lou. In an account of Gillot's lasting impact on her, Salomé attributed her preference for conceptual work over literary writing to the specific effects of her love for Gillot:

> When I did conceptual work, I experienced myself as strengthened in a feminine activity, in contrast to everything that turned into the literary, which felt like a masculine enterprise; it is for that reason that most of my female figures are viewed through the eyes of a man. The explanation for both reaches back into my adolescence. In the conceptual work to which my friend educated me, my love of him was a feminine love, whereas everything that set fantasy into motion fell under his prohibition and could only free itself from obedience to his rules by way of a masculine-oriented attitude of defiance. (172)

Salomé locates the source of her relation to different kinds of work in love. In so doing, she challenges any conception of the "objective" or "neutral" sources of knowledge and writing, and she inverts the usual connection of the conceptual with masculinity and fiction with femininity.

In the chapter "The Experience of Love (Hendrik Gillot)," Gillot becomes the occasion for more general reflections on love. Salomé writes of three different kinds of fulfillment in love: marriage, motherhood, and purely erotic bonds. She discusses her relationship with Gillot as a kind of unrealized marriage and suggests that her loss of God had something to do with her having never "dared" to bring children into the world. "God," she writes, "was much more familiar to me than the stork—children came from God: who, other than God could have made them possible?" (36). Though she refuses to attribute her childlessness completely to her loss of faith, she suggests that " 'birth' necessarily changes its meanings completely, depending on whether a child is assumed to come from nothingness or from plenitude" (36). What helps other women take the risk of motherhood, she muses, "in addition to their personal feelings and wishes," is their unquestioned, undoubting acceptance of what is generally assumed and expected. Salomé's loss of God rendered such general assumptions and expectations impossible.

The purely erotic bond, which Salomé considers very rare, consists of an erotic attraction between two lovers which is mediated by their shared devotion to a third object of desire, located in an intellectual or spiritual sphere. Her relationship with Gillot, she writes, had something of that kind of eroticism. But in herself, she says, the purely erotic, like the other kinds of love, remained unrealized. Characteristically, however, she concludes, "That's not what matters, as long as whatever we embraced was life, and lived, and we, as living beings, remained creative in it from the first day to the last" (39).

After leaving Gillot and St. Petersburg, Salomé mirrored the decision of large numbers of young Russian women to pursue their university studies in Zurich. Most of these women, as Salomé points out in her memoirs, intended to use what they learned in the service of the Russian people and their revolution. For Salomé, however, the passage to Europe opened up worlds of possibility for the intellectual, psychological, and emotional life she sought. It would become more and more important to her that the relationships she forged opened onto the social, instead of containing her within the closed space of the couple, of heterosexual complementarities and domesticities. She continued to envision the ideal relationship as two people who knelt before "God," her symbol of a desire that could not be fulfilled by any human relationship.

Because biographers and critics have made so much of what they suppose to be Salomé's fixation on her actual father, it is worth noting that the memoirs locate the experience of family after the experience of God and the experience of love. Salomé explicitly states that she was not intensely engaged with her parents, either positively or negatively. That claim fits the pattern of family life in the class to which the Salomés belonged, in which children were often entrusted to the care of nannies, nurses, and tutors. Salomé was the only girl in the family and was convinced she was a disappointment, that her mother had wanted a boy. From the first, therefore, she had defied her mother's expectations and wishes. Her family was part of the German-speaking colony in St. Petersburg, a city "exceptional" within Russia for its cosmopolitan and European character. Her father was a general in the Russian military, and the Salomés lived in the Generals' Quarters across from the Winter Palace, very much at the center of St. Petersburg and on the margins of traditional Russian life. Salomé remembered her childhood as a time of isolation in her own fantasy world, apart from the realities of Russian life. She would later have recourse to her knowledge of the Russian people and the Russian soul to explain her attraction to psychoanalysis. Yet though she figured for others and sometimes represented herself as Russian, Salomé's childhood and adolescence were largely insulated from, albeit influenced by, Russian political and social life.

The chapter on the experience of family begins with an account of her life among her brothers and describes her parents with significant distance. Salomé effectively eradicates hints of conflicts with her brothers and traces her later "brotherly" relations with men back to her relations with her siblings. She recounts an obligatory oedipal story by remembering her affection for her indulgent father and her resentment of her mother and even recalls telling her mother that she wanted her to die, to disappear. According to the memoirs, Louise Salomé made possible the kind of life her daughter led, and yet she was its biggest threat.

Salomé describes her mother as religious, even pietistic, and conventional, the picture of feminine domesticity and constraint against which Salomé would define herself. She remembers her mother as unaffectionate and concentrates her characterization on the particular ways in which her mother channeled her masculinity into domestic control. But she also explains that with age, she finally realized how much her mother had actually indulged her and how loyal she had remained, even though her daughter's choices could not have been farther from her expectations.

Salomé argues it was only by separating and distancing herself from her mother that she finally achieved her appreciation of Louise Salomé. She describes the last time they saw each other as the first and only time they were able to express intimacy directly:

She did not say a word. She just snuggled up to me. Although she had remained slim and upright, she was exactly my height now that she had become just a little smaller overall in her old age, so that now her delicate body with its thin limbs could completely cuddle up in me. But when had she ever had this bearing before? It was as if she lifted herself out of the most deeply buried parts of herself for just this moment, as if she had not grown to this way of being until her final years, grown to a final sweetness, the way sweetness collects in a fruit that has hung in the sun just long enough before it finally falls. And perhaps in the stillness of this freely given, tender sweetness the same thought went through us both, the same pain, the same heartache: "Oh why, why—only now?" This was my mother's last gift of life to me. Dear Muschka. (58)

Salomé's father, who died in 1879 when she was eighteen years old, necessarily figures far less concretely in her accounts of her life. It is clear that his death enabled her to refuse confirmation in her parents' church and removed the obstruction of the actual father's demands, leaving her to pursue her own intellectual and interpersonal passions. With the death of this actual father, she left the family church and took up her studies with, and her idealizations of, Gillot.

The memoirs give the most space to Salomé's relationships with Rainer Maria Rilke, Sigmund Freud, and F. C. Andreas. In her address to Rilke, "April—Our Month, Rainer," Salomé explains that the much younger Rilke was the first man who was "real" to her, the first with whom she achieved a love relationship that did not contain her in her own desire or subordinate her to his. Salomé and Rilke met in 1896 when he sought her out after reading "Jesus der Jude." After a somewhat slow beginning, Salomé and Rilke became intimate friends and grew somewhat more distant only after their second trip to Russia, in 1900. Salomé makes it clear in a number of published sources that it was Rainer the human being and not the poet that interested her. In fact, she disliked his early work, which she found overly sentimental and affected, just as she disliked his overly feminine name, René, which he changed to Rainer at her instigation. After the break in 1901, several years elapsed before they resumed their correspondence and contact, but then they remained close until his death in 1926. Salomé was drawn to his sexual ambiguity; Rilke seemed both masculine and feminine at once, exemplifying for her the basis of creativity in a primary narcissism and fundamental bisexuality.

Salomé suggests that age had a great deal to do with her capacity to love Rilke differently. In a passage from her diary of 1888, in which she compares Rée and Andreas, Salomé distinguishes her youthful love for Gillot from her relationship with Andreas in terms that are not altogether convincing as explanations of her marriage but make interesting claims about outliving the conflicts of youth:

The one person whom I loved and yet never criticized was Gillot, although, at least in my sense of the word, I really loved in him an ideal. The difference between that and what is now the only possible mode of feeling for me lies in the years between: in our youth, the ideal to which we aspire embodies itself directly in a person, and we love that person because of the equation. Later, when we are better able to separate people and ideas more precisely, we no longer seek a god-man; rather we unite with that person in a shared inner devotion to that which we revere and admire in common. No longer one person who kneels before the other, but two who kneel side by side. (289–90)

Though she was his lover, Salomé was primarily Rilke's anchor, friend, and analyst. Despite the amount of time they spent with other friends—Frieda von Bülow, August Endell, and even F. C. Andreas—and despite their involvement with the notoriously homosexual Atelier Elvira in Munich, their own stylizations of the relationship and the critics' isolation of it from the rest of their lives have ensured the assumption of an exclusive heterosexuality on both sides.[10]

Salomé's discussion of Rilke in the memoirs consists primarily of her analysis of the psychic dynamics and complexities that underlay his creativity and his problems. Her analysis makes of him not only the singularly creative artist but another modern religious genius, with conflicts similar to those she had identified in Nietzsche. What makes a Rilke or a Nietzsche creative, according to Salomé, is a capacity for an objectless religiosity and access to that realm of psychic life out of which religious feeling emerges. Rilke was what Salomé called the "repressionless artist"; Heinrich von Kleist was another. The artist personality, she believed, had access to psychic material that remains inaccessible, though operative, in other human beings. She stressed Rilke's consequent receptivity to experience, his capacity for surrender to external impression, his difficulties in adapting to external realities, and the conflict within him between

[10] For more information on Salomé's and Rilke's interactions with other friends and associates, see Rudolph Binion, *Frau Lou: Nietzsche's Wayward Disciple* (Princeton: Princeton University Press, 1968); and Ursula Welsch and Michaela Wiesner, *Lou Andreas-Salomé: Vom "Lebensurgrund" zur Psychoanalyse* (Munich: Verlag Internationale Psychoanalyse, 1988).

what she called the human (feminine) receptivity to experience and the artist's drive to master experience and give it external form.

Rilke exemplified what she considered to be the artist's capacity to heal himself and to overcome this conflict through his work, where the conflict between receptivity and the drive to give form to impressions found at least momentary resolution.[11] In almost all these qualities, Salomé subtly and perhaps even unconsciously identifies with such artists. The primary difference, once again, expresses itself most pointedly in what she sees as a feminine lack of anxiety; she does not suffer from as sharp a distinction between receptivity and creativity as men do. Woman's receptivity becomes creative within her and does not require the kind of mastery expressed in the compulsion to give impressions external form. Rilke's particular conflict bears the same structure as the conflict between woman's conflictual drives toward self-dissolution in her receptivity and toward self-assertion. Salomé represents woman, however, and herself, as simultaneously less irreparably split, with less need for visible objectifications of her creativity. This story puts her beyond, rather than behind "man." Woman is simultaneously less and more evolved than man and can act as witness and reminder to men of their former beliefs and current anxieties.

These particular narratives of difference have the effect, if not the intent, of making the lack of creativity often attributed to woman into the mark of her superiority. They remove Salomé from competition with men and generate positions for her that are neither outside male intellectual and artistic circles nor inside in their terms. Woman, though less differentiated, is not undifferentiated but has simply made the passage differently, has never renounced her roots, however refined her sublimations, and does not share the tragic and heroic sense of the poet and philosopher who suffer from the "modern loss of transcendence."

In the memoirs this difference emerges from the contrasts Salomé

---

[11] For the best recent interpretation of Salomé's understanding of Rilke as artist, see Welsch and Wiesner's *Lou Andreas-Salomé*, particularly the section titled "Lebensmitte," pp. 161–213; and Ursula Welsch, "Das leidende Genie: Lou Andreas-Salomés Einschätzung von Rainer Maria Rilkes Problematik," in *Lou Andreas-Salomé*, ed. Rilke Gesellschaft (Karlsruhe: Von Loeper, 1986).

sets both implicitly and explicitly between Rilke and herself. One of the central metaphors used to articulate their differences is that of "home" and "homelessness." Woman remained "at home" in exile, because she carried a sense of home around with her, as a snail carries its shell on its back wherever it wanders.[12] Salomé attempts to avoid reference to fixed or real "homes" without abandoning the possibility of a sense of security in the world, now a security in mobility itself. "Man," on the other hand, suffers from the loss of fixed, absolute homes, from a kind of inner homelessness that emerges from his renunciations. Such inner homelessness, born of anxiety over the loss of an external object, accounts for Rilke's psychic dilemma, according to Salomé, caught as he was in the conflict between the "human capacity for receptivity" and the "artist's compulsion to produce." The loss of God, she writes in the first section on Rilke, doesn't change Rilke's or Nietzsche's religious bearings or devotion and doesn't change the desire to create even a contentless god.

"For Rainer," she writes, "the object of art was God himself, or that which expressed his relation to the innermost ground of life, that anonymity beyond all conscious ego boundaries" (124).[13] To fulfill his project as a form-giver, she writes, "the artist has to reach into his innermost being, and when the project fails, it threatens his very being itself, because with the death of God, the inner self has become one with the object of creation" (124). The loss of God turns the artist in on himself; without an external object, his own psychic workings become his object or material. Now, according to Salomé, the receiving being comes into conflict with the compulsion to give his impressions form, and this conflict accounts for the way that Rilke experienced his calling as artist, "as a seduction or a temptation to aspire to heights that then necessarily wrenched him away from the deep, nourishing ground that underlies everything" (125). "Rainer's angst," according to Salomé, "was not simply the fearfulness of a fragile type of person about object loss in life, nor was it the

[12] Salomé develops this metaphor in an 1899 essay on woman titled "Der Mensch als Weib," which I treat in detail in Chapter 6.

[13] For the entirety of Salomé's analysis of Rilke's "psychic problems," see *Lebensrückblick*, pp. 113–50.

fearfulness of all truly artistic people, faced with an interruption in their capacity to produce, over which they have no control; rather, it was that *absolute* fear of being sucked into the abyss" (124).

Salomé then contrasts Rilke's religion of self-abandonment with the desire to be loved and its implied dependence on an object. Feminine, narcissistic love serves as the basis and model of religion and religiosity, she argues, and so explains Rilke's fascination with feminine love stories and fates. For Salomé, feminine narcissism, or objectless love, underlies all object choice but remains more apparent in woman than man. She credits Rilke with having understood that "however painful feminine love stories might have been, they led to a true loss of self as to true self-possession" (132). The model for true religiosity is the lover who may try over and over to free his passion from illusions, but whose "creative, emotional powers must appear more and more powerful, more and more fruitful, the less legitimated they seem by their object" (133).

Salomé most pointedly develops this distinction between object-less love and dependence on an object in her efforts to differentiate her narrative of human subjectivity and her concept of narcissism from Freud's, but it preoccupied her throughout her intellectual life.[14] She used it to explain the implications of both Nietzsche's and Rilke's fascination with "feminine love stories."

Salomé's view of the contrasts between Rilke and herself emerges most clearly in her descriptions of their different experiences of Russia, where they traveled twice, once in 1899, with F. C. Andreas, and again in 1900, in the company of friends for at least part of the journey. For her, these trips were a return, a memory, and a completion; for him, they were opportunities to produce and to work. Salomé describes the beginning of the second trip as a kind of paradise for Rilke before the unrest, before "the uncertainty over whether the compulsion to produce would come into conflict with the desire for the selfless receptivity to everything that was to be formed" (143).

[14] The concept of objectless love is, of course, often attributed to Rilke. It is clear that they shared an interest in that concept and developed it together. Rilke, as we remember, sought out Salomé after reading her essay "Jesus the Jew," in which the notion of an objectless love figures centrally in her understanding of the psychology of religion.

Traveling to Russia allowed Salomé to "grow up into her youth" and become completely herself. She wished the same for Rilke, the same return to his childhood, the same process of becoming himself, the same healing from anxiety and the compulsion to master experience. Her perception of his "paradise" before the storm is linked again to her conceptions of femininity and her conviction that experiences that prove to be creative within the self cannot then go into the work. When he was abandoned to his experiences, rather than producing works, Rilke's creativity took the form of a transformation of his entire being. Initially, Ursula Welsch maintains, Salomé diagnosed Rilke's problem as lack of the technical mastery required to give expression to the impressions to which he was so open; later, however, according to Welsch, Salomé began to believe that no art form was adequate to the task of expressing the psychic material to which Rilke had access.[15] Whereas *he* remains divided and achieves a kind of unity only in the act of creating, *she* combines the capacity for surrender with the feminine tendency to absorb it and have it become creative as self-transformation or enhancement.

When Salomé broke off their relationship during the second trip to Russia, she explained her decision in part on the basis of her strong belief that Rilke could heal himself only through his work and could work only if his creativity were not invested in dependence on an object, in this case her. He could be cured only by "objectless love." But she also noted that her desire for him had slipped away as her worries about him "placed her outside what unites man and woman, and that then never changed for me again" (146).

She resisted the idea of analysis for Rilke because she believed that his suffering and potential healing were both rooted in his access to preoedipal psychic material that might be damaged by analysis. Wiesner points out that Salomé's opposition to analysis for Rilke precedes her more intense involvement with psychoanalysis.[16] Still, she never abandoned her positive view of an unconscious mental life that was not entirely the product of repression but linked with

---

[15] Welsch, "Das leidende Genie," p. 58.
[16] Welsch and Wiesner (*Lou Andreas-Salomé*) provide the most exhaustive interpretation and account of Salomé's stance on analysis for Rilke.

primary narcissistic experience. She also never gave up her belief that there was something positive and creative in unmastered unconscious life; indeed, that belief became the primary difference between Freud's narrative of psychic development and her own.

In the memoirs, Salomé explains her receptivity to Freudian psychoanalysis on the basis of her experience of "the unique psychic fate of a single individual [Rilke]" and her experience growing up among "the Russian people, with their rich and self-evident inner nature" (151). The Russian people, according to Salomé, were more immediately analyzable and more honest in their relations to themselves because the layers of repression remained thinner, looser. They were, to put it another way, closer to what Salomé conceived as the feminine, by virtue of having not yet been forced into the sacrificial order of the individualistic West. In the years between 1897 and 1910, the period of Russia fascination in Germany, Salomé wrote extensively about Russian literature and "the Russian soul." As Angela Livingstone points out, Salomé's work on Tolstoy and Russian religion predated some of the later more influential and supposedly original writings on Russian literature.[17] After her notorious liaison with Nietzsche in the 1880s, her timely books on Ibsen and Nietzsche in the mid-1890s, and her work on sexuality and eroticism in the late 1890s, her work on Russian literature and psychic life in the first decade of the twentieth century kept her squarely at the center, if not at the beginnings, of evolving intellectual and cultural currents. Salomé figured for Nietzsche and others as "the Russian" and was rendered "exotic" by virtue of that difference.[18] The convergence of European fascination with Russia and Salomé's representations of Russian literature installed her, once again, at the center of a collective fetishization.

Salomé's efforts to resist confinement on one or the other side of the divisions with which she operated necessarily relied on welltrodden discursive and political terrain. Her passage between Russia and Europe included the naïve appropriation of stereotypes of the

---

[17] For more information on Salomé's contribution to the Russia fascination in Germany, see Angela Livingstone's account in *Lou Andreas-Salomé: Her Life and Work* (Mount Kisco, N.Y.: Moyer Bell, 1984).

[18] For more information on the reception of Nietzsche in Russia, see *Nietzsche in Russia*, ed. Bernice Glatzer Rosenthal (Princeton: Princeton University Press, 1986).

depths of the Russian soul, the simplicity of the Russian people, and the solidity of their faith. Such stereotypes and cliches and their exclusively psychological focus are most evident in her accounts of her travels in Russia with Rilke in 1900, which turn the Russian people into a naïve, pious peasantry, museum pieces for aesthetic appropriation. Sofya Shil, a St. Petersburg intellectual and Tolstoy devotee, commented on Rilke's and Salomé's glorifications of Russia's backwardness:

> Our friends from abroad experienced the journey to Russia as a festival of the spirit. How should one not be glad of such sympathy. But they sought and saw in our country an idyll, while storm clouds were gathering there and the first dull peals of thunder were rumbling. They saw in the people everything pure and bright, and this was the truth. But they did not want to see the other truth, just as true—that the people were perishing without rights, in poverty, in ignorance, and that the vices of slaves were growing in them: laziness, filth, deception, drunkenness. When we spoke of this with deep sorrow, we felt it was unpleasant to our friends; they wanted (very legitimately) gladness and miraculous peacefulness.[19]

Salomé's chapter on Freud and psychoanalysis suggests that she found "gladness and miraculous peacefulness" in them. She begins by stressing that psychoanalysis provided the rational approach she needed to the foundations of consciousness in a material unconscious. When she came to the new discipline, psychoanalysis had already made it clear that the conditions of neurotics could reveal the psychic functioning of "normal," healthy individuals, had begun to challenge the boundaries erected between the normal and abnormal, healthy and sick, rational and irrational. What bothers people about psychoanalysis, writes Salomé, is the bleak picture they think it draws of a humanity that no longer transcends its origins in animality and sex. Invoking Mephistopheles' assessment of reason, Salomé suggests that civilization "may lead us away from our animality, but not without diminishing the drives and our own powers so much that in the end we become an impoverished human

---

[19] Quoted in Livingstone, *Lou Andreas-Salomé*, pp. 111–12.

being in comparison to which the animal, with its undiminished lack of culture, impresses us like a great landowner" (152).

People resist psychoanalysis, as they resist sexuality, Salomé continues, because they do not want to be reminded that we extraordinary human beings are actually part of what appears to our conscious interiority to stand outside of us—the body. "The body," as Salomé insists, "is the most undeniable piece of external reality in us" (155). What bothers us most is not sexuality per se but being forced to see our dependence on the body, which accounts for our existence but which we are unable or unwilling to unite with our intellectual and spiritual selves. "The more finely developed our consciousness, the more everything becomes an other and is only approachable as something external to us—this includes the body, or our materiality, and accounts for its devaluation" (155). Freud, according to Salomé, challenges the opposition between inside and out, an opposition that was once conceived to be more of an exchange before modern consciousness divided the two. Freud's discovery of infantile stages disturbs people not because of the alleged pansexuality of children but because childhood is revealed as the ultimate source and ground out of which our entire inner development is nourished. The blurring of boundaries between inside and out, between animal and human, between child and adult puts Freud in the tradition of Darwin, but with a difference. For Salomé, psychoanalysis blurs the conventional distinctions between sexuality and spirituality, between our basest instincts and the achievements that we like to imagine as sublimations that float far above our primal roots. For Freud, all sublimations are a diversion of sexual drives from sexual to other goals. Thus, we can say that sexual perversions occur at the same site as the most valued sublimations: "What we call 'objectivity' instead of 'love' is nothing other than the fact that our consciousness willingly opens itself, with *its* methods, to the disclosure of the unconscious, where we have never ceased to deny our isolation or to know our shared connection with everything" (156).

The experience of sexual love makes us most aware of the instability of our most treasured oppositions, according to Salomé. We can think of sublimation, she writes, "as if even sexual goals were just a kind of embarrassment for the solitary, corporeal human being

who tries to convince another solitary being that we transcend ourselves and the body in each other's embrace, whereas the other is
actually only like us in the very realm of the body, and the bond
can only be celebrated and realized productively within that cor-
poreality" (157). In psychoanalysis, then, Salomé finds her own, and
Nietzsche's, critique of the leveling effects of civilization, its horror
of the body. She prefers Freud's fluid dualism between rational and
irrational to what she saw as Nietzsche's ultimately monistic celebration of instinct and will.

In her account of psychoanalysis, Salomé continues to pursue the
significance of religious faith and the creation of gods. "God," she
writes, "means both that which is most intimately us and that which
most exceeds us at the same time. God represents a *Notgriff* for the
most underworldly. We refuse to call it worldly because that would
sound too specific for something that in fact exceeds us and hence
expresses us more powerfully than the usual opposition between
inside and outside" (157). Salomé then reminds her readers that
"the very power of sublimation depends on how deeply it is guaranteed in this native soil, the primal ground of our sexuality, how
effective, how strong those drives have remained in everything we
do. The more powerfully erotic a person is, the greater the possibilities for sublimations, the longer he can hold his breath for the
demands that sublimation makes on us without letting the fulfillment of the drives and adaptation to reality come into conflict" (157).

She moves immediately to the personal significance to her of Freud
and psychoanalysis and emphasizes his "refusal to be influenced by
conventional reservations over the potentially disturbing results of
its explorations" (153). Salomé celebrates the unabbreviated, un-
aborted commitment of psychoanalysis to an exact, concrete investigation of the individual case, whatever the outcome. And that,
according to Salomé, was exactly what she needed: "My eyes, still
full of foregone conclusions, . . . had to force themselves to attend
rationally and concretely to the objectively human. They had to do
this in order to escape the danger of falling into a blind, because
blinded, reverie, the reveries of the pleasant psychologies that cannot lead to reality but allow us instead to tumble around in our own
garden of wishes" (153). Salomé had to turn away from her own
previous conceptions of a more primitive humanity that "remained

as our own ineradicable childhood—as a secret treasure—behind all maturity" (153).

As always, Salomé stresses the significance of the particular personality responsible for psychoanalysis and the love for him that underlies her own education in it. She emphasizes the "incurable rationalist" in Freud. "He named the newly discovered element the unconscious, ostentatiously in the name of a negation. But these two letters un always appeared to me as a positive, as a personal resistance to . . . everything that could turn discoverers into inventors" (154). According to Salomé, Freud taught us the importance of overcoming our need to bring everything under one hat. His exclusive emphasis on formal methods and ever-increasing analytic differentiations did not banish the need for what Salomé calls a unifying point, but it cured her of the illusion that such total explanation is possible without romantic obfuscation of what is empirically observable.

The chapter ends with a renewed emphasis on Freud the man and the significance of Freud's particular brand of thinking. Freud the thinker and Freud the man conflicted with each other and were united, according to Salomé, by way of a struggle and a sacrifice. The capacity to leave things hanging, rather than indulge in useless "brooding" over the inaccessible, was Freud's most important legacy (161):

Our formal thinking, in the end, is a kind of symbolization—a means with which to bring the inexpressible to intelligibility by way of its conversion into language. Reason is our trick.

Most people decide to enhance their knowledge of what can actually be proved . . . with that which they assume to be true. . . . About this indulgence of ours, about this leap from physics to metaphysics, Freud would say we abuse the very methods we created for use in the physical world. It is precisely at the point that separates physics from metaphysics that Freud came to his discoveries, to things that had been covered over up to that point, because they had been held prisoner or obscured by the metaphysical assumptions we put in their way. What made Freud a fighter against such leaps of faith was the seriousness of the scholar in him, the same scholarly seriousness, without retreat or concession, that brought such unintended results to light in the first place and had no tolerance for covering them up again. This ought not to be confused with the aggressiveness of the missionary, which emerges from the drive or compulsion to convince or to teach (for example, a Nietzschean "Bleibt mir der Erde treu" [Remain true to the earth!] or any other such desire to proclaim). (162–63)

Freud's work demands "that we remain more patient and hesitant at the point of decision," Salomé contends. "Freud's tendency was to subject us to the things themselves so that we first admit the ways in which we are part of everything, as the same, before we interest ourselves in how we might fundamentally differ. Knowing then becomes acknowledgment" (163).

For Salomé sociality and adaptation to reality are decisive in her assessment of the differences between Nietzsche and Freud. Two remarks clarify her respect for Freud and for psychoanalysis, in opposition to her prior attempts to come to terms with the "meaning of life." She notes that Freud was so important for the development of psychoanalysis because, unlike various other turn-of-the-century scholars, who complacently rationalized the enormous philosophical implications of a critique of metaphysics, Freud

> was the only one who brought the necessary degree of disinterest to the project—not to care about whether he would come upon something repulsive or offensive—not some kind of overcoming achieved through struggle or, on the other hand, some sort of pleasure in the disgusting. This means, quite simply, that his joy in thinking, and his intellectual curiosity drew so powerfully from his capacity to love, and his drive to mastery drew so powerfully from his very being, that the question of where the usual values and judgments should fall never became a question for him at all. (154)

In the second Freud section in the memoirs, "Memories of Freud," Salomé recalls her exchange with Freud over a poem, "Prayer to Life," which she had written as a student in Zurich. Nietzsche had loved that particular poem so much that he put it to music, but the sentiments expressed in it held little appeal for Freud. According to Salomé, "His emphatic sobriety of expression could hardly be impressed with what I, as a blood-young thing—inexperienced and untested—had achieved, cheaply enough, in enthusiastic exaggerations" (168). Salomé then quotes the one verse that Nietzsche put to music:

For thousands of years to think and to live
Throw in all you contain!
If you have no more happiness left to give me
Well, then! You still have your pain.

Jahrtausende zu denken und zu leben
Wirf deinen Inhalt voll hinein!
Hast du kein Glück mehr übrig, mir zu geben,
Wohlan—noch hast du deine Pein

Salomé became herself, against an initial containment in her own fantasies, by pursuing a life of intellectual work, but one in which she was able to invest her "religious affect" without metaphysical substitutes for belief in God. What she applauds in Freud she would also say about herself, that he worked against an inner resistance, rather than indulge that resistance as Nietzsche did, and he achieved the particular kind of synthesis that lives, rather than one that obscures and kills with mere pretense.

Salomé notes that her failure to be either intellectually or personally loyal to the men in her life gives rise to the two related charges that she was a destructive seductress and a dilettante. To constitute herself in relation to others, and to father figures in particular, without being caught in the daughter's submission or the son's renunciations is the challenge Salomé formulated for woman. The movement in and out of what appeared to be contradictory positions was as essential to her theoretical and literary work as it appears to have been to her relations with others. She insisted always on the importance of dualism, as opposed to the various monisms that characterized the philosophical reductions of the time. Salomé saw in Freud a crucial resistance to the monisms in Nietzsche's work. She also made her strongest critiques of Freud's work in those instances in which he seemed to her to privilege a single term over a consistent dualism. In her diaries and her tribute to Freud, she frequently complains that he had overemphasized or privileged the sexual to the virtual exclusion of the significance and strength of the ego in his early work on hysteria. She herself insisted that her belief in the positivity of the unconscious, as opposed to what she saw as Freud's emphasis on its dangers, most distinguished their views of culture. Pfeiffer reports:

A word in conversation with Lou Andreas-Salomé clarifies the similarity and the difference from Freud: "It was his accomplishment that he put the person back together in all his unity, with all his life, not intuitively but rationalistically. His difference from me from the beginning was that he would rather have taken the individual completely out of this dangerous connection with the One, whereas I experience the most powerful part of people at precisely those points where that connection has pushed through at the wrong place, in the manifestations of illness.[20]

Her emphasis throughout on the feminine, the unconscious, and the narcissistic could be read as a resistance to masculine renunciations of pleasure, the mother, and the body.

The memoirs are structured in such a way that Salomé's work on psychoanalysis ends a development that begins with the regressive creation of God and with a childhood locked in fantasy. The memoirs enact the movement from presymbolic groundedness in materiality to intellectuality that elaborates but never departs from its grounds in love. Having established the ultimate unity of her passion for life, for God, and for intellectual work, Salomé is able to present the course of her life as the manifestation of inner necessities and inner goals. There is nothing here of striving, of struggle, and very little of conflict or *ressentiment*.

The exception to the at least structural unity of the memoirs is her account of her marriage to Andreas. Even if Pfeiffer is ultimately responsible for the order of the chapters, it is fitting that Salomé's chapter on Andreas should appear at the end. Her account of her marriage wavers between regret, on the one hand, and an attempt, on the other, to make the relationship coherent with her self-representation as neither conscious chooser nor determined victim. She says that the chapter on Andreas the man is based on the perceptions of his students and colleagues. She begins by defining significant people as multi-dimensional, complex, and contradictory and by attributing Andreas's gifts to his inner conflicts or drama. "The so-called harmonious personality, to which we all aspire," writes Salomé, "usually represents either a premature contentment with a cheap sense of peace, achieved through a reduction of human

[20] Quoted in Pfeiffer's notes to Andreas-Salomé, *Lebensrückblick*, p. 219.

possibilities, or a merely schematic completeness of the kind that we project onto the nonhuman and against which we then measure our far greater complication" (185). In Andreas, the split between the primal and the conscious which is born into us all, was particularly strong, she writes, and accounted for both his talent and his limitations. He was, according to her, caught between his own intuitive, visionary sense of things and his commitment to a thorough research method that could never approach or satisfy the visionary part of what he knew. What got lost in the middle, according to Salomé, was the ability to complete a project.

Andreas was forty years old when Salomé, then twenty-four, met him in 1885. He was an orientalist, one of the best Iranologists of his day, and was made professor of west Asiatic languages at the University of Göttingen in 1903. Reputedly a charismatic and inspiring teacher, he was well known and respected despite his apparent inability to write and publish, a problem for which Salomé is blamed in at least one biography. Andreas's mother was German-Malayan, and his father was Armenian. Salomé draws on prevailing stereotypes about the East and the South when she repeatedly describes Andreas as dark, mysterious, passionate, even violent and remote. As both Rudolph Binion and Angela Livingstone have suggested, Salomé attributed to Andreas's influence a number of her own habits that others perceived as "exotic" or "Eastern," including vegetarianism; dressing in natural, woven fabrics; walking barefoot in woods and forests, even in the dead of winter; and attempting to communicate with the nonhuman life forms of plants and animals. The repeated description, even construction, of Salomé by others as the *harem Frau* certainly emerges in part from her association with Andreas and what he came to represent.

As a way of introducing her characterization of Andreas, Salomé draws on well-established oppositions between the European and the non-European, the primitive and the civilized, the West and the Orient. She is careful, as always, to insist that the cultural constitutes not a loss but an elaboration of the primitive, as she suggests that Andreas reflects something that is true of "the person from the East," namely, that that which grounds the intellectual is more visible in him than in "the person from the West, for whom the idea, the ideal, or the ideological always signifies a distance from something above or below it" (195). For the person from the East, Andreas, "the intellectual is given expression in a way that speaks the body and the physical; the corporeal takes on meanings beyond itself" (195). And for that very reason perhaps, in his teaching Andreas's vision and erudition came together to produce something awe-inspiring for his students. As a writer too, Andreas was haunted by extreme forms of frustration, restlessness, and what Salomé calls a "lack of Sundays." Andreas, according to Salomé, was given to extremes of anger and tenderness and lived out of a sense of compulsion, rather than conscious choice.

In "What's Missing from the Outline," at the end of the text, Salomé attempts to explain their relationship. The narrative suggests that their attraction for each other was itself of the order of compulsion, a confrontation with destiny. Having already established Andreas's compulsive and conflicted nature, Salomé finds it difficult not to portray herself as a victim of his will. The chapter itself is set up as an explanation for her separation from Paul Rée, whose friendship she assesses as the most significant in her life. She presents the loss of this relationship as one of the few instances in her life when she did not actually choose what she felt to be natural and right. Rée disappeared after her engagement to Andreas, she says, and she explains his departure by emphasizing his insecurities and his inability to believe in his importance to her. For her part, she was unable to make the nature of her relationship with Andreas clear to Rée, or to explain its limits. Though freedom to continue her relationship with Rée was part of the contract she made with Andreas, Andreas would not allow her to explain it to Rée. Rée had no idea, writes Salomé, that she needed him more than ever, when she entered into the relationship with Andreas, "because the compulsion, the coercion under which I took that irrevocable step separated me not just from [Rée], but from myself" (199).

Only those who knew Andreas well, according to Salomé, could begin to understand what she meant by compulsion and coercion. The compulsion came from what she called the violent force of the irresistible to which Andreas succumbed, irresistible because "it did not begin with the force of wish or impulse, but suddenly appeared as an unchangeable, given fact" (200). With the benefit of hindsight, she came to see that Andreas was completely oblivious to or unaffected by her feelings, her state of mind, and her lack of erotic attraction to him. She responded to Andreas the way she had responded to Gillot, she writes, "not at all as a woman." Neither of them understood how she actually worked, but Andreas assumed that what he took to be her "girlish notions" would disappear. His sense of inevitability about their participation in a life larger than both of them intrigued her. In retrospect, she finds his belief and his certainty about their belonging together all the more monstrous considering how much older and more experienced he was than she, and how much more childlike and naïve she was than other girls her own age.

If their coming together and staying together belonged to the order of necessity, so too did her refusal to consummate the marriage. Salomé explains that her preservation of self and her freedom depended on that refusal. It was not grounded in "girlish views" or in principles of any kind, according to Salomé; such things were never decisive for her. Instead, her motivations and behaviors were based in the revelation to her of a will or desire that emerges from unconscious knowledge, rather than carefully considered conscious or moral choices.

She gives two examples. The first is her refusal to be confirmed in her parents' church after a dream in which she hears herself say no. She is careful to distinguish her refusal from an act of defiance or some kind of fanatical commitment to "Truth." She even reports fighting against her own impulse, but like other involuntary acts and choices, this one was absolute and irrevocable because it came from her innermost being. "It is impossible, ultimately, ever to unravel our motivations and valuations; however hard we try to pin them down, they elude us," she writes in explanation of her sense of the involuntary. "And to suddenly realize that fact can completely change our lives forever" (202).

Salomé then provides a much more dramatic example of the revelation to her of "involuntary" choices, this one about her decision not to consummate the marriage. Once again, it is a story of sleep. As she lay sleeping outside on a cot one afternoon, Andreas came and lay beside her. He must have decided to overwhelm or to conquer her. She did not wake immediately, but when she did, she heard a strange guttural sound that she could not identify. She was aware of being unable to find her arm until she realized that it was at his neck and that she was choking him. The sound was caused by Andreas's efforts to breathe. This "instinctual response" to what she clearly takes to have been his attempted rape of her becomes a moment of revelation. She realizes that her refusal to consummate the marriage comes from an undeniable and irretrievable decision made deep within her. The text continues with a description of the evening before their engagement, when Andreas grabbed a knife on her table and stabbed himself in the chest with it in order to convince her that they had to marry. Salomé notes that the doctor who was called to attend to Andreas obviously suspected her, and she follows with the observation that there were other times that the two of them "stood before death, having finished with life and having made arrangements for the future; this was the sign of their utter desperation and confusion" (203).

Nevertheless, Salomé succumbed to Andreas's, and perhaps her own, sense of necessity about staying together. She notes that she was prepared to adapt to his situation and work conditions and would even have left Europe with him when it looked as though he would be located in Armenia-Persia. She would have been able to adapt because she lacked ambition, goal orientation, or any sense of what she required or needed. She then quickly turns that lack into a privilege, of sorts, by explaining that particular goals were unnecessary, since she firmly believed that whatever she took up, if she went about it right, would lead to the center. Again, as if aware of a slight contradiction, Salomé adds that she acted out of a certain secret resignation, a sense that she had nothing more to lose, that the days of deliberation and choice about what she wanted and with whom she wanted to spend her time were over, replaced by her embeddedness in responsibilities she could never escape. At this point she emphasizes the importance of her work and the independence she found there.

After what she characterizes as months of pain-filled togetherness and sporadic separations, she became involved with the socialist journalist Georg Ledebour. In this period she learned that she could not continue the relationship with Andreas in the same form. Despite the misunderstandings between Ledebour and herself about the nature of their relationship, Salomé makes it quite clear that the event itself produced a "new perspective" for her. "Externally," she wrote, "nothing changed, but internally, everything" (210). And in the years that followed, she continues, there were many many trips.

At the end of this section of her account, Salomé suggests somewhat cryptically that the struggles and strains that worked against sexuality in her marriage may have contributed to the great stillness and self-evidence of love when it finally met her. Pfeiffer's footnote assures us that this observation refers to her love for Rilke, but Salomé is not so explicit. Anticipating her readers' desire for a more clear-cut explanation of her marriage and her sex life, Salomé reminds us that she has merely tried to express something of what lies behind the terms in which we ordinarily judge and explain such things. These hints at the unexplainable reflect her ultimate attempt to locate this relationship beyond good or bad, and beyond causal explanations. "We know so little about the whole secret of love because of our limitation to the purely personal—because our grasp extends only along that line. The whole play of what is all too human about us and what is a passionately directed superhumanness gets entangled with our judgments and valuations of something that no human heart has ever really submitted to reason" (211–12).

Her marriage had nothing of the expected or conventional about it, according to Salomé, no sexual relationship, no shared work, and no confrontation of the one by the other with their perceived knowledge of each other. They shared a love of the animal world, a sense of immersion in it, and Salomé tells us that she learned and adopted a simplicity in dress, food, and habits from Andreas, together with a sense of the physical and its relation to the intellectual. After the violence and desperation that marked the beginning of their relationship, they settled into a side-by-side that had the quality of a kind of ground for both of them, a togetherness that allowed them to share in each other's joy and to develop a keen knowledge of each other from a distance. "Ultimately," she tentatively suggests, "he might have been right all along in his certainty that we belonged together" (216), but in fact—and she apologizes for her uncertainty— she remains unsure whether he was right or not.

Salomé explains her resistance to Andreas through her experience of Gillot. She reemphasizes her fear of losing herself to her own "feminine" capacity for submission and loss of self and to his desire to make her in his own image. Salomé's early fiction and the essays she wrote between 1899 and 1910 focus on the danger sexuality posed for women, whose desire for self-assertion and knowledge was as strong as their desire to lose themselves in love. Salomé shared a critique of conventional conceptions of marriage and a commitment to experimentation with her unconventional contemporaries. Like many of her friends and acquaintances, she formulated her views on sexual relations, friendship, and marriage in the language of post-Darwinian biology, suggesting that psychic life lagged behind biological differentiation, so that human beings continued to seek unicellular fusion despite its impossibility. For men in particular, "woman" continued to operate as the instance and object of that desire. The question for Salomé's fictional women was how to avoid being reduced to male fantasy, how to resist their own desire to submit until submission no longer meant the total subordination of self to another, or to convention. In fiction and in her essays, Salomé plays with the possibility for women of episodic sexual passion, the possibility that sexual love might constitute but one, even provisional facet of women's lives, rather than their entire essence. In her own life, Salomé organized enormous mobility for herself, combining her home in Göttingen with Andreas, where she lived and worked for several months of every year, with her extensive travels in Europe and Russia, her friendships, her cultural, intellectual, and even sexual liaisons with writers and thinkers in Munich, Berlin, Paris, Vienna, and St. Petersburg.

At least two biographers have suggested that Salomé's "sexual problems" can be traced to unresolved incest fantasies and fears, and they explain her "narcissism" as a displaced incestuous and fundamentally oedipal desire. Of course, it is also possible that she dealt with the effects of actual incest. It is not my purpose here to "diagnose" Salomé: I want to explore the discursive structures that inform her self-representations. Her efforts to expose the fundamental eroticism at the core of the structure of knowledge and pedagogy and, at the same time, to avoid the reduction of all psychic and intellectual life to sex produced "incest" as an at least constant conceptual suggestion, and Salomé uses the figure of incest to explore intersubjective relations in her fiction. Her efforts to conceive an elaboration, rather than repression, of desire were part of her attempts to imagine ever finer differentiations that allowed for the highest intellectual development without "falling out of love." That fantasy, given the hierarchical relations that structured the social world in which she loved, required constant vigilance. Ultimately, she comes under the auspices and protection of an assumed, removed father, who protects her autonomy from empirical men. In this effort to locate the paternal function in a symbolic, as opposed to empirical, realm and to redefine that function in terms of the father's yes, Salomé intended to open up the possibility of a feminine subject based in affirmation, rather than renunciation.

Her memoirs situate her life in the center of what have come to be read as the typical problems, questions, and crises of modernity. From her first chapter, which deals with her loss of God, through her discussion of psychoanalysis, she repeats the range of bourgeois-antibourgeois responses to the situation of the intellectual and the artist in Wilhelminian Germany. She moves from a childhood refuge in fantasy and myth, from Russia, that symbol of the not yet fully conscious, through the philosophical idealism and rationalism of Hendrik Gillot, the positivism and accompanying pessimism of Paul Rée, the antimetaphysical "metaphysics of the self" she saw in Nietzsche, the pragmatism of the Berlin circle that surrounded her in the 1880s, the naturalism of Berlin, Munich, and Paris in the 1890s, the revolts of Wedekind and the bohemian circles of Vienna and Munich at the turn of the century, the aestheticist retreats of Rilke, to Freud, who offered her a conceptual "home" for her own ideas and work, a conceptual home that did not reduce the double directionality of desire at the expense of what she called "woman."

2.

Salomé, Rée, and Nietzsche

Like other conventions at the end of the nineteenth century, friendship became an increasingly unstable category by virtue of its supposed exclusion of what was assumed to saturate male-female interaction, namely, sexuality.[1] Salomé and her post-Darwinian contemporaries participated in the destabilization of boundaries as they assumed a fundamental undifferentiation underlying all human intercourse, all human difference. For Salomé, friendship and intellectual community with men were vital to her escape from the constraints of family and the insularity of the couple; they were crucial to the separation of sexuality from marriage. Above all, however, Salomé stressed the separation of woman's agency and desire from its containment in "sexuality."

In this chapter I focus on Salomé's negotiation and representation of her intellectual and personal relationships with Paul Rée and Friedrich Nietzsche.[2] Salomé had a plan, revealed to her in a dream,

---

[1] For a provocative discussion of the implications of Darwinian thought for conceptions of sexual difference, see Lawrence Birken, *Consuming Desire: Sexual Science and the Emergence of a Culture of Abundance, 1871–1914* (Ithaca: Cornell University Press, 1988). For a feminist formulation of the effects of the increasing "saturation of woman with sex" in the nineteenth century, see Denise Riley, *"Am I That Name?" Feminism and the Category of "Women" in History* (Minneapolis: University of Minnesota Press, 1988).

[2] For a recent attempt to substantiate claims that both Nietzsche and Rée were homosexuals, see Joachim Köhler, *Zarathustras Geheimnis: Friedrich Nietzsche und seine verschlüsselte Botschaft* (Nördlingen: Greno, 1989). Köhler bases his argument almost exclusively on circumstantial evidence, and his interpretations are at times too facile. Nevertheless, his work does help create the conditions that enable us to consider not

to live and work with like-minded male intellectuals. Initially, her plan involved only herself and her new friend, the positivist philosopher Paul Rée, but soon it also included Friedrich Nietzsche, Rée's longtime friend. It is difficult to think about the relationships among these three as mere friendship, if friendship is defined as the exclusion of sexual desire and marriage, for sexual desire, the rhetoric of romantic love, and marriage proposals intrude onto this scene despite attempts of Nietzsche apologists to deny, diminish, or contain them by attributing all such intrusions to Salomé, to woman, to her sex.[3]

It is not surprising that so much ink has been spilled in the effort to prove that it was Salomé who desired and seduced Nietzsche; that it was she who gained more from the relationship, both intellectually and personally; that she was, in effect, his product, "Nietzsche's wayward disciple," in the words of Rudolph Binion. Nietzsche is restored to the position of Master, saved from the contamination of his own desires, and rendered over and over as a victim of either Salomé or his sister, Elisabeth Förster-Nietzsche, or both.[4] All the efforts to banish sexuality and love from the scene

---

only homosexuality but plural sexualities. Though I am not particularly interested in documenting the "homosexuality" of any of the figures involved, I am interested in opening discussion to more than the one heterosexual possibility.

[3] In his study of Nietzsche's encounter with Salomé, in *Chance and the Text of Experience: Freud, Nietzsche, and Shakespeare's Hamlet* (Ithaca: Cornell University Press, 1986), William Beatty Warner offers a sophisticated reading of just such intrusions and the efforts of both Nietzsche and his guardians to contain them.

[4] For a discussion of the earliest accounts of the relationship between Salomé and Nietzsche, see Erich Podach, *Friedrich Nietzsche und Lou Salomé: Ihre Begegnung, 1882* (Zurich: Max Niehans, 1937). Podach considers two alternative accounts in the early literature, one of which blames Salomé and the other Elisabeth. Podach is interested in the structural similarity of the two accounts, both of which seek to save Nietzsche, to restore him to the position of a "victim turned wise man and judge." See also C. A. Bernoulli, *Franz Overbeck und Friedrich Nietzsche*, 2 vols. (Jena: Diederichs, 1908); Henry Walter Brann, *Nietzsche und die Frauen* (Leipzig: Felix Meiner, 1931); Karl Schlechta, *Der Fall Nietzsche: Aufsätze und Vorträge*, 2d ed. (Munich: Carl Hanser, 1959). Among more recent Nietzsche scholars, Walter Kaufmann presents a notable example of only apparent fair-mindedness in his efforts to diminish Salomé and her place in Nietzsche's life in *Nietzsche: Philosopher, Psychologist, Antichrist* (Princeton: Princeton University Press, 1974). Kaufmann relies on Binion's reduction of the complexities to the simple "truth" that it was Salomé who had the greater investment in the relationship with Nietzsche, that it was she who benefited more intellectually, that it was the relationship with Nietzsche and her exploitation of it that made her famous, that it was Nietzsche who ended the relationship and she who suffered

bypass what is most interesting about the conceptual and intersubjective negotiations among these three late nineteenth-century figures, namely, their common interest in the evolution of the intellectual out of the physical origins of life, their interest in the implications of the now-blurred boundaries between the physical and the intellectual or spiritual, their anticipation of what would come to be called "the new woman" and new relations between the sexes, conceived in terms of differentiation rather than absolute difference. One of the most interesting aspects of their comings-together and their misunderstandings lies in the metaphoric conflation of intellectual and sexual seduction. It is this conflation that accounts for the tenuous status of intellectual life, which, in Salomé's case, is suspected again and again of being a mere pretext for more essential underlying sexual designs. Salomé's contemporaries accused her of sexually motivated designs and opportunism whenever rules of propriety and decorum were violated, and critics continue to repeat these charges. She herself would make this reduction of intellectual passion to sexuality an epistemological preoccupation.

Salomé has provoked the ire of more than one commentator and biographer for subordinating her relationship with Nietzsche to her friendship with Paul Rée in the chapter of her memoirs titled "The Experience of Friendship." Most of Salomé's own biographers have succumbed to the pressures of Nietzsche's monumentalization by organizing her life around her relationships to Nietzsche, Rilke, and Freud. But as Salomé wrote to Gillot in the spring of 1882, after she had decided to live with Rée and his friend Nietzsche, whom she had not met, Rée was the one person who was important to her personally.[5] Her representations of her connection to Nietzsche consistently imply that her interest in Nietzsche was profoundly intel-

---

more from its ending. Subsequent Salomé biographers have treated the "affair" much more evenhandedly, but only Ursula Welsch and Michaela Wiesner, in *Lou Andreas-Salomé: Vom "Lebensurgrund" zur Psychoanalyse* (Munich: Verlag Internationale Psychoanalyse, 1988), succeed in granting that personal relationship as little space as Salomé herself granted it in her memoirs. For a recent critique by a Nietzsche scholar of the limits of all moralistic accounts of the Nietzsche-Salomé relationship, see Mazzino Montinari, "Zu Nietzsches Begegnung mit Lou Andreas-Salomé," in *Lou Andreas-Salomé*, ed. Rilke Gesellschaft (Karlsruhe: Von Loeper, 1986), pp. 15–22.

[5] In her biography, *Lou Andreas-Salomé: Leben, Persönlichkeit, Werk* (Frankfurt am Main: Insel, 1986), Cordula Koepcke gives a detailed account of Salomé's relationship with Rée and their importance to each other.

lectual and spiritual and never involved the kinds of intimacy she established with Rée. Her relationship with Rée, with whom she lived for four years in Berlin and whose loss she grieved throughout her life, was the one that fulfilled her dream of a passionless intimacy with a male intellectual, surrounded by books, flowers, and friends.[6]

The relationship between Nietzsche and Salomé, about which so much has been written, was actually a brief and limited acquaintance. Here, I have no wish to produce the definitive historical account, but I do want to explore the interpretive possibilities in the accounts that have survived. Salomé and Nietzsche met in Rome in April 1882, and she and Rée enlisted him for their plan to live and study together in a holy trinity, or in what Nietzsche would call their Pythagorean friendship. The three spent a few days in one another's company in Rome before Salomé and her mother left for northern Italy. Nietzsche and Rée later rejoined the Salomés there, and after Nietzsche's side trip to Basel to visit friends, they met again in Lucerne. Finally, against all odds, Salomé persuaded her mother to allow her to stay in Germany at the Rées' estate in Stibbe, rather than return to St. Petersburg. She spent the first part of the summer with Rée's family there, then left for the opening of *Parsifal* in Bayreuth; from there she traveled to Tautenburg, where in August she spent three weeks with Nietzsche, chaperoned by his sister. Rée, Salomé, and Nietzsche met again in October in Leipzig, where they spent several weeks together, but they parted ways in November without having made firm plans to rejoin each other for the winter, and they were never to see each other again.

Nietzsche and Salomé were introduced to each other in Rome by their friends the post-48er and idealist Malwida von Meysenbug and Paul Rée. They were also prepared by their friends for what they then experienced as a profound intellectual and spiritual convergence, a convergence that they both, but Nietzsche in particular, formulated in the rhetorical terms of romantic love.[7] From the be-

---

[6] For Salomé's account of this dream and its significance, see her *Lebensrückblick: Grundriß einiger Lebenserinnerungen*, ed. Ernst Pfeiffer (Frankfurt am Main: Insel, 1968).

[7] In his reading of Nietzsche's relationship with Salomé (*Chance and the Text of Experience*), Warner attends to this very rhetoric and contests the efforts of Nietzsche apologists to deny or suppress Nietzsche's emotional investment in his relationship with Salomé. Though Warner's emphasis on the love that intervenes in Nietzsche's

ginning, the question of friendship involved a marking out of boundaries from within what was taken to be a marriage of minds and
souls, a union of two fundamentally religious natures, as Salomé
put it, or free spirits in the most extreme sense. Salomé's and
Nietzsche's attitudes, both conscious and unconscious, to that presumed unity would diverge, however. For her, at both the personal
and intellectual levels, mediation would be essential, but Nietzsche's
project, as she saw it, was the denial of just such mediation, both
intersubjectively and epistemologically. Hence, for her, the friendship failed, and intellectual collaboration became impossible.

When Nietzsche and Salomé met in Rome in 1882, he was thirty-
eight, Rée was thirty-two, and she was twenty-one. Salomé had
arrived that winter in the company of her mother after giving up
her studies in Zurich because of failing health. Her health problems,
which began during her studies with Gillot in St. Petersburg,
seemed, at one level, to confirm the popular nineteenth-century
antifeminist view that study and the development of the mind damaged women's physical and mental well-being and, on another level,
to elevate her, in Nietzsche's eyes, for example, to the lofty heights
of "an almost" masculine heroism in the pursuit of knowledge and
truth. On the recommendation of Gottfried Kinkel, Salomé and her
mother sought out the progressive idealist and Wagnerian von Meysenbug, whose popular *Memoiren einer Idealistin* (Memoirs of an idealist) Salomé had read and greatly admired. Meysenbug found an
idealist outlet for her feminism in her efforts to provide an environment in which young women might benefit from the intellectual
stimulation of noble male minds without the suspicion of contamination by sexuality. The exclusion of suspicion demanded constraints on male-female social intercourse which Salomé was to
transgress immediately upon meeting Paul Rée.

Rée burst into Meysenbug's salon unexpectedly one April evening, in need of money, claiming to have lost heavily at Monte Carlo.
According to Joachim Köhler, he had actually just spent over two
months in Genoa with Nietzsche, who had given up his professor-

---

will to live out his ethos of aesthetic affirmation allows for a suggestive reading of
the shifts in Nietzsche's theory of will after 1882, it also tends to consolidate an
exclusively heterosexual and psychologically insular reading of their historical and
rhetorical encounters.

ship in Basel and gone to Italy in the hope that his poor health might improve in the more benign climate. Köhler suggests that Nietzsche had also gone there to participate in the Platonesque all-male communities in Italy. Rée and Nietzsche had been close friends (and perhaps lovers, according to Köhler) since 1873, when they met in Basel where Rée was working on his dissertation and attending Nietzsche's lectures. Nietzsche had published *The Birth of Tragedy* just a year earlier, a work still under the influence of Wagner and Schopenhauer. Rée's thought combined the pessimism of a Schopenhauer and the skeptical positivism of the French materialists. His collection of aphorisms, *Psychologische Beobachtungen* (Psychological observations), was published in 1875 and met with Nietzsche's enthusiasm and approval. They became friends and spent much time together, including the winter of 1876–1877 in Sorrent, where they had been invited by Nietzsche's friend, Malwida von Meysenbug.

Meysenbug described Rée over and over as a kind of son, for whom she felt a great sense of protectiveness despite her strong aversion to his way of thinking. Her account, like others, characterized Rée as suffering from extreme forms of Jewish self-hatred, which have often been taken to be the basis for his generosity, tenderness, and sensitivity toward others.[8] Most of these accounts consider Rée's supposed self-hatred a purely psychological problem and make no mention of the growing anti-Semitism in German culture, but the Rée-Nietzsche-Salomé friendship felt the virulence of that anti-Semitism in the person of Elisabeth Förster-Nietzsche, wife of the popular anti-Semite Bernhard Förster, with whom she lived for years in his Aryan colony in Paraguay. Elisabeth Förster-Nietzsche did her best to present Salomé, incorrectly, as Jewish and to make her Jewishness part of the case she built against her in trying to have her deported to Russia. Förster-Nietzsche's diatribes against Rée also had anti-Semitism at their base. It is no surprise that contemporaries who viewed themselves as guardians and heirs of Nietzsche and who dwelled in the same anti-Semitic milieu con-

---

[8] Cordula Koepcke provides the most lucid account of this particular analysis of Rée in her biography of Salomé. Joachim Köhler, *Zarathustras Geheimnis*, suggests that Rée's self-hatred involved both internalized homophobia and anti-Semitism.

sistently downplayed Rée's influence on Nietzsche and were infuriated when Salomé accorded Rée a significant place in the development of Nietzsche's thought.

Salomé felt an immediate affinity with Rée. She persuaded him to meander with her on moonlit nights between midnight and two o'clock through the streets and the coliseum of Rome in defiance of what was supposed to be a straight line from Meysenbug's salon to her mother's hotel. Meysenbug was scandalized when Rée, supposedly in love but feeling guilty, finally reported the walks to her. Meysenbug believed it to be crucial that women who aspired to the cultural ideal of intellectual companionship with men avoid any hint of flirtation or romance. To Salomé, however, Meysenbug's sense of propriety seemed to allow for a mere extension, but no real defiance, of conventional relations between the sexes and conventional divisions between private and public worlds. She had developed her own critique of Meysenbug's brand of idealism and held to her own already-emerging conception of radical individualism. Before she either met or read Nietzsche, she replied to a letter from Gillot, who had written at her mother's urging to set his young disciple straight:

> Malwida is also opposed to our plan, and I am truly sorry about that. I am enormously fond of her. But it has been clear to me for a long time that we mean something very different even when we appear to agree. She has the habit of formulating things in terms of "we"—"we" mustn't do this or that, "we" ought to do this—and I have no idea who this "we" really is—probably some ideal or philosophical party—but I myself know only of an "I." I can neither live according to models, nor will I ever serve as a model for anyone else, but I will structure my life in accordance with my self, no matter what the consequences. And in that I am not advocating any principle, rather something much more wonderful—something that is buried deep within one, hot with life, which seethes, and wants out.[9]

Salomé formulates her resistance to both Meysenbug and Gillot in the discursive terms she will share with Nietzsche, a commitment to "life," to eternal transition, to the disavowal of principles and

[9] My translation of part of Salomé's letter to Gillot from Rome, March 1882. The entire letter in the German original is reproduced in *Lebensrückblick*, pp. 77–79.

causes, a willingness to take risks and the courage to live from the depths of oneself, as opposed to convention or superficial ego needs. These formulations also point to the instabilities built into the plans for the threesome. Salomé's radical individualism is formulated in terms that (con)fuse life, inner self, and sexuality, making the setting of boundaries a matter of choice and negotiation, not convention or principle. Her general resistance to Meysenbug's principles and causes included at least partial resistance to the older woman's feminism. In a letter to Alois Biedermann written shortly after her arrival in Rome, Salomé writes:

> I think that we still have to, and should, overcome a lot of prejudices against it [women's emancipation], but such an extreme advance may do less good than it does harm by giving the upper hand to false distortions. No one is less opposed than I to the emancipation of women, when it comes to their intellectual education, but I think that the most important thing, that one should put everywhere in the foreground, and that is forgotten in the heat of battle, is *this*, that we are still and always above all women.[10]

Salomé certainly shared the anxiety of many of her antifeminist contemporaries that women's emancipation would make women into men, even as she refused to accept Meysenbug's constraints on what it meant to be the women "we still and always above all" are. In the reply to Gillot, Salomé reports that Meysenbug viewed her attempt to win Rée over to her plans during their midnight meanderings through Rome as a scandalous seduction. Rée too, she says, despite her efforts and to her dismay, did the conventional thing: he fell in love with her and asked her mother for permission to marry her. After a time, Salomé reconciled Rée to her refusal, just barely in time for the arrival of Nietzsche, to whom Meysenbug had written of Salomé's brilliance and "her preparation for his way of thinking." In a letter dated March 27, 1882, for example, Meysenbug had told him that this "very unusual girl seems to me to have arrived in her philosophical thought at about the same results as you have to this point, i.e., to a practical idealism, leaving aside all metaphysical presuppositions and concerns about the explanation of

---

[10] Quoted in Koepcke, *Lou Andreas-Salomé*, pp. 57–58.

metaphysical problems. Rée and I are in agreement in our wish to see you together with this unusual being."[11]

So in the spring of 1882, Nietzsche entered the scene. A number of Nietzsche scholars have emphasized the significance of that spring in Nietzsche's life, and his perhaps consequent readiness for the encounter with Salomé. Having given up his professorship in Basel, he was isolated from any possible students, disciples, or heirs. The public had not yet begun to read or to celebrate his work. Nietzsche had just completed *The Gay Science*, the last work in what Salomé (and others after her) called his positivist phase, during which Rée had been particularly important to him. In his important study of the mutual interventions of life and writing, William Beatty Warner has given us a subtle and suggestive reading of Nietzsche's readiness for what Warner calls his "Lou experience." Warner's careful readings of *The Gay Science* and *Thus Spake Zarathustra*, as well as the documents that survived the events of 1882, lead him to suggest that "in writing the fourth book of *The Gay Science* in the first weeks of 1882, Nietzsche has developed an ethos of aesthetic affirmation, and made the decision (wearing the mask of Zarathustra) to 'go down among men.' These compositional acts create the space within which Lou Salomé can be met, experienced, and loved (as a contingent happening, a 'dear chance')."[12] Warner then reads the episode that unfolds in the space that was "invented for Salomé by the text of *The Gay Science*" not as a simple application of philosophy to life experience but "as what comes between *The Gay Science* and *Zarathustra*; not as a bridge, but as a fissure, a violent displacing, a challenge, a mockery and a joke." He goes on:

> By narrating these events, and reading the words and acts and philosophic texts of this period of Nietzsche's life in relation to one another, we will be able to do a critical articulation of the relationships of several pairs of terms which are not parallel in themselves, but which the contingent events of Nietzsche's life in 1882 make parallel: philosophy and love; writing and life; mind and body; man and woman; Nietzsche and Frau Lou. A sequential narrative of this epoch of Nietzsche's life will give us access to what is contingent, uncontrollable, and decisive in the

[11] Quoted ibid., pp. 71–72.
[12] Warner, *Chance and the Text of Experience*, p. 34.

encounter between the first and second of each pair. *The Gay Science* stages this encounter with a strong prejudice toward happy anticipation, aesthetic symmetry, and a philosophic commitment to affirm whatever comes of this encounter; the experiences of the year, as they unfold around the axis of the passion for Lou Salomé, test, confound, and displace the philosophic postulates of *The Gay Science*; and *Zarathustra* fulfills, short-circuits, and sometimes even reverses the themes and positions of *The Gay Science*, as they are refracted and realigned around a quite new and much more conflictual concept of the will operating within interpretation.[13]

Though Salomé's own accounts and analyses anticipate Warner's focus on the particular ways in which Nietzsche's "ethos of affirmation" involved the occulting of "the other," she, in contrast to Warner, laments, rather than celebrates, the turn Nietzsche takes in his work after 1882.

Before they ever met, then, Salomé figured for Nietzsche and for Meysenbug as the realization of his plans to end his isolation and to find not only intellectual companionship but practical help as well. "From what star have we fallen to each other?" were his first words to Salomé when they met in St. Peter's in Rome. According to Salomé's account, and to a number of others, Nietzsche was so taken with her that he had Rée propose to her for him soon after his arrival in Rome. Prior to his arrival in Rome, on March 21, 1882, Nietzsche had written to Rée: "Greet the Russian girl for me, if that makes any sense: I am greedy for souls of that species. In fact, in view of what I mean to do in the next ten years, I need them! Matrimony is quite another story. I could consent at most to a two-year marriage, and then only in view of what I mean to do these next ten years."[14]

---

[13] Ibid., pp. 122–23.

[14] Warner quotes Binion's translation, ibid., p. 172. For the German original, see *Friedrich Nietzsche, Paul Rée, Lou von Salomé: Die Dokumente ihrer Begegnung*, ed. Ernst Pfeiffer (Frankfurt am Main: Insel, 1970), pp. 99–100. In Karl Schlechta's edition, *Der Fall Nietzsche*, the (in)famous letter of March 21 reads as follows: "Grüssen Sie diese Russin von mir wenn dies irgend einen Sinn hat: Ich bin nach dieser Gattung von Seelen Lüstern. Ja ich gehe nächstens auf Raub darnach aus—in Anbetracht dessen was ich in den nächsten 10 Jahren thun will brauche ich sie. Ein ganz anderes Capitel ist die Ehe—ich könnte mich höchstens zu einer zweijährigen Ehe verstehen und auch dies nur in Anbetracht dessen was ich in den nächsten 10 Jahren zu thun habe." In *My Sister, My Spouse* (New York: Norton, 1962), H. F. Peters translates: "Greet this young Russian from me if you think it does any good. I am greedy for her kind of souls. In the near future I am going to rape one. Marriage is a different matter

The possibility of marriage, then, actually preceded Nietzsche's introduction to Salomé. As a number of commentators have suggested, it is very possible that Nietzsche automatically assumed that only marriage would enable the plans for an intellectual threesome, indeed, that marriage was the only proper response to the plans, given the scandal that their living arrangement would otherwise cause.

Both Rée and Nietzsche at least nominally accepted Salomé's refusals of their marriage proposals and contented themselves with the plan for close intellectual friendship. Nietzsche apologists have long claimed that his proposal, if there was one at all, was based on his sense of propriety and his perception of the young Salomé's wishes. On this view, a marriage proposal was the proper response to Salomé's desires. Her resistance to this as to other conventional conclusions was articulated in the same letter to Gillot already quoted. In his letter, Gillot had insisted that he intended Salomé's passionate pursuit of self-becoming to be a mere transition on the way to a presumably conventional end. Salomé replied:

> Just what do you mean by "transition"? If some new ends for which one must surrender that which is most glorious on earth and hardest won, namely, freedom, then may I stay stuck in transition forever, for *that* I will not give up. Surely no one could be happier than I am now, for the gay fresh holy war likely about to break out does not frighten me: quite the contrary, let it break. We shall see whether the so-called "inviolable

altogether. At the most, I could agree to a two-year marriage, and even that only because of what I have to do in the next ten years." Rudolph Binion, on the other hand, in *Frau Lou: Nietzsche's Wayward Disciple* (Princeton: Princeton University Press, 1968), translates: "What pleasures your letters give me! They draw me in every which way—and to you in the end, come what may. . . . Greet the Russian girl for me, if that makes any sense: I am greedy for souls of that species. In fact, in view of what I mean to do these next ten years, I need them! Matrimony is quite another story. I could consent at most to a two-year marriage, and then only in view of what I mean to do these next ten years." None of the translations is perfect, of course. At issue is the question of Nietzsche's fantasies about and his investments in Salomé before and immediately after he meets her. Those critics who stress Nietzsche's *Wirklichkeitsfremdheit* (Podach, Brann, Peters) use this letter as evidence of Nietzsche's unrealistic fantasies and demands. Others, Nietzsche apologists above all, read it as an indication that Nietzsche simply assumed that social convention required marriage if he or Rée were to work closely with Salomé. Only Köhler suggests that Nietzsche and Rée would have perceived a marriage to Salomé as a protection from the rumors (circulating in Bayreuth, for example) of their "perversion." By including the first portion of the letter, Binion avoids the complete heterosexualization that other translations imply.

bounds" drawn by the world do not just about all prove to be innocuous chalk-lines.[15]

After a brief time in Rome, Salomé and her mother traveled north to the Italian lakes, where Nietzsche and Rée soon joined them. Nietzsche and Salomé escaped their two chaperones and spent a now infamous afternoon alone on Monte Sacro which left them both with the impression of great intellectual, philosophical, and spiritual affinity—and left Rée, who had stayed behind with Salomé's mother, disgruntled. Nietzsche, who had initiated Salomé into the secret of the eternal return, would later thank her for "the most charming dream of my life." And Salomé, when asked at the age of seventy whether she had kissed Nietzsche on Monte Sacro, replied that she couldn't remember.

Nietzsche traveled on alone to visit his friends Ida and Franz Overbeck in Basel, where he sang the praises of the "young Russian," whom he later described to Peter Gast as "as shrewd as an eagle and as courageous as a lion, and ultimately still a very girllike child," a "young, truly heroic soul" in whom he wished to have a disciple and heiress.[16] Salomé had come to Nietzsche, as she came to any number of others, already figured as something both exotically other and absolutely the same, his auto-reflection. The constant designation of Salomé as the "young Russian" suggests the degree to which she was cast and cast herself in the romanticized and stereotyped role of the Russian, characterized by great depth of soul, by a certain "primitivism," by what George Kline lists as "passion, eloquence, powerful commitment to a cause, and 'maximalism' or 'extremism' in cultural and intellectual matters"—the very same cluster of national characteristics that Kline says Fedorov invoked when he later called Nietzsche "a Russian among the West Europeans."[17]

Shortly after the afternoon on Monte Sacro, Nietzsche, Salomé, and Rée met in Lucerne. There, in the Löwengarten, Nietzsche either proposed anew or explained away the first proposal. Salomé's account emphasizes the relief they felt when they had cleared the air.

---

[15] *Chance*, p. 162. For the German original, see Pfeiffer, *Dokumente*, p. 103.
[16] Pfeiffer, *Dokumente*, pp. 159–60.
[17] Quoted in George Kline's Foreword to *Nietzsche in Russia*, ed. Bernice Glatzer Rosenthal (Princeton: Princeton University Press, 1986), p. xi.

In Lucerne, Nietzsche orchestrated the infamous photograph of the threesome taken by Jules Bonnet, which depicts the two men pulling a small cart driven by Salomé, who is half perched on the seat of the cart with a whip in her hand. The photograph clearly played with the then-scandalous suggestion that this young woman controlled two rivalrous suitors, one twelve and the other seventeen years her senior. It became a true scandal when, some say, Salomé showed it around at the premiere of *Parsifal* in Bayreuth in July.

It took all of Salomé's skill and finesse to persuade her mother to return to Russia without her in June 1882, leaving her in the care of Rée's family in Stibbe and in close proximity to her brother Eugène, who had come to Germany to study medicine. Salomé spent the first part of the summer on the Rée estate, where she and Rée consolidated their unusual friendship, and then traveled to Bayreuth in July to join Meysenbug and Wagner's inner circle. The intimacy between Salomé and Rée is evident in the language they used to talk about the relationship and in the names and nicknames they assigned one another. In dialect Rée describes himself as her *Husung*, "her house, her shelter," and her as his *Schneckli*, his "little snail." The conception of a freedom from within a secure and protective relationship occurs over and over in Salomé's characterization of both an ideal and a set of realities in her life. And the figure of the snail occurs at other points as well, in her 1899 essay in which "woman" is likened to the wandering snail who carries her home around with her on her own back rather than be confined to home as the cult of domesticity demanded. Rée also referred to himself and Salomé to him as her brother, pointing to her preferred conception of her relationships to men as sibling relationships, as what she characterized over and over as two kneeling side by side before a higher purpose or ideal. Salomé represented herself to herself as either daughter to a removed father or as a sibling, though not explicitly a "sister," to men. These are the terms in which she managed to figure herself as "woman" without succumbing to the position of wife or mother.

In her biography of Salomé, Cordula Koepcke offers the most succinct and convincing account of what Salomé and Rée meant to each other when she, too, emphasizes the importance to Salomé of Rée's "shelter" and the significance to him of her faith in and genuine

Lou Salomé, Paul Rée, and Friedrich Nietzsche, 1882. Photograph by Jules Bonnet affection for him.[18] What she emphasizes less is that Salomé's friendship with Rée offered not only the security from which she could go out into the world but also an escape from her family and from generalized familial demands. However painful the effort to "invent new values and new social forms" might have been to Rée, whom most commentators assume to have been in love with Salomé, they managed to make their unconventional connection work for four years in ways that were irreducible to middle-class moral and social conventions and also to the anticonventionality of the bohemian circles in Berlin, the city in which they lived for those four years. Again, Salomé cannot have been oblivious to the discussions among young Russians of a revolution in the relations between the sexes, of new forms of marriage. At this time, Salomé's efforts to live different social forms were, at least at the conscious level, in the service of her intellectual life. Sexuality figured for her, as for many other women of that period in Germany, as the potential nemesis, even if it also figured for her as the ultimate ground of such pursuits.

In July, Salomé left Stibbe and Rée, for whom she kept a diary of her subsequent experiences. She met Nietzsche's sister, who was to accompany her to the Tautenburg Forest, where Salomé and Nietzsche planned to spend several weeks after the opening of *Parsifal* in Bayreuth. In Bayreuth and immediately after in Jena, Förster-Nietzsche's hostility toward Salomé emerged in full force. She felt that Salomé was humiliating her hero-brother by consorting with his enemies in Bayreuth, participating in their degradation of him by spreading rumors of his designs on her. Salomé offended Förster-Nietzsche's sense of propriety by attending séances in which she was the only woman present and by commiting such "indiscretions" as having the designer-painter Paul von Joukovsky design a dress on her body. When Salomé apparently unveiled the Lucerne photograph in Bayreuth, Förster-Nietzsche took it as proof that Salomé was blatantly misrepresenting her brother's character and intentions.

Certainly, Nietzsche would have considered any friendly contact with Wagner's inner circle to be potential, if not actual, disloyalty to him, for he and Wagner had repudiated each other. Nietzsche's

---

[18] Koepcke, *Lou Andreas-Salomé*, p. 87.

sister had been part of the Wagner circle since 1876, the year in which she met her future husband, the "blond, colossal, patriotic, mercilessly anti-Semitic [Bernhard] Förster with his grandiose plans for the rebirth of the German spirit," as Klaus Goch describes him. "Elisabeth proved to be impressed with this 'idealistic man,' whose propaganda activities (against an intellectual, destructive professoriat and for a vegetarian, natural lifestyle, against Jewish infiltration and for an Aryan Christianity) had caused such a sensation in the German Reich." Goch reports that in 1880 she had joined Förster's campaign to collect signatures on a petition to the emperor which demanded "protection from Jewish contamination, an end to the immigration of Eastern Jews, control of the Jewish influence on the press, banks, and stock exchange."[19]

In Jena, where Salomé and Elisabeth Nietzsche waited out bad weather before moving on to Tautenburg, the two women came to figurative blows. Salomé left no account of what actually happened there and never publicly either confirmed or refuted Elisabeth Förster-Nietzsche's version, the only one that survives. Förster-Nietzsche describes the conflict in a letter to her friend Clara Gelzer. "I want to explain to you," she wrote,

> that Fritz got acquainted with this Russian woman in Rome in response to her passionate wish. Now I want to acknowledge her intellectual talents right off, but you know the main thing is that she is really, I cannot deny it, my brother's philosophy personified: this raving egoism that mows down everything that gets in its way and this total lack of morality. . . . But when I met Lou Salomé I saw immediately, although I liked her at the time, that the plans to live together were totally absurd, even assuming that the girl had completely pure sensibilities, but her living habits were so different from ours. Fritz is after all painfully and completely conscientious and tends toward the ascetic.[20]

Salomé, Förster-Nietzsche continued, had suddenly given vent to a diatribe against her brother, calling him a "madman who doesn't

[19] Klaus Goch, "Elisabeth Förster-Nietzsche: Ein biographisches Portrait," in *Schwestern berühmter Männer: Zwölf Portraits,* ed. Luise F. Pusch (Frankfurt am Main: Insel, 1985), pp. 375, 377.
[20] Pfeiffer, *Dokumente,* p. 252.

know what he wants," who intended to exploit her intellectual talent, and who, like all men, was really mainly interested in sex. Förster-Nietzsche closed the letter with an expression of horror at Salomé's total lack of morality and at her brother's philosophy, of which Salomé becomes the clear personification.

As Warner maintains, whatever Salomé said about Nietzsche's designs and intentions, or her own, offended not only Förster-Nietzsche's sense of decency but also her idealized image of her brother and her relationship to him. She soon made Salomé's supposed outbursts a scandal of "truly European dimensions" as she took up the task of protecting her brother's reputation and reasserting her own control. In the short term, her interference would create an irreparable rift between her and her brother after the breakup of the threesome. Eventually, however, his illness and institutionalization would put her in control of his image.[21] As Warner suggests, the text of Förster-Nietzsche's letter depicts more than a struggle over interpretations of Nietzsche. In effect, Nietzsche "also simply offers the occasion for each woman to assert the kind of person she intends to be."

In the battle, Lou Salomé makes use of the shock value of direct disclosure, so as to unmask the social properties Elisabeth Nietzsche so values. Without the counterpressure of Elisabeth's sense of virtue, much of what Salomé says here might have gone unsaid. Elisabeth counters with all the force of outraged modesty; her censored and delayed disclosures will help make this scene of Salomé's anger into a scandal. . . .

Salomé's tirade brings to the fore what is contradictory and symptomatic about the whole living scheme, and subsists as a problem in her relationship with Nietzsche. When the plan for a trinity is formed, sex is quite explicitly left to one side. To conceive the "holy trinity" is for Salomé and Nietzsche and Rée a critique of the way marriage turns relations between men and women into a crude material and sexual transaction. It is also an assertion of faith in a particular ideal: that men and women can know each other in and through a shared intellectual quest. This idealism is implicit in Salomé's judgment of Nietzsche for

---

[21] For Förster-Nietzsche's accounts of Nietzsche's encounter with Salomé, see her biography, *Das Leben Friedrich Nietzsches* (Leipzig: Kröner, 1904). Her accounts would play a dominant role in shaping the views of the Nietzsche-Salomé relationship.

"soiling" the study plan with "low designs." But the "trinity" is also flirting with becoming a *ménage à trois*—and a rather kinky one at that.[22]

Of course, this was not simply a clash between the kinds of people that two different women "intended to be"; it was a conflict between contending constructions of gender, sexuality, family, race, and nation. When Förster-Nietzsche went after Rée and Salomé, it was not only because she felt they had denigrated and rejected her brother, or her, but because she perceived them as incarnations of larger threats to bourgeois respectability and Germanness. As Russian and Jewish, they represented political radicalism, contamination, impurity, and danger.

Förster-Nietzsche's disapproval was not the only problem with the relationship. Apparently, during the months they were making plans to live and study together, Salomé also worried about Nietzsche's strong desire to have her as follower and heir, and perhaps wife. Surviving letters from Nietzsche to Salomé contain revealing responses to her obvious reservations about what he had in mind. A letter of June 26, 1882, provides one such example:

> If we fit each other, then our health will fit each other too, and there will be a secret gain in that. I have up till now *never* imagined that you should "read aloud and write for me"; but I very much want to be permitted to be your *teacher*. Finally, to tell the whole truth: I am now looking for people who could be my heirs; I am carrying something around with me that certainly cannot be found in my books—and I'm looking for the most beautiful, fruitful, and arable land for it.
> Look at my *selfishness!*
> When I think now and then of the dangers of your life, of your health; my soul is completely filled every time with tenderness; I don't know of anything that could bring me close to you as quickly.[23]

The suggestion that illness could bring them closer contrasts sharply with Salomé's later assertion that her pursuit of both literal and figurative health and fresh air made it impossible for her to stay with Nietzsche. Ultimately, not only the apparently banished sex-

---

[22] Warner, *Chance*, pp. 171–72. I take issue with Warner's characterization of the tendency toward the ménage à trois as particularly "kinky."

[23] Pfeiffer, *Dokumente*, p. 152.

uality but also, as Warner concludes, "social law," in the form of Förster-Nietzsche's outrage, intruded to expose the instabilities built into this radical individualism and "practical idealism."[24]

Despite the tensions that emerged full-blown in Jena, Salomé and Nietzsche were able to patch up their differences for their three-week stay in Tautenburg in August 1882, and both remained committed to the plans to live and work together. In Tautenburg the two talked and studied from morning to night, interacting with an intensity that by many accounts, including Nietzsche's own, gave birth to his *Zarathustra* and gave her work direction and force. Nietzsche spoke with greater confidence of their intellectual and psychic similarities. He wrote to his friends in terms that sustained, even enhanced, what Warner has characterized as the rhetoric of coincidence and the typology of love. To his composer-friend Peter Gast, for example, after comparing Salomé to an eagle and a lion, Nietzsche wrote: "I am indebted to Frl. Meysenbug and Rée for her. . . . She is most remarkably prepared for my way of thinking and my ideas. . . . Dear friend, you will surely do us both the honor of keeping the idea of a love affair from our relationship. We are *friends*, and I shall keep this girl and this trust in me sacrosanct."[25]

Yet even when their relationship was at its most intense, when Salomé was most enthralled by their similarities, she also began to record their differences. Her writing mediated the relationship, exposing how her view of it differed from Nietzsche's and maintaining her distance from him. In the journal-letter to Rée she engaged in continuous analysis of his thought, his psyche, and their relations. At Tautenburg in August she wrote: "In the quiet, dark pine forest alone with the sunshine and squirrels. . . . conversing with Nietzsche is uncommonly lovely. . . . There is quite special charm in the meeting of like thoughts and like emotions; we can almost communicate with half words. . . . Only because we are so kindred could he take the difference between us, or what seemed to him such, so violently and painfully."[26] The same entry continues with a comparison between her friendship with Rée, the apparent addressee, and her

---

[24] Warner, *Chance*, p. 168.
[25] Pfeiffer, *Dokumente*, p. 159.
[26] Warner, *Chance*, pp. 178–79. For the German original, see Pfeiffer, *Dokumente*, pp. 181–82.

friendship with Nietzsche. Precisely because of their fundamental differences, she and Rée are able to experience and to take pleasure in the points where they connect. A general dissimilarity, even contrast, between two people can, according to Salomé, produce both sympathy and antipathy. But isolated differences in a relationship that is based on underlying unity are experienced as "interrupted and broken sympathy and are always embarrassing."

Salomé believed their great similarity was based in what she called their fundamentally religious natures. In an entry from August 18, discussing the coincidences of their natures, Salomé mentions her early conviction that Nietzsche was deeply religious. She goes on to explain the relationship between religious character and the ethos of the free spirit, or *Freigeisterei:*

> The characteristically religious aspect of our characters is what we share; it has perhaps burst forth so strongly in us because we are free spirits in the most extreme sense. In the free spirit, religious feeling can no longer refer to anything godlike or to any heaven outside itself, to anything in which the forces that create religion, such as weakness, fear, and greed, might find some advantage. In the free spirit, the religious need engendered by religions—the nobler remnants of particular forms of belief—can be thrown back on itself, as it were, and become the heroic strength of our being, it can become the impetus for submission to a great goal.
>
> There is a heroic bent to Nietzsche's character, and this is the essential thing about him, which gives all his features and drives their form and unity. We will live to see the day that he steps forward as the prophet of a new religion, and it will be of a kind that engages heroes as its disciples.[27]

After claiming the religious character for both of them, Salomé attributes the heroic character to Nietzsche alone. Indeed, it was precisely this heroic bent that she would come to see as a significant distinction between them. The same diary entry ends with an assertion of her difference from Nietzsche and suggests that they diverge at a profound level. It is conceivable, she writes, that they could one day be enemies. The basis for their identification and attraction seemed to her to lie in those aspects of their thought and

[27] Pfeiffer, *Dokumente,* p. 184.

their experience which were hostile to reality and to the reality in each other.

In other entries, Salomé focuses on the differences between Rée and Nietzsche and among the three of them. She saw herself as standing between two philosophical and psychological extremes, between what she considered to be Rée's arid rationalism, and Nietzsche's romantic mystifications, between Rée's refreshing detachment of self from his work and Nietzsche's genial but suffocating confusion of self and idea. Salomé quite concertedly worked out her own philosophical positions and psychic dynamics in her fascination with and analysis of theirs.

> Nietzsche relates to his intellectual goals as the believer relates to his God and the metaphysician to his metaphysical ontology; he puts his mind and the force of his character in their service. What is still at stake for him in all this is recognizing himself as he would *like to be* in the eyes of his intellectual god, and for that reason he is not nearly as honest with himself as you are. . . . Like Nietzsche, you have put the force of your character in the service of knowledge, but whereas this service has a religious tenor for him and does not therefore exclude an ultimate self-appreciation, you relate to yourself purely intellectually, indifferently, i.e., as a mere object of knowledge.[28]

Salomé goes on to suggest that it would be very difficult for someone with as rich an emotional life as Nietzsche's to observe him / herself purely as an object of knowledge, and she ends by reemphasizing her fascination with Nietzsche: "As I said, such an emotional life is opulent plunder, philosophical plunder, above all for the psychologist who cannot feel and experience deeply or widely enough to achieve an All-Understanding. I would like to have been in the skin of every human being."[29]

The subtle identification of herself as psychologist, perhaps as his psychologist, at the end of this passage prefigures the approach she will take to Nietzsche's work in her book, completed some ten years later. It is this assumption of the position of analyst / interpreter which Nietzsche guardians have considered the ultimate presumption. Salomé maintained a sense of distance from Nietzsche "in

[28] Ibid., p. 186.
[29] Ibid., p. 187.

reality," a reality represented by the positivist Rée, with whom she had what she described as a passionless friendship. In her relationship with Nietzsche, she encounters once again the conflict between passion and self-development in the world.

Their childhood experiences of the loss of God became paradigmatic for Salomé not only of the similarities between them but also of the differences, the specific ways in which religious feeling affected their approaches to themselves, to knowledge, and to reality. For Nietzsche, she says, "because of his disposition, his intellectual goal took on what I would call a Christian-religious character, in that he grasped for it as a kind of self-salvation from a painful state, from which he needed to be freed." Her own reaction was different. "My completely similar intellectual goal took hold of me in a complete state of happiness: it is this difference that is most apparent between us, and can be seen in all of our developmental struggles."[30] According to the accounts they constructed together, Nietzsche threw religion overboard when he ceased feeling anything for it, and he longed for a new goal or object to fulfill him in this moment of complacency and emptiness. Her realization that God did not exist caused emotional trauma when her reason challenged what she clung to emotionally. But according to their accounts, Salomé never lost the sense of emotional security that her early belief had created, whereas for Nietzsche, pain and suffering became the spur for each new developmental phase, and he experienced this pain passively, as if each new ideal were something external, something he was forced to endure. As Binion suggests, "she would struggle painfully toward her one (unspecified) goal felt to be an innermost necessity."[31]

Only a short time later Salomé would pinpoint their differences as the tragic in Nietzsche, his ultimate inability to live without God, despite his own pronouncements on the death of God. Instead, he created surrogate gods when he subordinated himself to goals, and eventually to ideas, that only seemed to lie outside of him. What he perceived as external and coercive goals were actually warring oppositions within himself. What for her were only various forms

[30] Ibid., p. 188.
[31] Binion, *Frau Lou*, p. 83.

or manifestations of self-expression were forms of self-immolation for Nietzsche, who misread the transferential character of his idealizations. Salomé states the differences between them even more explicitly at the end of a diary entry from August 21:

> And while I consider what Nietzsche said of me to be entirely accurate: "that for a being as *concentrated* in itself as I am, one that develops in accordance with its own natural necessity, we would have to think of an ultimate goal as one that externalizes itself in activity..." and that he imagines his own goals as something to be endured.
>
> I find the explanation for Nietzsche's conception of the heroic in these two points, first, that, for the reasons given above, his goals appear to him to have been thought outside him, to have a separate existence, and to have to be suffered by him and, second, that the submission to those goals takes the form of self-immolation.[32]

Salomé continues by emphasizing the heroism involved in "the creative power for which even the hardest and most unyielding material is not too hard or too unyielding because it is nonetheless superior to it, still capable of carving its god-images out of it." She concludes by returning to a "we" to suggest that "for us free thinkers who no longer hold anything sacred, anything that we could worship as 'great' in a religious or moral sense, there is nevertheless still greatness that moves us to wonder and to veneration."[33] She then reminds Rée that she had sensed such greatness in Nietzsche almost from the beginning. She combines respect and appreciation for his greatness with the assertion of their differences and with regret over the direction his work has taken.

The distance Salomé established between herself and Nietzsche reflects the conflicts she identified as intrinsic to feminine psychology and, therefore, also the difference between masculine and feminine responses to modernity. These converged with distinctions between "man" and "woman" which she would later work out more explicitly. While in Tautenburg, Salomé began work on an essay on "woman," of which only Nietzsche's comments and suggested outline remain. The short piece was to emphasize the significance and implications for women of both men's and women's belief in female

[32] Pfeiffer, *Dokumente*, p. 189.
[33] Ibid., p. 190.

weakness. "To feel weakness—that is for woman not only to feel a lack of strength but, more important, to feel a need for strength."[34] Woman's need for strength and power is satisfied by projecting strength onto everything outside herself, with the consequence (so Nietzsche) that she believes in her own weakness. Woman is consequently trapped in a world of illusion and dependence. The piece was to end by suggesting that woman, or perhaps femininity, was essential to the emergence of religion. According to Rudolph Binion, who has found evidence of disagreement in Nietzsche's and Salomé's interpretations of these theses, "only when Lou called woman's very frailty woman's greatness because of its religious signification did Nietzsche dissent."[35] If, as Binion suggests, Salomé saw woman's greatness in her capacity for self-subordination, she also saw the dangers of her projection of strength onto something or someone outside herself. The point in the Tautenburg essay would not have been to reduce femininity to weakness and illusion but to lament the tendency to live through the other, a tendency that has its source in distortions of woman's positive capacity to give herself, to submit, to desire.

The aphorisms Salomé wrote under Nietzsche's tutelage in Tautenburg and after her visit there show once again the similarities in their interests and perspectives. Nietzsche is said to have been enthusiastic about Salomé's aphorisms; she, far less so. The following examples demonstrate her preoccupation with the psychology of religion, its relation to love and eros, her self-stylization as a free thinker and free spirit, and the critique of marriage and sexual relations she shared with Nietzsche.

The poorest person is the one who never had an illusion to destroy.

The drive for knowledge is not the drive for truth.

A great, life-fulfilling, shared interest is perhaps the only thing that ensures a lasting attraction, because personalities, even the rich ones, exhaust themselves.

---

[34] Ibid., p. 215. Both Binion and Koepcke document Nietzsche's interest in having Salomé write an essay on femininity. Nietzsche's outline for such an essay, as Nietzsche would have it, can be found in Pfeiffer, *Dokumente*, p. 215.

[35] Binion, *Frau Lou*, p. 82.

People must love one another, as the Christians said, "in God."

There is no path from physical passion to a fundamental intellectual sympathy, but certainly from the latter to the former.

Keeping friendship between the sexes pure requires either a little physical antipathy or a great spiritual-intellectual understanding.

To be religious means that one's happiness requires great feelings.

Greatness lies not the direction but in the force.
The power of evil is the criminal's greatness.

There is nothing wrong with being godless, if one is really rid of God.

The idea of having to expose prejudices can also become a prejudice.

Metaphysics fills our gaps in knowledge with gods; it is the deification of a lack of understanding. Religion is the deification of the lack of power.[36]

These aphorisms, written in and after her stay in Tautenburg, and edited by Nietzsche during their visit in Leipzig in October, were the only ones she ever wrote.

When Salomé left Tautenburg, the plans to live together were apparently still intact, and the three friends intended to meet again in October, when she and Rée would join Nietzsche in Leipzig. By the time they made their rendezvous, relations were strained. They spent the month reading, discussing, and enjoying Leipzig. Salomé showed Nietzsche an early draft of her sketch of him which met with his approval, and Nietzsche continued to coach her on style, correcting and rewriting her aphorisms. But the plans for the winter were never consolidated, and Salomé and Rée left for Berlin, where they would live together for the next four years. Nietzsche left for Italy, never to see his two friends again.

It is not at all clear what happened in Leipzig or after to end the plans for the winter. Some evidence supports the view that Nietzsche gave up on the plan, having realized in Leipzig that he would always be an outsider to the intimacy between Rée and Salomé. Other evidence suggests that Salomé and Rée aborted the

---

[36] See Pfeiffer, Dokumente, pp. 190–213. See also Angela Livingstone's translations of selected aphorisms, Lou Andreas-Salomé: Her Life and Work (Mount Kisco, N.Y.: Moyer Bell, 1984), pp. 48–50.

plans by simply neglecting to consolidate them, in part because Nietzsche's attempts to diminish Rée led Salomé to the conviction that the "trinity" could not work. Few commentators have suggested that Salomé resisted what she considered to be Nietzsche's pathology. Yet evidence in Nietzsche's letters to Salomé and in her later study of Nietzsche indicates that they shared at least the question of his sanity. Because her study of Nietzsche's "pathology" was the basis of efforts by Nietzsche guardians to malign and discredit her, her supportive biographers have been understandably reluctant to suggest that she simply found him intolerably self-absorbed and emotionally tortured.

Whatever the reasons for the break or on whose initiative, Nietzsche's hurt was the most obvious, revealed in letters and drafts of letters to Salomé, to Rée, and to Rée's family written throughout the winter and spring of 1882–1883. Nietzsche spent the following year in pain and rage, encouraged by his sister to believe that his friends had betrayed and humiliated him. His drafts and letters manifest a fury so primitive as to suggest that much more was shattered for him than friendship or intellectual exchange. Although none of Salomé's letters to Nietzsche survive, Nietzsche apologists have been satisfied to assume from Nietzsche's letters that she offered what Nietzsche considered to be only "schoolgirlish defenses" of herself and her choices, rather than genuine apologies, explanations, or even regrets that she was, as Nietzsche maintained, settling for pleasure instead of heroic greatness. Nietzsche's diatribes include the ironic accusation that Salomé had failed to live up to what he perceived to be her potential:

> I have never fooled myself about a person: and in you there is that drive toward a holy self-seeking that involves the impulse toward obedience to what is highest. You have apparently confused it, through some kind of curse, with its opposite, the self-seeking and the pleasure in exploitation of a cat that wants nothing other than life. Accept that the cat's egoism, with its inability to love anything anymore, its life-feeling in nothingness, to which you now commit yourself, is exactly what I find most disgusting in people: worse than anything evil: of all things, to conceive knowledge as simply one pleasure among other pleasures.[37]

[37] Quoted in Brann, *Nietzsche und die Frauen*, p. 154.

These are outraged responses to her difference from his image of her and anger at a real or perceived rejection. Nietzsche's charges against Salomé, here and elsewhere, of settling for pleasure rather than greatness, of failing to sacrifice herself to higher goals, precisely intersect with the differences between them that Salomé recorded in her diary and developed in her later work. She would come to identify the specificity of "the feminine" with "woman's" greater capacity for pleasure. In "Der Mensch als Weib" (The human being as woman), which I discuss in detail later, Salomé writes that "woman is the more hedonistic person." Man is more ascetic and self-sacrificing, renouncing himself in pursuit of goals that he perceives as external to himself. Whatever Salomé had become, or proven herself to be, in defiance of Nietzsche's conception of her, what seems to be at stake for him in these drafts and letters is control, not only over her but over what he had fantasized her, and himself, to be.

But Salomé was beyond the control and the safety of his idealized image, and no appeal to her potential for greatness could induce her to make the sacrifices he would have demanded of her. Again and again in accounts of Salomé's relations with men, "her problem" would be characterized as narcissism, evidenced by her supposed inability to love or to sacrifice, and all too evident in those criticisms would be what Salomé came to theorize as unacknowledged male narcissism. Even in later more positive memories and accounts of her, Nietzsche would betray his regret that she did not become what he saw in her, that she did not become his mirror. A letter to Ida Overbeck refers to Salomé as "a first-rate being about whom it is a shame forever. Given the energy of her will and the originality of her intellect, she was destined for something great. I miss her. . . . I have never found anyone as free of prejudice, as modest, and as prepared for my kind of problems." And in another letter, written early in 1883, he writes: "I had the best intentions of remaking her in the image I had formed of her." But perhaps the most revealing was the letter he wrote to Rée soon after the final meeting in Leipzig, in which he expressed his wish that he could erase the painful memory of the entire year, "not because it offends me but because it offends the Lou in me."[38] Salomé remained silent throughout the

[38] Pfeiffer, *Dokumente*, pp. 338, 326, 273.

months of accusation and turmoil, apparently protected by Rée, who kept much of what transpired secret. Even late in her life, even in response to Freud's suggestion that she set the record straight about the events of that year, Salomé refused to answer Förster-Nietzsche's defamations.

There has been a great deal of speculation about the break-up of the so-called trinity, but few serious analyses and few accounts that escape moralistic judgment. Though all three participants, with the possible exception of Rée, seem to have successfully overlooked or suppressed them, from the first they had obvious and not so obvious conflicts of interest. Despite idealistic hopes that the triangle would bring them closer, confused intentions and seemingly endless permutations of competitiveness and rivalry were built into the plan. As Warner has demonstrated most convincingly, both Salomé's and Nietzsche's denials of sexual or marital interests were couched in the language of intellectual, spiritual, and psychic convergence, in the language of romantic love. As noted, both formulated their dreams for a community of like-minded intellectuals in terms of seduction. Salomé defied the warnings of elders and friends and the moral outrage of her critics, but eventually she saw the impossibility of the rivalries she had had a part, however inadvertent, in setting up.

Conflicts over the relative openness of their unconventional plans and arrangements also introduced a significant source of tension from the outset. For Nietzsche as thinker, privacy, not public display, was crucial. Nietzsche was interested for a variety of complicated reasons in turning the relationship into his own aesthetic as well as personal experience, a testing ground for his ethos of aesthetic affirmation, developed in the just-completed *Gay Science*. Salomé, on the other hand, sought access to intellectual life and community and escape from familial control over her sexuality, thought, and life. It was important for her that the relationships she forged open onto the social, even establish for her both a network and a reputation. Hence, it was essential to resist the closed space of the couple, whether intellectual or matrimonial, and the secrecy Nietzsche would have preferred to impose on the plan for a passionless threesome. This Salomé-Nietzsche-Rée triangle was not the first and would not be the last time that a third term would help

Salomé avoid isolation in a couple, in which she was expected and may have desired to be the subordinate term. She displayed a photograph of Gillot in her living quarters with Rée, a picture of Rée on her dresser in Tautenburg. Later, she had Gillot preside over her marriage to Friedrich Carl Andreas; then she refused to consummate that marriage. She had her most satisfying sexual relationships with third parties, outside her marriage, but never left Andreas to marry any of her lovers.

At the same time, Salomé also mediated the personal, erotic, and intellectual tensions between Rée and Nietzsche; indeed, each of the members of the threesome helped to mediate the relationship of the other two. Salomé later remarked of friendship between men and women that only slightly homosexual men could see the human qualities in women and appreciate them. It is possible that the break occurred because of the ambiguities of Nietzsche's relationship with Rée, which left Salomé open to misunderstanding both men's desires and intentions.

Salomé and Rée lived their passionless intellectual friendship among philosophers, sociologists, and scientists for the next four years in Berlin. Then, when Salomé married Andreas, Rée left Berlin and Salomé never saw him again. She later wrote that she had had a true friend in Rée, both because of the lack of sexual attraction between them and because they were so far apart intellectually. Their distance had allowed them to appreciate their points of convergence and had allowed her to breathe.

Salomé continued to maintain that she was philosophically and psychologically much closer to Nietzsche than to Rée. Her book on Nietzsche, the first major study of his work, published in 1894, can be read as her negotiation of intellectual distance from within what she had taken to be a powerful convergence. Despite what she would continue throughout her life to call their fundamental similarity, their religious natures, their *Freigeisterei*, Salomé also continued to claim that to have followed Nietzsche in his totalizing critique of reason, his contempt for the *Mensch des Geistes* (Man of the Mind), and his appeal to unmediated instinctual life would have taken her back in the direction from which she had been moving, back into an exclusion from the social, into isolation and containment in desire. For Salomé, the loss of God and the recognition that desire could not be satisfied by any object or contained within any relationship freed women from their masochistic projections of their own desires, thoughts, and powers onto deified men. And it unmasked any man's fraudulent claims to satisfy and speak their desire. Acknowledging the impossibility of unity, of complementarity, of that romantic dream of heterosexual union was the key to "affirmation without dread." Thus the discourses of apocalypse and heroism which she saw in Nietzsche, particularly in his later work, had no appeal for her. Friendship required the distance he sought to remove, and thought required the mediations that his late work, in her view, defied.

In *Spurs: Nietzsche's Styles*, Jacques Derrida reads Nietzsche's figures of woman as questions of style, as radical elaborations of the untruth of truth, of its impossibility, as a challenge to the imposture of those who claim to know or who believe in the referent. On Derrida's reading, Nietzsche's texts figure woman as lie, as veiled truth, and as the affirmative displacement of that opposition. *Spurs* ends by suggesting of Nietzsche, "He was, he dreaded this castrating woman. He was, he loved this affirming woman. At once, simultaneously or successively, depending on the position of his body and the situation of his story, Nietzsche was all of these. Within himself, outside himself, Nietzsche dealt with so many women. Like in Basel where he held council."[39] Woman as deception, or the castrated woman, and woman as truth, the castrating woman, are displaced by the dionysiac, the affirmative woman, who refuses castration and exposes the blind spots of the metaphysical philosophical enterprise that Nietzsche's writing subverts.

Nietzsche's relation to Salomé, whom he figured as heroic and affirmative soul, was, of course, more than a question of style. For here Nietzsche could be said to have posed as the subject who knows, who knows even that it is impossible to know, to have posed as the teacher who desires to contain that figure of affirmation, woman, by denying her a place in a scheme or reality outside his own.

For Salomé, as we shall see, woman's passage into modernity was

---

[39] Jacques Derrida, *Spurs: Nietzsche's Styles*, trans. Barbara Harlow (Chicago: University of Chicago Press, 1978), p. 101.

different, less apocalyptic and heroic than it was for Nietzsche's man, without the radical break that many would see her and other modern women as representing. Salomé represents herself as the more perfect realization of her own and Nietzsche's conception of the affirmative, noble personality. As such, Angela Livingstone points out, Salomé figured woman as the enactment of, but also as a threat to, Nietzsche's philosophy:

It has been suggested that, in creating the Superman, Nietzsche was merely translating Lou into the masculine, since she had, simply and without any fuss, that "feeling of life amid the nothing" which was really the state he most longed for. Yet this would mean a consequence worse for Nietzsche than the failure to win over a brilliant and beloved female mind. It would mean that Lou's existence undid his very philosophy. If by mere fortune, by the generosity of nature, she could be it all—vital, self-creating, unconventional, happy; the *opposite* of the mediocre, unimpulsive type he loathed—and yet live as if there were nothing to "overcome," she would be an annihilating caricature: the Overman without the Overcoming![40]

[40] Livingstone, *Lou Andreas-Salomé*, pp. 57–58.

3.

Salomé as Nietzsche Analyst

Salomé considered Nietzsche's response to the crisis in post-Hegelian thought to be more original and promising than those of any of the utilitarian rationalists and positivists who surrounded them, most notably, of course, her friend Paul Rée. Later publications, such as her 1896 essay "Jesus der Jude" resonate with Nietzsche's virulent critique of the rationalists' attempts to suppress the implications of the "death of God" by substituting practical morality for the thornier problems of human subjectivity. Her critique of Wolfgang Kirchbach's "Book of Jesus" in "Aus der Geschichte Gottes" ("From the history of God") echoes Nietzsche's polemic against David Strauss in the first of his *Untimely Meditations;* her review of the history of interpretations of Jesus converges with Nietzsche's attacks on Christianity in the *Antichrist.*[1] Both attack the distortions, the flattening out, of the significance of the figure of the son of God. For Nietzsche and for Salomé, Jesus represents precisely that which cannot be adequately represented, namely, the unconscious roots of the construction of gods. In "Jesus der Jude," Salomé celebrates the courage and the naïveté in early Judaic confrontations with the absence of God, the failure in that tradition to explain away doubt with the postulate of an otherwordly afterlife. Salomé argued that Christian rationalizations had substituted practical morality for religious experience, for the primordial confrontation with the anx-

---

[1] See Lou Andreas-Salomé, "Aus der Geschichte Gottes," *Neue Deutsche Rundschau* 8 (1897): 1211–20.

iety of individual existence and the terror and intimation of a lost unity. In her later essays on the psychology of religion, Salomé suggests over and over that the methods employed by scholars of religion "leave off at precisely that point where the 'loot' becomes most interesting, where the secrets of the now highly individualized and concentrated religious feeling are most inaccessible to scientific scrutiny."[2] Salomé goes on to insist that religious affect can now be grasped only in personal life or in the finest psychological monograph, the kind of study she offers of Nietzsche and later of Rilke and Freud.

Salomé's *Friedrich Nietzsche in seinen Werken*, published in 1894,[3] expanded the sketch of "the man in his work" she had shown Nietzsche for his approval back in 1882 in Leipzig. It explores the imbrication of Nietzsche's psychic dynamics with his work. And that very structure, which, Anna Freud would remark years later, anticipated psychoanalysis, enraged Förster-Nietzsche, as well as other guardians of the Nietzsche archive, and has provoked not only Nietzsche scholars but at least one of Salomé's own biographers as well.[4]

Salomé set out quite explicitly to counter what she saw as misunderstandings and distortions of Nietzsche's work by his self-styled followers. At the beginning, she argues that "a genuine Nietzsche study" would have to concern itself with the psychology of religion, for Nietzsche was, she believed, a fundamentally religious personality, a religious genius confronted with the death of God. Nietzsche typified what "moves [our time] most fundamentally," the " 'anarchy in the instincts' of creative and religious powers, whose desire for fulfillment is too powerful for them to be satisfied with the crumbs that fall to them from the table of modern knowledge" (41). According to Salomé, "That they can neither be satisfied with what is left for them nor give up their relation to knowledge, that is the

---

[2] Lou Andreas-Salomé, "Jesus der Jude," *Neue Deutsche Rundschau* 7 (1896): 342–51.

[3] I use my own translations of Salomé's *Friedrich Nietzsche in seinen Werken* (Vienna: Carl Konegen, 1894), citing this edition in the text. For an alternative translation, see Salomé, *Nietzsche*, trans. Siegfried Mandel (Redding Ridge, Conn.: Black Swan Books, 1988).

[4] I refer, of course, to Rudolph Binion's reading of Salomé's book on Nietzsche in *Frau Lou: Nietzsche's Wayward Disciple* (Princeton: Princeton University Press, 1968).

great and moving feature in the picture of Nietzsche's philosophy" (41–42). It is completely obvious that Salomé writes from within an implicit presumption of convergence. She inhabits Nietzsche's own words by quoting him in such a way and to such a degree that it is often difficult to discern where his ideas leave off and hers begin. She sustains her view of their common interest in subjectivity and psychic life over against the various empiricisms that surrounded them. Nevertheless, writing is an act of separation and difference, and I am interested in how the differences emerge, how Salomé positions herself in relation to Nietzsche, and how "femininity" figures, both implicitly and explicitly, in her efforts to negotiate a relation to him.

According to Salomé, Nietzsche "recognized that in religious affect, we live out the immensity of our most individual demands and our will to the most intense possible self-bliss" (40). In a gesture that characterizes all her writing on the psychology of religion, she stresses that the "sublime egoism" that "radiates freely and naïvely from everything religious is the core of all religion" (40). In a "knowing" Nietzsche, and in Rilke, Salomé argues, that egoism circles back on the self as object with enormous gains in psychological knowledge but with tragic consequences for the individual. In both cases, increasing isolation and frustration follow from the failure or refusal to recognize and respect the importance of mediation through a "presumed exterior life force," presumed even in the face of the death of God.

Nietzsche typified modernity because his religiosity manifested itself in his desire for knowledge, but according to Salomé, and here we get an implicit attempt to differentiate herself from him, Nietzsche, because of the time in which he lived, was able to satisfy his religious longings "only by way of a turn back to the self, instead of toward an exterior life force that lay outside and encompassed him. And so he achieved exactly the opposite of what he sought: not a higher unity of his being but its innermost split, not the integration of all feelings and drives in a unified individual but their split into a 'dividuum' " (35). The consequent psychic dynamic of self-deification and its twin, self-immolation, was a problem from which "woman" was exempt because she never committed the "father's" murder, never forfeited the basis of knowledge in love as

man did. For Salomé, Nietzsche's isolation and his failure or unwillingness to act on the psychological necessity for external investments and idealizations were the key both to his suffering and
to his genius. Ultimately, she differentiates woman's capacity for
self-dissolution from what she saw as Nietzsche's self-elevation in
the very moment of self-immolation. Nietzsche achieved self-loss
only by way of a pathological, self-induced pain put in the service
of negation and transformation.

The book begins with a letter from Nietzsche to Salomé in place
of a preface. By virtue of its location in the text, this letter comments
on the epigraph on the title page, which is taken from Nietzsche's
Human, All-Too-Human: "A person may puff himself up as much as
he wants with his knowledge and fancy himself as ever so objective;
in the end, he comes away with nothing other than his own biography."[5] According to Ernst Pfeiffer, the letter that follows was probably sent to Salomé in September 1882 at the Rée estate in Stibbe.
It begins with this address: "My Dear Lou, Your idea of reducing
philosophical systems to the personal dossiers of their originators
is truly an idea that arises from a 'sibling brain.' In Basel I myself
explained the history of ancient philosophy in just *this* sense. The
system has been refuted, and is dead, but the person behind the
system is irrefutable and cannot be killed, Plato, for example" (v).

The juxtaposition of the letter to the epigraph establishes a particular convergence between them, figures her as his sister or brother
brain, his confidante, and if not the origin, then at least the affirmation and enactment of his ideas. As I suggested in the previous
chapter, the personal and intellectual relationship between
Nietzsche and Salomé presented Nietzsche with the conflict between
his conceptions of her as sister brain and as the location of his ideals.

In the second paragraph of the letter, Nietzsche reports that Professor Riedel has shown interest in his music, the music to which
he had put her "Prayer to Life." And he notes, "That could indeed
be one small path by which we would reach the afterworld *together*—
without precluding other paths." The third paragraph, positioned
as it is as an introduction to her book, underwrites the ensuing

---

[5] Friedrich Nietzsche, *Menschliches, Allzumenschliches,* in *Werke,* ed. Karl Schlechta,
4 vols. (Frankfurt am Main: Ullstein, 1969), 1: 697.

analysis: "As for your 'characterization' of me—as you put it—it is true, and so, I recall my little verses with the heading, 'Request' in *The Gay Science.* . . . Can you guess, my dear Lou, what I am requesting?" The little poem reads as follows:

> The minds of others I know well:
> But who *I* am, I cannot tell:
> My eye is much too close to me,
> I am not what I saw and see.
> It would be quite a benefit
> If only I could sometimes sit
> Farther away; but my foes are
> Too distant; close friends, still too far;
> Between my friends and me, the middle
> Would do. My wish? *You* guess my riddle.[6]

Whatever the solution to the riddle or wish, Salomé sits here between Nietzsche and his friends and foes as his sibling brain, his confidante, the site of his idealizations, and in this particular book his analyst.

Nietzsche ends his letter to Salomé by describing an afternoon in the Rosenthal listening to *Carmen* and reflecting "naïvely and devilishly about whether or not I had some predisposition for madness." "Finally," he continues, "I told myself *no.* Then the *Carmen* music began, and for half an hour I was overcome by tears and by the beating of my heart. But when you read this, you will in the end say *yes!* and make a note of it for your 'sketch' of me." This final paragraph anticipates Salomé's analysis of both Nietzsche's genius and his demise.

Salomé identified the period after their break in 1882 as his most complete turn inward toward the madness that follows. In that periodization Rudolph Binion sees at least a suggestion that his loss of her represents his failure to find himself by way of a relation to the world. None of these implications were lost on Förster-Nietzsche and her supporters, who accused Salomé of falsifying or exaggerating her privileged access to his innermost thoughts and feelings and the significance of their relationship to each other. Some of these

[6] Friedrich Nietzsche, *The Gay Science*, trans. Walter Kaufmann (New York: Random House, 1974), pp. 49, 50.

accusations, including Binion's, have been based on what some have judged as a deliberate attempt to fudge the brevity and the limits of their friendship by neglecting to date the letters, for example, by leaving the unsuspecting reader with the impression that their friendship spanned a much longer period of time than it actually did. Yet this book is no different from any number of her other works, which also lack a clear sense of temporality or history. I read her inclusion of his letters and of anecdotal accounts of his revelations to her as strategies of authorization and identification.

Salomé's view of Nietzsche's "madness" and his "predisposition" toward it was not based in the still-popular assumption of physiological predisposition or degeneracy. Nor does she reduce his thought to his biography as some have suggested. She shared Nietzsche's view that, in the words of Alexander Nehamas, "the goal of every philosophical view is to present a picture of the world and a conception of values which makes a certain type of person possible and which allows it to prosper and flourish."[7] Salomé did believe that Nietzsche's search for a nonmetaphysical basis for subjectivity led him into the depths of his own psyche, from which there was no return. Or to put it in other terms, Salomé was convinced that sanity required the mediations, despite the inevitable limits, of reason. But for her, his "madness" was inextricably bound up with his genial descent into the chaotic life of the drives. Anticipating the concerns of psychoanalysis, Salomé searched for what she could learn about subjectivity in general, about "normal processes," from a study of what was unique, genial, and pathological in Nietzsche's psyche and his work. Ultimately, Salomé based her resistance to his plunge into the abyss, to that threat of "falling out of the world," on a "feminine advantage." This structure of advantage and envy is implicit in her resistance, and I will return to a discussion of it at the end of this chapter.

Salomé located Nietzsche's originality in the interrelations between his rich inner life and his writing. In Nietzsche, according to Salomé, "external intellectual work and the inner picture of his life coincide completely" (4). Leaning on Nietzsche's own distinctions

---

[7] Alexander Nehamas, *Nietzsche: Life as Literature* (Cambridge: Harvard University Press, 1985), p. 128.

and on their shared ideas, Salomé emphasized his "fertilization," rather than his "invention" of ideas. Her critics, who continue to define creativity as literal, unparented originality, have accused Salomé of willfully diminishing his stature as a theorist. Yet Salomé enjoined her readers again and again to direct their attention away from Nietzsche the theorist, away from the abstract or theoretical frame of his writings, and toward the human being, the psyche at work in the writings. She argued that Nietzsche had taken an unfortunate turn when he tried to systematize his thought in his late work; she argued that his "fertilizations" of ideas and his imprint were always preferable to system building.

As she so often does in this book, Salomé relies on quotations from Nietzsche's own writings to support the view that his creativity was a kind of feminine geniality. "With regard to theory," she writes, "he frequently leans on unfamiliar models and masters, but at the point at which they achieve their maturity and productivity, they become the mere occasion for him to attain his own productivity. The slightest touch of his intellect sufficed to call forth a wealth of inner life, of thought-experience. He once said, 'There are two kinds of genius: one that, for the most part, begets and wants to beget, and another that is happy to be fertilized and give birth.' He belonged unquestionably to the latter. In Nietzsche's spiritual nature there was something—in heightened form—that was feminine" (43). In a footnote to this observation, Salomé tells us that at times, "when he was particularly conscious of this, he tended to consider feminine genius as the true genius" (43–44). The very concept of "thought-experience" expressed for Salomé the ultimate indivisibility of thought from emotional, even bodily, experience, an indivisibility that was most obvious in woman and in the creativity of feminine thinkers and artists.

In the brief biography of Nietzsche at the beginning of her study, Salomé presents what even her critics have called a sensitive and loving portrait, one that ultimately rests on both his own and her interpretations of his eyes, his hands, and his ears. The photographs included in the book were all taken during the last ten years of Nietzsche's life, the time, according to Salomé, "in which his physiognomy, his entire appearance was most characteristically marked by his deeply stirred inner life" (11). Salomé recalls her initial impressions of Nietzsche, when "this hidden element, the sense of a concealed solitude" made its impact through his appearance. He gave the impression, she writes, "of standing aside, of standing alone" (11). Nietzsche himself believed his hands and his ears revealed his inner life, and Salomé quotes from *Beyond Good and Evil* and from the preface to *Zarathustra* to stress the significance he attributed to them. But she thought his eyes, precisely because of the effects of his poor eyesight, revealed even more:

> Though half blind, they nevertheless had nothing of the peering, blinking, unwanted intrusiveness that so many nearsighted people have; they looked instead like the guardians and protectors of their own treasures, their own mute secrets, not to be touched by the unauthorized. His defective eyesight gave his features a very particular kind of magic because they mirrored only that which made an internal impression on him, instead of reflecting changing external impressions. These eyes looked into the inside and, at the same time, beyond the closest objects into the distance, or better: into the inside as into a distance. After all, ultimately, his entire research as a thinker was nothing other than an exploration of the human soul for undiscovered worlds, for "their yet unfinished possibilities" which he restlessly created and recreated. (12)

Nietzsche's face was no open book, certainly not for the unauthorized or uninvited. Nietzsche's eyes looked into their own interior as into a distance, and this gaze dissolved the split between inside and outside, probed into the human psyche as such by exploring his own. In this context, Salomé constructs herself as his interpreter, if not analyst, as one who is "authorized" but also perhaps as one who sees with Nietzsche's eyes. What we see of Nietzsche, she writes, are veils and masks and the joy he took in disguise. "In every period of his intellectual development, we find Nietzsche in some form or other of mask," but "the lonelier he became in his inner life, the more his outward bearing became mere appearance—a mere deceptive veil woven around the depths of his loneliness simply in order to become an intelligible surface for other people's eyes" (13). For Salomé, Nietzsche's masks or veils were related to his inner life not as falsehood is related to underlying truth but, rather, as the kinds of appearance which guarantee social intelligibility are related to the inexpressible depths of psychic life. "Nietzsche," she writes, "sank into a final loneliness with his last philosophical mysticism, in the stillness of which we can no longer follow him but are left with only his laughing thought-masks, with symbols and signs, and their interpretation" (15).

Having established the essence of Nietzsche's person and his characteristic thought-experiences, Salomé sketches and then interprets Nietzsche's "transformations" and, finally, his "system." Salomé was the first to divide Nietzsche's work into three distinct periods. His first transformation was his conversion away from Christianity, from a state of belief in which he felt completely at home. That transformation thus required the violent intervention of the self-induced demand to wander. She finds the seeds for what she calls Nietzsche's self-deification and self-immolation in this childhood experience of the loss of God, when he required a painful intervention in what had become the complacency of "home." Here again, we recall the distinction they established in Tautenberg between his and her experience of the loss of God. She experienced it as the painful intervention of reason in fantasy, without violation of her sense of security in the love of that idealized other. Fundamentally different was Nietzsche's need for the suffering that violently unsettled him in his health. To her own sense of security, Salomé juxtaposed Nietzsche's homelessness, attributing his need to "wander" to his dissatisfaction with and resentment of the solutions he found to the riddles that reason could not solve. Though she identified masochism in his need, she more often conceived it as the consequence of his religiosity, and the inner split and self-inflicted wounds that it necessitated. Salomé's "woman" remains at home not by virtue of immobility, but because she carries her home around with her. She combines what has come apart in man, namely, a sense of security and a freedom from metaphysical and conventional moorings.

The next transformation Salomé identifies took Nietzsche from a period of restrained philological work into his first philosophical phase with *The Birth of Tragedy*. That philosophical or so-called Schopenhauer-Wagner phase "provided him complete fulfillment of his deepest, almost feminine psychic need to adore, to look up to someone. However deep the happiness Nietzsche got from the Wagner-Schopenhauer philosophy, and its entire point of view, still the most valuable thing for him was his personal relation to Wagner, his unconditional admiration of him. His enthusiasm was kindled by a personality that stood outside of him, one in whom he believed the ideal of his own being was embodied" (76). Salomé emphasizes Nietzsche's desire for discipleship in what she calls a religious sense. Once he abandoned his masters, that desire required him to unite "disciple and master in himself" (80). She would figure her own self-becoming in terms of the feminine art of finding oneself by way of the adoration of something taken to be embodied and idealized in another, but Wagner and Nietzsche needed discipleship in a more traditionally religious sense, in a way that necessitated the split between master and disciple within the self, rather than a more harmonious integration. "Others have assessed Nietzsche's turn from Wagner as either a purely intellectual move or an exclusively human-emotional one" (81), according to Salomé. For her, the two are as intertwined at this moment as they were in Nietzsche's first conversion from Christianity.

In *Human, All-Too-Human*, according to Salomé, Nietzsche became the fledgling positivist; he completed another conversion and rejected Wagner and his own earlier convictions with the violence typical of the convert. Typically, she stresses, his inner change proceeded from a personal relationship, this time with Paul Rée—a relationship she characterizes as intellectual companionship rather than a discipleship. Letters from Nietzsche to Rée, quoted in the text, underscore how significant Rée's work and his companionship were for Nietzsche. The letters stress what Nietzsche learned from Rée, and how intensely he longed to be at his side. Salomé quotes from two letters written in 1879 in which Nietzsche's rhetoric of coincidence is directed to his friend Rée. In May Nietzsche wrote: "In my mind, I always tie my future to yours," and in October he suggested that he had "had to give up a lot of wishes, but never the wish to live together with you, my 'Epicurean garden!' " (100). By way of *rée*-alism, according to Salomé, Nietzsche took up philosophical realism and buried the old idealism. In fact, she suggests that Nietzsche overvalued Rée's first book, *Psychologische Beobachtungen* (Psychological observations), and took Rée's favorite authors—the French aphorists La Rochefoucauld, La Bruyère, Vauvenargues, Chamfort—as his own. Rée's second work, *Der Ur-*

sprung der Moralischen Empfindungen (The origin of moral sentiments), published in 1877, had even more influence on Nietzsche's
work during this period, leading him to the English positivists and
to the tools he needed to challenge the notion of altruism in Schopenhauer's and Wagner's ethics, to turn "his entire philosophizing
into an analysis and a history of human prejudices and errors" (103).
"The metaphysician," Salomé writes, "became psychologist and his-
torian and planted himself on the ground of a sober and consistent
positivism" (103). After her study of psychoanalysis and work with
Freud, Salomé wrote that she preferred this middle period in
Nietzsche's work because of his success in grounding his intellectual
passions in concrete and systematic observation.

Daybreak (1881) and *The Gay Science* (1882) were, for Salomé, the
most important works of Nietzsche's middle period, for in these
works "he succeeded practically in overcoming the exaggerated
intellectualism to which he had still subjected himself through
voluntary self-martyrdom in *Human, All-Too-Human* . . . without
loosening the rigor of the method with which he pursued problems"
(130). Nevertheless, Salomé suggests that Nietzsche's passionate
inwardness and his impatience with the limits of the empirical and
experiential began to break through in these works in their anticipation of new values.

Salomé organizes her discussion of the pivotal year 1882 by po-
sitioning herself, once again, as Nietzsche's confidante by mail. She
quotes from a letter written to her "a year after the publication of
Daybreak," in which he shared with her "his new philosophical hopes
and his future plans" (136). In an excerpt from a second letter,
Nietzsche identifies the ground they share as "the golden dawn on
the horizon of all my future life" (137). Salomé then suggests that
"when Nietzsche completed *The Gay Science* in 1882, he was already
certain about his India: he believed he had landed on the shore of
a strange and as yet nameless and monstrous world, of which nothing was known except that it must lie beyond everything that could
be challenged by thoughts, and destroyed by thoughts" (137). The
movement back and forth between a moment just prior to their
meeting and a set of moments after they had met, coupled with the
total silence about the personal events of 1882, both minimizes and
mythologizes her significance. She is both absent from the discussion

of direct influences on Nietzsche and yet always already there for his discovery, figured in the rhetoric of his letters and in their strategic insertion into the text not only as privy to his thoughts but, perhaps, as what he perceived to be the embodiment of "his India." In this way, femininity comes to figure as the location for the origins and the future of his hopes.

What Nietzsche imagined to be the shore of the new world was actually a return to his point of origin, according to Salomé, who argues that Nietzsche's late work "grew out of the old (metaphysical) soil" (153–54). By then, "his different philosophies are, for him, just so many god substitutes, meant to help him do without a mystical god-ideal outside of himself. His final teachings," she argued, "contain the acknowledgment that he was unable to do this" (147).

In her third chapter, "Nietzsche's System," Salomé works through what she takes to be the direction and basic tenets of Nietzsche's post–1882 turn toward a form of mysticism, in which the philosopher-creator becomes the inventor of values, rather than their discoverer. In her later work with Freud, she repeats this distinction between the discoverer and the inventor of truth and value when she explains not only her own preference for the discoverer, Freud, but the greater epistemological value of his work compared to that of the would-be inventor, Nietzsche.

Salomé opens "Nietzsche's System" with a fragment of a letter to her from Nietzsche, one of those he wrote after the break in October 1882.

Intellect? What is "intellect" to me? What is knowledge to me? I treasure nothing except *impulses*, and I would swear that that's what we have in common. Look straight *through* this phase I have lived through for the past years—look behind it! Do not deceive yourself about me. Surely you don't believe that "the free spirit" is my ideal?! I am—Forgive me! Dearest Lou—F.N. (153)

Inasmuch as Nietzsche writes explicitly against what he obviously assumed was her image of him and against what had united them, Salomé's strategic use of the letter here suggests that Nietzsche's "system" and his mysticism were their point of divergence. The reader who has any knowledge of the biographical significance of the year 1882 and the period between the publication of the *The Gay Science* and *Thus Spake Zarathustra* (which is how Salomé identifies the letter), brings an even more textured reading of the significance of that divergence to this section of Salomé's book.

Nietzsche's letter and its disavowals of knowledge in favor of impulse not only counter what he takes to be her assumptions but also suggest that she shares those impulses, that they remain united, regardless of her conscious apprehension of their differences. Nietzsche's demand that she look through and behind the phase through which he had just lived authorizes the very method she has employed, for she has read Nietzsche's "free spirit" phase as a sort of reversal of his earlier positions in the service of a peculiar return, with a twist, in his late work. In Salomé's words: "In Nietzsche's entire final philosophy, in the ethics and the aesthetics, we once again find the continuous theme that decline through excess is the condition required for a highest, new creation. And therefore, Nietzsche's theory of knowledge opens onto a kind of horrible personal mysticism, in which the concepts of madness and truth are inextricably linked" (170). This personal mysticism, this madness, this pleasure in excess threatened not only Nietzsche but Salomé as well.

Salomé lingers on the implications of Nietzsche's view of philosophy as a kind of atavism, quoting Nietzsche:

"In fact, it is far less a discovering than it is recognition and remembering again, a turn and return home to a distant and primeval, common household of the soul, out of which those concepts grew long ago. From that perspective, philosophizing is a kind of atavism of the highest order." Everything highest as a kind of atavism—therein lies the curious *reactionary* character of Nietzsche's entire final philosophy, which distinguishes it most sharply from his earlier periods. It is an attempt to replace metaphysical glorification of particular things and concepts with a glorification of their age and their origins in a very distant past. (184)

Not surprisingly, Salomé preferred Nietzsche's earlier conception of the untimely genius who showed the human being to be increasingly rational, despite the ultimate inseparability of human from animal. For Salomé, who will write of "woman" as the "regressive without a neurosis," Nietzsche's later conception of the untimely genius is disturbing because of its radical renunciation of reason and its celebration, in what she will see as a monistic sense, of the instinctual. Here again, it would be fair to note a resistance on the part of the interpreter Salomé to what she sees as Nietzsche's dismantling of the difference between the animal and the human, or between sex and intellect. She perceived that the stakes in such a total dissolution of boundaries would have been quite different for her as a woman from the stakes for Nietzsche.

It was not so much the erasure of the boundary between animal and human, however, as the relation between the decline of man and his apotheosis in the *Übermensch* which she lamented in Nietzsche's late work. His solution to the conflict between "needing God and having to disavow him" was what Salomé considered to be a profoundly religious, even mystical, opposition that Nietzsche set up in himself between man and overman, self and God. "He is the one as creation, the other as creator, the one as reality, the other as a mystically conceived superreality. 'The sacrificial animal as God' is truly a title that could stand over Nietzsche's entire last philosophy and illuminate most clearly the inner contradiction contained within it—that exalting of pain and bliss in which the two flow indistinguishably into each other" (147–48).

Salomé saw her response to Nietzsche's conception of the *Übermensch* and the eternal recurrence as a critique of his tendency to elevate aesthetics above all else, a critique that anticipates many later philosophical, political, even literary-critical responses to Nietzsche. Salomé sets out to demonstrate that there was no simple bridge, no dialectical movement for Nietzsche from man to *Übermensch*. The *Übermensch* emerged out of the decline of man through excess. In other words, the ideal was attained only through the sacrifice of the self and only in the realm of aesthetic illusion. In his critique of dialectics, Salomé could see only asceticism and self-inflicted pain. She reintroduces Nietzsche's revision of Schopenhauer to explain the antimetaphysical twist in his elevation of the aesthetic:

The mystical and ascetic significance of the aesthetic is no less important in Nietzsche's system than it was in Schopenhauer's; in both, it coincides with the deepest ethical and religious experience. And it is not accidental that Nietzsche relies on thoughts and images from *The Birth of Tragedy* in order to elucidate its importance. But in Schopenhauer, the aesthetic view was conceived as a mystical glimpse into the metaphysical background of things, into the essence of "the thing-in-itself," and to a certain extent, the solace provided by all spiritual life presupposes a casting off of everything earthly. In Nietzsche, however, where there is no metaphysical background, and where a substitute has to be *created* out of the midst of a superabundance of earthly life forces, the psychic presupposition is just the *opposite:* the beautiful should arouse the life of the will in its depths, it should release all powers, "should make them ardent and stimulate them to procreation," because it is not a question of the metaphysical revelation of some eternal beingness but of the mystical creation of something that does not exist. (216–17)

In this passage, Salomé emphasizes Nietzsche's insistence on imagining the creation of the beautiful out of an excess of "life forces," rather than viewing it as a product of their desexualized sublimation. The aesthetic emerges out of, and stimulates, the forces of will when Nietzsche dissolves the structure of surface and depth implicit in metaphysical approaches to the beautiful. On Salomé's reading, Nietzsche's conception of the creation of beauty out of its opposite necessarily involves a mysticism that sets the ideal over and beyond what exists. In their view of "the tragic," then, Schopenhauer and Nietzsche meet, according to Salomé, because "through the tragic both enter into the rapture of their mysticism" (217). Nietzsche's paradoxical thinking allows the decline of life and of the human to be "experienced as the bliss of an inexhaustible fullness of life from the standpoint of existence itself, or from the standpoint of one who identifies with it and who triumphs over himself by intensifying it in himself to the point of excess" (217–18). Salomé's later figuration of woman's participation in the fullness of life requires no such decline into excess since, once again, she has never completely forfeited the soil that Nietzsche's inventor seeks to regain by way of self-elevation and self-destruction. Here, too, Salomé's woman operates as a protection from the threat of falling out of the world, and from Nietzsche's genial but tragic descent.

In the "turnabout from pessimism to optimism," Nietzsche avoids the asceticism of a Schopenhauer or of Hindu philosophy; it is "not freedom from the coercion of the recurrence but a joyous conversion to it" (229) which he desires. At the center of this turn stands

Nietzsche's philosopher-creator Zarathustra. Salomé characterizes the relations between Nietzsche and Zarathustra in the following terms:

> Because this creation relied exclusively on [Nietzsche], it stood and fell with his own confidence—in and of itself, it did not exist at all. For that reason the doubts that tortured him must have been a thousandfold as soon as his mood sank even for a moment; his need to differentiate himself in his vacillating, doubting humanness from a self-confident, already-knowing being was relentless, to differentiate Nietzsche from Zarathustra. Even if the most horrible fate fell to him in his earthly given downfall, for Zarathustra it remained a sign of election and elevation; even if Nietzsche were to fall into the most horribly chaotic condition, to the point of animality, for Zarathustra it was just the expression of the All-Encompassing, which absorbed even the lowest and most profound. It is in this sense that we read in *Twilight of the Idols* that the philosopher of the highest order is a kind of combination of animal and god. (246–47)

Salomé then points to Nietzsche's "peak to a self-destructive deed," as she calls it: "Zarathustra's divine right to interpret life and to transvalue all values is achieved only at the cost of entering into that primal ground of life which expresses itself in Nietzsche's human existence as the dark depth of madness" (248). Here Salomé most explicitly differentiates herself from Nietzsche, not, as some have assumed, by suggesting that Nietzsche's decline came as the inevitable result of some inherent madness but rather by introducing a clearer resistance to his critique of rationality and his entry "into the primal ground of life." "The image of madness stands at the end of Nietzsche's philosophy," she writes, "like a shrill and terrible illustration for the execution of theoretical knowledge on which he bases his philosophy of the future because the point of departure produced the dissolution of everything intellectual through the dominance of the chaotic and drivelike" (251). Here Salomé suggests that Nietzsche could not have done otherwise, that his insights required his descent.

She draws different emotional and intellectual conclusions about the limits of knowledge and represents herself, in contrast to Nietzsche and other men of knowledge, as capable of accepting that limit, rather than suffer the self-ravaging that comes of an inability to "do without God." In the only passage in which she identifies herself with those outside Nietzsche's realm, she writes:

> For us, the outsiders, he was shrouded in total darkness from then on; he entered into a world of the most individual inner experience, in the face of which the thoughts that accompanied him came to a halt: a deep, disturbing silence spreads out over him for us. But it is not just that we cannot follow his mind any farther into the final transformation that he achieves by giving his entire self over to it; we shouldn't follow him: for therein lies the proof for him of the truth that has become completely one with all the secrets and concealments of his subjectivity. (252)

Salomé's analysis of Nietzsche's figurative and literal "decline" and "elevation" contains an explicit "ought not" in this passage, and the prohibition against following him shows once again her sense of the danger implicit in his total turn inward as well as her emphasis on Nietzsche's individuality and unique trajectory. She concludes by comparing Nietzsche's end with "the return of a tired child to its original religious home in which understanding was still not necessary for participation in the highest blessings and revelations. After the intellect has run full circle and has exhausted all possibilities, without finding satisfaction, it finally buys itself satisfaction with the highest sacrifice, the sacrifice of the self" (254). And here she cites Nietzsche's own formulations of a return to "Catholic belief" for the second time in the book: "When everything has been covered—where does one run to then? What? Would one not arrive again at belief? Perhaps at a Catholic belief? *In any case, the circle would still be more plausible than standing still*" (254).

Nietzsche's philosophy becomes absolute and reactionary when he returns to his disavowal of reason, against "his own and earlier individualism," a return in which his self-deification repeats a kind of religious absolutism. And this return, she suggests further, reflects a typical psychological dynamic:

> When the religious drive is forced by free thinking to live itself out in a strictly individual way and creates something godlike out of the self, then it claims for itself the most absolute and reactionary powers that were ever open to an objectively thought god—to the point at which it *deposes* reason itself and cuts off any further appeal, even though reason's drive to knowledge originally gave it its direction. (255)

This passage sustains some of the oppositions with which Salomé approaches Nietzsche, dissolution / individuality, drivelike chaos/intellectuality, decline into animality/idealization. Here Salomé resists the dissolution of self which she understands not as selflessness but as absolutism that takes its pleasure from an excessive investment in the self, paradoxically, from self-inflicted pain and self-deification. She resists what she sees as the decline of the individual in favor of a superindividual ideal.

For Salomé, Nietzsche's will to power, to be God, to parent himself, is associated with what she sees as his abandonment of the contingencies of the social and the materiality of the present. The inability to do without God is reflected for her in the question of influence and Nietzsche's ultimate denial of the influence of others. In his "moral for a builder of houses" in *The Wanderer and His Shadow*, Nietzsche suggests that "one should remove the scaffolding after the house is built" (quoted on 257–58). Salomé notes that this moral typified the new definition of independence in Nietzsche's late work. Nietzsche, says Salomé, was unjust to his former colleagues and teachers (Wagner, Schopenhauer, Rée) both in rejecting them when his thought turned in a new direction and in later attempting to claim that all his travels had simply led him back to himself, whence all his thoughts had emerged in the first place.

In a diary entry from 1911, Salomé recorded a retrospective account of Nietzsche's place in epistemological developments of their time, representing him as "a personal formula for the past thirty years of philosophical life: first, metaphysics, then empiricism, stocked full of an idealistic dedication and submission to truth for which only the metaphysical period could have prepared him and which was out of proportion to the empirical goals. A refinement of the scientific method of research, with a consequent narrowing of focus and of 'truth,' led, then, to what Salomé calls a practical or aesthetic need for more, to the reemergence of idealism, and with it the power of the drives, *Triebkraft*."[8] She characterizes *Human, All-Too-Human* and *The Gay Science* as the most successful expressions of Nietzsche's capacity to infuse precise analytic thought with life:

[8] From Pfeiffer's notes to Lou Andreas-Salomé, *Friedrich Nietzsche in seinen Werken* (Frankfurt am Main: Insel, 1983), pp. 358–59.

"This is what Nietzsche brought to the most beautiful and remarkable expression—these instinctual reactions, which were grasped as ideals within a thinking that remained cool and exact. For my taste, those remain his most beautiful and important works, those in which he was tamed by a scientific theory that, in fact, did not appeal to him."[9]

The next epistemological period, which she associates with Freud, is the development that Nietzsche could not make, the one that claimed "even the life drive as intellectual drive," that reinstated a consistent and fluid dualism, that theorized the coimplication of the rational and the irrational, of "life drives" and intellectual drives. She characterizes Nietzsche's ultimate turn to mysticism and the overman as theoretically and philosophically flat. In an almanac excerpt written on May 6, 1926, edited and published by Ernst Pfeiffer as a second addendum to the 1983 edition of *Friedrich Nietzsche*, Salomé explicitly compares Nietzsche and Freud:

> Nietzsche's entire trajectory, even into this final heights, led him through areas of psychic discoveries of the most illuminating kind—often, one might even say, of a psychoanalytic kind. The sterility of school psychology was overturned by the sheer wealth of material on which the human psyche, freed from all prejudices, began to feast itself with incomparable depth and insight. Whoever experienced it could certainly sense this was the spot on which we ought to settle intellectually: with daring *and* patience; here it would be important in practice to linger a long time under the guidance of the scholarly precision that had been achieved in the meantime, instead of taking a precipitous turn to a renewed theory. In the process, of course, the problem necessarily arises: how to approach this most living material with scientifically sure levers and screws without damaging the material precisely in its aliveness. This is the riddle to which Freud brought us the solution.[10]

Freud's "solution" enables what Salomé comes to figure as femininity, the reciprocal relationship between the unconscious with and its basis in the materiality of life, on the one hand, and the intellect or rationality, on the other. What she resisted in Nietzsche was the tendency in his late work to privilege the radical negativity of the

[9] Ibid., p. 359.
[10] Ibid., p. 360.

drives over reason on the basis of a paradoxical renunciation of pleasure, of sociality and contingency. To have gone with Nietzsche, as Salomé said, would have meant returning to the world of the drives or their manifestations in fantasy, to a literally selfless suspension. She resisted just such a total dissolution in the name of woman, who had never separated so radically from her materiality, from her mother, whom she preserved by way of her idealization of that removed father-God. In relation to Nietzsche, Salomé would seem to have protected woman from her historical containment in desire. To exempt her from the world of reason would have been to continue depriving woman who had been protected from engagement in reality by other fathers in the name of other truths and styles for too long. Salomé resists the split she sees in Nietzsche between drive and reason and rejects any assumption of the fundamental asociality of sexual drives.

Salomé and Nietzsche discussed an essay on woman soon after Salomé had read *The Gay Science*. Her essay "Der Mensch als Weib" (1899) ends with a passage that shows the effects of *The Gay Science* at least at the level of metaphor:

> And when the man then slowly descends from these heights into daily life and the loud workday and sees *woman:* then it must appear to him as though he saw eternity itself in the form of a young, kneeling being, of whom it is impossible to know whether it kneels in order to be closer to earth or more open to heaven. Indeed, the two are so unified in their expression, as if there were something embodied in the expression that exalts all humanness and makes a symbol out of the old biblical words: Everything is yours! You, however, are God's.[11]

Again we encounter Salomé's oft-repeated pattern of ideal love between man and woman as a shared love for and dedication to a third instance, to something that exceeds them both and to which each has the same access. In fact, the structure of the passage stresses woman's inaccessibility or immunity to man's desire to possess as he idealizes her. For as much as he, she belongs to "God." The lure of woman for man, but also her distance, recalls Nietzsche's aphorism "Women and their action at a distance" in *The Gay Science:*

[11] Salomé, "Der Mensch als Weib," *Neue Deutsche Rundschau* 10 (1899): 311.

Do I still have ears? Am I all ears and nothing else? Here I stand in the flaming surf whose white tongues are licking at my feet; from all sides I hear howling, threats, screaming, roaring coming at me, while the old earth-shaker sings his aria in the lowest depths, deep as a bellowing bull, while pounding such an earth-shaking beat that the hearts of even these weather-beaten rocky monsters are trembling in their bodies. Then, suddenly, as if born out of nothing, there appears before the gate of this hellish labyrinth, only a few fathoms away—a large sailboat, gliding along as silently as a ghost. Oh, what ghostly beauty! How magically it touches me! Has all the calm and taciturnity of the world embarked on it? Does my happiness itself sit in this quiet place—my happier ego, my second, departed self? Not to be dead and yet no longer alive? A spiritlike intermediate being: quietly observing, gliding, floating? Like the boat that with its white sails moves like an immense butterfly over the dark sea. Yes! To move *over* existence! That's it! That would be something!

It seems as if the noise here had led me into fantasies. All great noise leads us to move happiness into some quiet distance. When a man stands in the midst of his own noise, in the midst of his own surf of plans and projects, then he is apt also to see quiet, magical beings gliding past him and to long for their happiness and seclusion: *women*. He almost thinks that his better self dwells there among the women, and that in these quiet regions even the loudest surf turns into deathly quiet, and life itself into a dream about life. Yet! Yet! Noble enthusiast, even on the most beautiful sailboat there is a lot of noise, and unfortunately much small and petty noise. The magic and the most powerful effect of women is, in philosophical language, action at a distance, *actio in distans*; but this requires first of all and above all—distance.[12]

For some feminist critics, Nietzsche's aphorism figures woman's inaccessibility in a way that exposes the philosopher's envy but also reproduces his privilege. In her Introduction to *Die imaginierte Weiblichkeit*, Silvia Bovenschen uses this same aphorism to analyze the "double form of woman," her fantasmatic and her everyday appearance. Bovenschen suggests that that fantasmatic "woman," who is the product of male projection, cannot stand the light of day. She attacks Nietzsche's apparent regret that proximity necessarily disappoints by shattering the fantasmatic illusion:

Nietzsche is completely right in pointing out that this image of the feminine has this quality only at a distance, one between desire and the

---

[12] Nietzsche, *The Gay Science*, pp. 123–24.

everyday—that it dissolves as soon as we approach it; but he is wrong to blame women for the disappointments that follow from proximity to women, who, after all, were not even a party to the desire and wish production and whose unhistorical existence inevitably provides the occasion for such imaginings.[13]

Bovenschen uses the Nietzsche passage to demonstrate the relationship between the absence of empirical women and the cultural production of femininity. She relies on too easy a distinction between representation and empirical reality and comes to the problematic conclusion that women can and should represent themselves as they really are. The suggestion that women should tell the truth of woman or the truth about women risks the ultimately repressive trap of empiricism, which operates on the basis of such conflations of representation, reality, and truth.

As we saw in the last chapter, Derrida has read the Nietzsche passage for its deconstructive possibilities. On Derrida's reading, Nietzsche "revives that barely allegorical figure [of woman] in his own interest. For him truth is like a woman."[14] Nietzsche, he says, is interested in the complicity for the philosopher between woman and truth, their seduction, their veiled and veiling effects. Man has to keep his distance from this distance, leave truth in suspension:

If it is necessary to keep one's distance from the feminine operation, from the *actio in distans*, . . . it is perhaps because the "woman" is not a determinable identity. Perhaps woman is not some thing which announces itself from a distance, at a distance from some other thing. In that case it would not be a matter of retreat and approach. Perhaps woman—a non-identity, a non-figure, a simulacrum—is distance's very chasm, the out-distancing of distance, the interval's cadence, distance itself, if we could still say such a thing, distance *itself*. . . .

There is no such thing as the essence of woman because woman averts, she is averted of herself. Out of the depths, endless and unfathomable, she engulfs and distorts all vestige of essentiality, of identity, of property. And the philosophical discourse, blinded, founders on these shoals and is hurled down these depthless depths to its ruin. There is no such thing as the truth of woman, but it is because of that abyssal divergence of the

[13] Silvia Bovenschen, *Die imaginierte Weiblichkeit* (Frankfurt am Main: Suhrkamp, 1979), p. 59.
[14] Jacques Derrida, *Spurs: Nietzsche's Styles*, trans. Barbara Harlow (Chicago: University of Chicago Press, 1978), pp. 49, 51.

truth, because that untruth is "truth." Woman is but one name for that untruth of truth.[15]

So Derrida, following Nietzsche, subverts the Western philosophers' obsession with truth by exposing the equation of "woman" and "truth" or "lie." The affirmative woman who has no use for truth, who challenges the hierarchy of values in Western philosophy, who refuses castration—she is the woman the antimetaphysical philosopher loves and is.

Mary Ann Doane addresses relations between seeing and knowing in psychoanalysis, philosophy, and film in a way that opens up the structure of envy in the philosophers' and the psychoanalysts' investment in "their" woman. Though Nietzsche dissolves the distinction between surface and depth, which woman, truth, and the veil have so systematically upheld in Western philosophy, he does not do away with the category of deception.

> Deception, from this point of view, is not defined as the noncoincidence or incompatibility of surface and depth (appearance and the truth), but as the very posing of the question of truth and its hiding place—the gesture indicating truth's existence. Deception, far from distorting truth, operates a double negation by, as Derrida will point out in another context, concealing the secret that there is no secret. . . . in Nietzsche's view, woman epitomizes the pretense of essence.[16]

"In Derrida's text," Doane writes, "the woman no longer figures the veiled movement of truth but the suspended veil of undecidability. She comes to represent the limit to the relevance of the hermeneutic question" (125–26). Deception is not a negative value in Nietzsche or in Derrida's figurations of woman as "exemplar of instability." Nonetheless, Nietzsche's woman must remain naïve, innocent, unconscious of her own operations in order to remain "the projection of Nietzsche's own epistemological desires, his will to *embody* the difficulties, the impossibilities of what remains a tantalizing truth" (123). This exclusion of woman from knowledge robs

---

[15] Ibid., pp. 52–53.

[16] Mary Ann Doane, "Veiling over Desire," in *Feminism and Psychoanalysis*, ed. Richard Feldstein and Judith Roof (Ithaca: Cornell University Press, 1989), p. 121, hereafter cited in the text.

her of subjectivity, as Doane points out, but woman's exclusion from the position of conscious master of her "operations" is not the primary problem for Doane:

> Nietzsche's woman, closing her eyes to herself, and Lacan's woman, who doesn't know (who has *jouissance* without knowledge), have something in common. Yet, knowledge, like truth, is a peculiar term in the work of both Nietzsche and Lacan. The subject's position outside of knowledge is not necessarily to be lamented. In these theories, therefore, it is a question not so much of depriving the woman of subjectivity (a term psychoanalysis problematizes in any event) as of making her a privileged trope, a site of theoretical excess, an exemplar of the philosophical enterprise. (133)

Doane, drawing on the work of Luce Irigaray, argues that woman remains "the fetish of philosophy," that "the given symbolics of a patriarchically ordered sexual difference" are maintained (135).

Doane is interested in the male theorist's relation to woman, which "oscillates between fear and envy of the feminine." What the theorist envies is the "woman" he himself has created as outside his theory, the woman "who most fully embodies a 'completeness closed upon itself' " (134), the woman who, as Doane stresses, supports his theory by virtue of the fact that she marks its limit:

> In effect, what the male subject of theory here envies is the woman whom he has constructed as inhabiting a space outside his own theory—nevertheless supporting that theory through her very absence. "You only have to go and look" to see that she is not of this world. As Lacan himself points out, the Latin *invidia*—envy—is derived from *videre*, to see. What we witness here is the displacement of vision's truth to the realm of theoretical vision. The psychoanalyst sees immediately that to see the woman is to envy her, to recognize that what she represents is desirable. The "seeing" is often on the side of the theory that hopes to disengage itself from the visible, from the seeing/seen nexus. (134)

The antimetaphysical philosophers' and psychoanalysts' distrust of the visible and of Truth have not sufficed to challenge the sexual politics of traditional philosophy fundamentally, according to Doane; in fact, she argues, "the idea that the visible is a point of crisis seems to be conveniently forgotten when theory contemplates its own limits" (134). What distinguishes Salomé's woman from Nietzsche's or Derrida's philosophical de(con)structions is her insistence on a figuration of woman as "divergence of truth and identity" in the interests of a different sexual economy, of woman's narcissistic, perhaps homosexual identification with "woman," an identification that challenges the theorist's exclusive or stable and possessive idealization of her. Salomé's "woman" confounds the structure of the knowing philosopher and the unconscious woman of his philosophy not by laying claim to his position of mastery for woman but by occupying both positions in that structure at once, positions that in their interrelation are Salomé's "woman."

4.

Salomé on Ibsen's Female Characters

Salomé believed that Nietzsche's fate illustrated the genial and pathological consequences of a total critique of reason and the refusal of an at least presumed exterior power through which desires are both mediated and unified. Ibsen's female figures, however, typified for her the dangers to women of locating that presumed exterior life force in actual, empirical male others, the dangers of literalizing the symbolic significance of the father. Salomé lamented Nietzsche's refusal of sociality in favor of a literal and figurative isolation in his own psyche; in Ibsen's female characters, she lamented women's containment in their own fantasy lives because of the socially imposed lack of access to purposeful activity. In *Henrik Ibsens Frauengestalten* (Henrik Ibsen's female characters),[1] Salomé presents a remarkable analysis of feminine subjectivity nearly twenty years before she began her intensive study of psychoanalysis.

The "problem of love" had preoccupied her for a long time and may have had particular urgency for her in 1891 when she wrote and published her book on Ibsen. Since 1886 she had been living

---

[1] Lou Andreas-Salomé, *Henrik Ibsens Frauengestalten nach seinen sechs Familiendramen* (Berlin: H. Bloch, 1892). Siegfried Mandel's translation was published under the title *Ibsen's Heroines* (Redding Ridge, Conn.: Black Swan Books, 1985). I prefer "Henrik Ibsen's female characters" because it is closer to the German original and truer to Salomé's stated intention to draw out the unity of Ibsen's work on the basis of his female characters, even where they appear to be secondary figures. I have provided my own translations of the 1892 edition of Salomé's text, citing page references in the text.

what she described as the tortured first few years of her marriage.[2] The conflict for the female figures in Ibsen's works, as Salomé sees it, emerges from the restriction of women's self-becoming by the constraining conventions of marriage, and from the tensions between unbound passion and sociality. The Ibsen book allowed Salomé to address the reduction of woman to mere half of man's whole in marriage and to draw out the implications of the heterosexual marital unit when it is secured as the apparently "natural bond." Rosalind Coward formulates the social and political implications of that unit in terms that make a fitting introduction to Salomé's study of Ibsen's wild ducks in the attic:

> In our society, the preferred unit is the heterosexually committed couple who are assumed to have children. Since the end of the last century, state intervention and social policy have constructed this unit which is not a neutral unit. For it is maintained by a definite ideology and concomitant practices which make women dependent on men. . . . This unit, which is to the direct disadvantage of women, works not through direct coercion, but because it appears to correspond to the sexual needs arising from the sexual identities of men and women. This social unit is maintained by appearing as the natural expression of sexual and emotional needs and activities. Because it is the only structure in which our society recognises dependency between individuals, it becomes the easiest way in which dependency can be expressed.[3]

Salomé shared with her middle-class intellectual and artistic contemporaries a concept of the modern individual for whom the old bourgeois forms and conventions had become meaningless, the individual capable of self-renewal and invention. Not only aesthetic but also social, intersubjective, sexual, and intrapsychic experiments were conducted in the name and for the benefit of this individual. Salomé put the invention of new forms, both psychic and social, at the center of her interest in Ibsen's work and its reception.

When Salomé wrote and published her study, Ibsen's renown and popularity were not yet firmly established in Germany. As Siegfried

---

[2] Lou Andreas-Salomé, "Gedanken über das Liebesproblem," in *Die Erotik: Vier Aufsätze*, ed. Ernst Pfeiffer (Frankfurt am Main: Ullstein Materialien, 1985).

[3] Rosalind Coward, *Patriarchal Precedents: Sexuality and Social Relations* (Boston: Routledge and Kegan Paul, 1982), p. 284.

Mandel notes in the introduction to his translation of Salomé's book, she was one of Ibsen's earliest "trumpeters" in Europe, along with Georg Brandes in Scandinavia, Otto Brahm in Germany, and George Bernard Shaw in England. In 1891 Salomé was living with Andreas in Tempelhof, one of those outlying areas of Berlin, those escapes from city life, like Schmargendorf and Friedrichshagen, where members of the avant-garde literary and critical political community gathered. Salomé's friends and associates included a number of figures who were connected with the Freie Bühne, the showcase of Naturalism in Germany. Salomé's memoirs and her unpublished diaries from that period attest to the importance of her friendship with her neighbors Gerhart and Marie Hauptmann. Wilhelm Bölsche, a novelist and popularizer of natural science, introduced Salomé to the group of Naturalist poets, critics, journalists, and activists in Friedrichshagen, including, among others, Arno Holz and the Hart brothers. Salomé moved to the center of Naturalist circles in Berlin socially, and she became a major contributor to the social and critical review *Die Freie Bühne*, the major organ of the Naturalist movement in Berlin. In contrast to what she saw as Nietzsche's irrationalism and isolation, the Naturalists' commitment to a collective project appealed to her. She had the opportunity to work, to participate in an intellectual and social community of the sort she had tried to create with Nietzsche and Rée. She began to realize the "dream" that would be fulfilled most completely in her involvement with psychoanalysis.

Salomé's involvement in Naturalist literary circles led to her first serious attention to literature. "Literature as such had never particularly interested me," she noted. "I was uneducated in it, even in the 'Schönfärberei' [whitewashing] of the preceding period, against which this fresh war now broke out."[4] In part in order to minimize the inevitable scandal of their living together, she and Rée had avoided moving in bohemian, artistic circles during their years together in Berlin. Instead, they had surrounded themselves with scholars in philosophy and the natural sciences. The Naturalists, who were committed to modernity and change, seemed refreshingly young to her: "What affected me most," she wrote, "was the human

---

[4] Salomé, *Lebensrückblick: Grundriß einiger Lebenserinnerungen,* ed. Ernst Pfeiffer (Frankfurt am Main: Insel, 1968), p. 97.

part of it: the joyful buoyancy, the tempestuous youth and conviction, neither of which were obliterated despite the fact that it was by way of the gloomiest and most dismal themes that they took it upon themselves to preach the new spirit."[5]

Salomé's treatment of Ibsen's female characters demonstrates the importance she ascribed not only to this "new spirit" but also to a sense of responsibility to a larger community. Her interest in, study of, and critical writing on literary developments in Germany, Austria, France, and Russia were inextricably linked with and sustained by her connections with major literary and intellectual figures and circles in Vienna, Berlin, Munich, Paris, and various parts of Russia (where she and Rilke visited Tolstoy on their two trips in 1899 and 1900). She conceived of commitment and responsibility in the limited terms of the bourgeois intellectual or artistic circles in which she moved, however, where the sovereignty of the creative individual was not to be diminished by the *ressentiment* that motivated political oppositions. She was not the only member of the Naturalist circles in Berlin to stay clear of the movement's initial political engagement.

In fact, Salomé's association with Naturalism was as idiosyncratic as her other involvements; she would not have considered herself a "Naturalist," nor would it be accurate to so consider her now. She participated, but she never "joined." The social and political commitments of Naturalist poets and philosophers held little interest or appeal for her. She objected to what she considered excessive realism in the new theater in Berlin, believing that it defeated the actual purpose of the movement, namely, its self-proclaimed desire for modernity and renewal. Far more appealing to her was the psychological focus of Ibsen's work, which she saw as its central moment. It is no surprise that her interest in literature would ultimately find its apotheosis in Rainer Maria Rilke and, even there, that her interest would be primarily psychological, not literary.

Salomé's interpretation of Ibsen's female characters is first and foremost a study in their psychology and an effort to work through certain key questions about love and sociality by way of a further proliferation of the stories already contained in Ibsen's work. Salomé begins with a set of short parables about "the wild duck" and its

[5] Ibid.

domestication, which call the concept of "nature" into question, even as they use it metaphorically to point to parts of the self which exceed and underlie what is allowed expression within the constraints of social convention and psychological normalcy. "Once there was an attic. . . . In the attic, people held all kinds of animals captive, and weaned them from their free life in nature by way of discipline and caretaking. [The basket in the corner] sheltered the noblest of all these creatures that had been robbed of their freedom, a wild duck and thus a truly wild bird. It seemed not only to be the noblest but also the most deserving of pity. Because even though its comrades willingly accommodated themselves to this artificial idyll—a wild bird in an attic? isn't that necessarily a tragedy?"(2) The "attic" can be read as marriage and family, as convention, but also as the socio-symbolic contract "as a whole" in its sacrificial logic. Salomé suggests that there might be something other than a tragic ending to woman's entry into that order.

Salomé follows her question with six answers, six stories, some of which suggest that there might be something other than a tragic ending to woman's entry into the social order. The first involves a small bird taken from the maternal nest and put among domestic animals; the bird finally remembers the wild. She "still does not know where her home is, but knows that it cannot be here; an irresistible instinct tells her so, as does the deep, powerful, longing that so commandingly sets her young wings into motion." This bird, this Nora, "silently spreads her wings and soars into the vast unknown" (3).

The second story follows a very different trajectory. This young bird is so successfully socialized that she comes to regard the attic world as "an unchangeable law of nature," rather than the construction that it is. She, too, finally awakes to the realization that her life in the attic has been predicated on illusion and forgetting. Without ever leaving the attic, she "dreams that she is inwardly united with the thousands of free-born birds that soar unfettered, in their native distance, over the earth and toward the light of the sun" (6). This, too, is a kind of liberation.

In the third story, Salomé posits yet another possible outcome. Here, the wild bird grows complacent, exploits and enjoys captivity by deceiving the other domesticated animals into admiring his mere "pretense to the drive for freedom." In the end, a blind songbird, the only animal in the attic who has really taken the bird's pretense seriously, sacrifices herself in the attempt to "teach him how to move his wings and win his freedom again" (9).

In the fourth parable the bird comes to the attic voluntarily, out of the will to dominate the other animals, but they take their revenge in the only way the weak can, they slowly bind the bird to themselves, to her own domestication, through love. "She lingers much too long in the anxious confines in which human discipline and control rule, in which all wild drives are eradicated, and all offenses have to be punished" (11). This Rebecca bird acquires the conscience characteristic of the domesticated animal and becomes an "insubstantial, gray ghost" (151). When she has been completely imprisoned by her own inner controls, and yet still senses freedom, she can find "no solution to the conflict between wild and tame, free and constrained, the natural world and the attic world." (151).

The fifth story comes closest to Salomé's ideal, something other than total domestication to conventions or total revenge against community and self. This wild bird suffers from enormous homesickness in the attic and is dominated by images of imprisonment. "In splintered, alluring images she conjures up [that distant wonderland] for them over and over again, tortured by the consuming tug of the unattainable and the boundless, and by the dread and terror of imprisonment and confinement" (15). Ultimately, the human beings and animals around her reluctantly grant her freedom, a freedom that allows this Ellida bird to avoid both escape and suicide, "for only her fear of being captive drove her away" (15). She is able to appreciate the possibility of protection, communality, and friendship, and to cease dreaming of escape, only when she can set her own boundaries voluntarily.

The sixth and final parable, the parable of the wild duck Hedda, may very well represent the fate that Salomé most resisted and dreaded. Here, the attic cannot "develop from a prison into an asylum of freedom" (16) because this bird is damned by its peers to homelessness. She is "capable neither of the struggle against the status quo nor of harmony in mutual support and must therefore abide forever in an impotent restlessness" (17). Though the attic world represents only confinement to her, she lacks the courage and will to seek anything else and is incapable even of "escaping from the world anymore" (18).

Salomé does not conceive of emancipation as permanent and total escape from the bonds of social order. Her excavations of the female characters in Ibsen's work take the form of a psychological tapestry. She begins with Nora, the woman who desires "the miraculous" but lives within the constraints of a conventional feminine upbringing and a conventional marriage, in which she figures as a plaything, an infinitely manipulable object in her husband's hands. The analysis does not move, as one might expect of a good feminist narrative, from this beginning in fetters, through Nora's "escape," toward examples of increasing independence and freedom. On the contrary, Salomé applauds Nora's decision to leave her marriage, but she does not hold it up as a model. It is a small change, which opens but in no way resolves the questions Ibsen's female characters raise. Salomé was interested not in women's emancipation from others but in a transformation that would restore both partners in a marriage to their fundamental bisexuality.

Salomé insistently questions any conception of freedom as total escape from constraint, responsibility, or sociality. The story with the most positive resolution, the story of Ellida, reverses a linear narrative of emancipation by showing that what Ellida must free herself from is a complete lack of boundaries; her "emancipation" requires her to enter into relationships involving commitment and responsibility, for the first time. Again, Salomé stresses that women must be freed from their long confinement in fantasy and desire. She is particularly critical of any pursuit of freedom that simply indulges ego needs, and therefore she expresses particular animosity toward Hedda Gabler, to whom she has been compared by at least one of her own biographers.[6] Salomé differentiates what she calls self-becoming from an ego-bound self-seeking, and she draws out the deep psychic contradictions and conflicts women encounter in search of self and sociality.

Salomé proliferates stories and draws out their complicated interweavings. Methodologically, she is concerned with neither an

[6] See Rudolph Binion, *Frau Lou: Nietzsche's Wayward Disciple* (Princeton: Princeton University Press, 1968), p. 145.

assessment of Ibsen's "images of women" nor an evaluation of the relationship between Ibsen's female figures and "real" women. Salomé pays little attention to the figures in isolation from one another. She draws out the psychic dynamics that underlie the tensions in each play and then connects one to the other. Such a strategy effectively eliminates the integrity of each individual work, the boundaries around it. In fact, Salomé eschews questions of fidelity to Ibsen's work. His work simply provides Salomé with the material for a subtle psychological investigation, which she conducts by proliferating her own stories with no apologies for her fabrications. Ibsen's texts achieve great richness in her analysis, but she is not interested in deriving his "meanings." Instead, Salomé inhabits Ibsen's figures in order to construct her own circuitous explorations of the psychology of women. Not only are the characters lifted out of their individual contexts, but they come to life in relation to one another. Each figure returns, as it is woven through the discussions of every other only apparently unique play, until the individual readings become a grand fabric of suggestion and commentary. What engages Salomé about the content, but also the structure of the plays, is the relation between freedom and necessity, between desire and sociality, and between the double directionality of woman's drive toward unbounded, self-effacing passion and purposeful self-assertion in the social.

The main body of the text begins with a story of escape, the Nora story. Nora is the "child-woman" who so intrigued turn-of-the-century writers and artists, in whom some male artists found the greatest seduction. For Salomé, the childishness of this woman illustrates the effects of feminine subjectivity formed so completely within the oedipal model of the nuclear family. Nora's sense of "the miraculous" "is grounded in a childlike quality that is nothing other than the child's deep sense of the ideals of life, which can elevate itself just as quickly and decisively to a strong, valiant virility" (46), to the strength to escape the bourgeois family and its crippling effects.

Nora's love for her husband, Helmer, parallels and reproduces her love for her father, "that familiar love that looks up reverently, fervently, with the wide, adoring eyes of the child" (22). That childlike quality, in its desire and capacity for something miraculous, is double-edged or, in Salomé's later terms, doubly directional. Nora conceives of her marriage, of Helmer's choice of her, as an "incomprehensible miracle, and she believes in it as a child believes in miracles" (22–23).

> With this sense of the miraculous a new world and development of her own awaken in her for the first time—a world of humility and pride; the unreserved devotion to her husband together with the first claims to, and search for, herself and her own worth. The first urgent stirrings of her latent strength are awakened. . . .
> What is roused in this way in Nora's innermost being remains temporarily hidden and not understood even by her. (23)

Salomé is interested in Nora's passion for life and change, however hidden it is in the encrusted forms of the bourgeois family and its oedipal scenarios. As always, Salomé searches for the dynamics that underlie woman's particular relation to man, rather than condemning and simply escaping the enduring psychic complexities that make change so difficult. For Salomé, the goal is not the rejection of femininity but the exploration of those positive forms of desire and pleasure that have been, as she put it, "emasculated."

Salomé then contrasts Nora's childlike sense of wonder to Helmer's masculine ego. Once again, the effects of modernity on men appear lamentable, even as modernity opens up the possibility of growth for women. Helmer is clearly the product of an impoverished reality, a man who has become one with his social role, whose self-satisfaction and self-assurance are bought at the expense of what Nora and Salomé call "the miraculous." The desire for the miraculous is constituted of the fundamentally erotic desire for a relation to the world that engages the deepest feelings and capacity for growth. For Helmer, whom Salomé describes as a "complacent, conceited adult who can no longer look up beyond himself" (25), Nora is merely a plaything, an adornment, a pastime between important business matters. Nora and Helmer experience life in two different registers:

> He doesn't give much thought to the fact that the impetus for this child-like being's development is given by love and that her life's horizons are

opened up to her for the first time through that love. His self-contained little doll's house was not well suited for being unsettled in that way.

Nora does not know that the two of them understand love and beauty in ways that are as diametrically opposed as a radiant miracle is to everyday life. . . . Helmer's joy in merriment and loveliness is, at the same time, the ordinary person's aversion to struggle and seriousness—to anything that could disturb the aesthetic comfort in which he enjoys himself and his existence.

The apparent moral rigor that helps Helmer gain prestige, his need to appear blameless and to keep his dignity unblemished—all this self-control in daily life ultimately arises out of the same egotistical perspective on pleasure. But it points every time, on the other side, to the petty human fear of coming into conflict. (26–27)

Nora's strength and her capacity to act independently express themselves initially in deceptions of her husband, but Salomé challenges the line between honesty and deception by pointing to the evidence of masculine will and strength in Nora's lies about her work and her earnings. Salomé also emphasizes Nora's continuing naïveté about her own strength, because Nora continues to think of her ability to earn money as a gift to Helmer: "For all the independence she had so happily achieved, she had little desire to use it as a trump card against him, or to transform her admiration of him into the direct, bold look of an equal partner. What she understands by the dream of a true marriage is not the dullness of an equality achieved through laborious work but rather the miracle of an incomprehensible love that raises her up to him and is all the more wonderful the higher he, a god, stands above her, the child" (31). In the next paragraph, Salomé stresses that "Nora's emerging individuality expresses itself in the recognition that expectation, longing, and faith have to transform themselves into creative action" (32), not remain invested in an actual other. When Nora says that she felt like a man when she took on the responsibility to work, it is at that point, according to Salomé, that she begins to develop a sense of her own strength and independence, to "secretly feel around in the dark for freedom" (30). Nora's desires for freedom initially take childish forms because she has been "left in the dark," but on Salomé's reading, the web of lies she spins represents "the first, unconscious protest against father and husband, both of whom kept her under the spell of childishness and ignorance" (30).

Questions about education arise over and over in Salomé's analyses. Here, she is concerned with the subordination of women through imposed naïveté and ignorance. Rather than figure women as passive tools or victims, however, Salomé insists on their strength and capacity for creative action, which too often find no other form of expression than in projection of their power onto the love object, a man or a child, through subordination and submission. Helmer sees only deceit in Nora's efforts to earn money behind his back, but Salomé reads these efforts as a manifestation of love and an unconscious protest against imposed dependence and passivity. Here we have two very different orders of ethics at work. Nora's ethics are indivisible from her love and her desire for independence, whereas Helmer follows the letter of a moral law set outside of him.

Nora learns about the social exploitation of woman's desire when she realizes that it has been evoked only to contain her within it. "The childlike visage with which she masks and hides things from others," according to Salomé, "is not a mask when it is donned for Helmer but the countenance of true and humble love" (30). Salomé describes Nora's ultimate disappointment in Helmer as an unmasking, a demystification, a loss of God. Only when she sees the reality of the man she had deified can she begin to come to terms with herself. Only that demystification can return her to herself:

What all the worries and experiences of the entire recent past had not taught her is now accomplished in one instant: she suddenly sees life as it is, as it stands before her in the shape of Helmer, an ordinary person, who is tormented by fear and selfishness. All her life and her thought were concentrated in him, it was in him that her life took on its truth and self-evidence—it could be demystified and destroyed only in him. Though she may have grown equal to the maturity and experience of this hour, her childlike heart, in its depths, remained full of faith, and her life full of wonder. . . .

Something strange and immense occurred in her. All her slowly awakened strength and independence, everything that she had so humbly and zealously collected as a present, a gift of love—her entire, inner being—now rears up and fights its way free from this love in an enormous protest. And now, free of that love, she is a new, strange, strong, proud human being . . . who no longer allows herself to be enslaved or deceived. (43)

Both the language and the ethical content of this passage cohere with Salomé's description of her relationship with Gillot and her own capacity both to break out of her deification of him and to sustain her sense of childlike wonder and faith. This trajectory, as she will explain in her psychoanalytic work, differs profoundly from the son's rebellions and separations from the roots of life in that erotic sense of the miraculous.

Salomé's conclusions introduce the language and the metaphors she shared with Nietzsche. Of Nora's first decisive conflict, she writes that Nora had finally "comprehended that the highest things in life, its miracles, do not come with the self-evidence with which the fairies come to deliver an enchanted existence in a children's story; in life, those things have to be earned" (47). Nora ventures forth into the "vastness of life," but

> nothing tells her yet whether she will find the way through this darkness, whether she will reach her goal. The "miraculous" is now no longer the blue sky, in which she always felt securely enveloped—it has blown up so high above her that a vast abyss seems to separate it from the ground on which she stands, abandoned and confused. Only far, far away at the outermost horizon of this incalculable desert can the image of promise and reconcilation appear in her mind's eye, like the thin line in which heaven and earth are so wonderfully united and flow together for the human eye. (48)

Salomé's attention shifts to Helmer and the effect on him of Nora's change. It now seems to him "as though the child in him had awakened again after a long, heavy slumber, the child that can still be" (49). "Out of all the corners and crevices of the abandoned room, out of its entire, cold isolation, it seems as if old forgotten fairy tales gather around him like childlike, playful mental figures, all the figures among which he had abided for so long, among which he had spent his entire marriage, without seeing anything deeper in them than playthings and amusements" (50). Man's reduction of what is profound to play, and his location of play in woman, impoverishes his inner life and ensures his conformity to social expectations.

The second parable and the second chapter of the main body of Salomé's text comment on the story of Helene Alving in Ibsen's *Ghosts*. When this wild duck awakens to her entrapment and her self-delusions, she seeks freedom in the kind of fantasy world in which she can imagine herself "being inwardly united with thousands of blissful, freeborn birds that soar unencumbered over the earth and toward the light of the sun" (6). Salomé contends, following Ibsen, that Helene Alving's tragic end and the damage she does to herself and to those around her result from the illusions and lies that she is forced not only to tell but to live. Salomé establishes subtle connections between Nora's and Helene Alving's worlds of illusion. Frau Alving lacks the strength or insight to challenge the conventions in which she is trapped. Her desire for life is distorted and ultimately suppressed by her inability to let go of convention and traditional morality. For Salomé, this inability expresses itself most tragically in Helene Alving's failure to understand what lay behind her husband's drinking and pleasure seeking, to see the desires and longings in him that could have led to a true marriage. Her eventual willingness to confront the conflicts and pain of her own childhood enable her to face the truth. Her son's madness, which Helene initially attributes to her husband's debauchery, serves as the concrete tragic manifestation of a failed marriage and failed lives, but also as the spur she needs to come to terms with her past:

> The tragedy of her past is realized in Oswald, and inexorably revives itself like a returning ghost, but it is also illuminated in all its depth and in its causal connections to the now-knowing mind. And therefore, it is also transfigured in him at the same time. . . . Her judgment of the past is no longer a condemnation; it is only an immense grief and compassion. She can forgive, without distorting the truth, because she can understand. (69–70)

In this passage, Salomé challenges biologistic degenerative theories of alcoholism and madness by suggesting that causation lies in family and personal histories and in the effects of an unconscious, or of a ghost of the past. With the outbreak of her son's madness, Helene Alving is "compelled to destroy with her own hand what she raised on a false foundation" (71). Salomé concludes by comparing Helene to Nora: "The ideal she assumes is no longer the same as what Nora, with her youthful readiness for action and her confidence of victory, sought. . . . For her, there is no future, no line on the horizon in which heaven and earth seem to melt so wonderfully together—just a vision of something beyond herself, and behind her, of the now-abandoned, victim-ridden battleground of her life. But instead of Nora's confident search for knowledge and growth, instead of her painful first separation from ideals she had believed in and loved, up to that point, Helene Alving has already entered the realm of truth, has experienced it and taken it into her strong hands. . . . She does not wander like Nora out into the unfathomable dark distance; she is allowed instead to stand still under a sky that has cleared above her, her face and arms raised upward to the sun that rises over her life" (71). Salomé, following Ibsen, turns a potentially congenital model of family illness, alcoholism, and madness into an analytic one. Her analysis demonstrates her unusual lack of moralism and her genuine psychological interests.

In the third section, Salomé develops her thoughts on the question of truth and illusion by reconstructing the relations among the figures in *The Wild Duck*. She suggests that the resolution of ideal and reality finds its expression in the female characters:

> And so, this time too, it is the female characters that take up and develop the basic, guiding idea of the previous works, the idea of a reconciliation of ideal and reality through the all-understanding, all-forgiving gentleness that follows the acceptance of truth. The ideal claim to truth itself may be embodied in Gregers's character—but it took Hedwig's life and death to add what it needed to change from an abstract dream to a force in human existence. (98)

Salomé criticizes the fanatical and necessarily abstract insistence on "truth" by the male characters, whose relation to everyday life and to "the average person" is either extremely arrogant or completely nonexistent. Their conception of truth as absolute objectivity, and their cynical rejection of man's need for illusion of any kind, kills not only God, according to Salomé, but the plenitude and the anxiety out of which "he" is born from the human psyche. Perhaps more important, this fanatical cynicism destroys the possibility of sociality or collectivity.

For Salomé, the Russian people represented the possibility of retaining the very human sense of responsibility and connection to something higher, to the life that precedes and outlives the destruction of myth, religion, and belief. The impulse to destroy narrative and all forms of intelligibility was purely reactive, she believed, and dominated by *ressentiment*. Two characteristic strategies emerge quite clearly from Salomé's critique: one, her methodological juggling of apparent contradictions in ways that avoid the arrogance and forgetfulness implicit in the complete renunciation of illusion; and two, her complex approach to individuality and subjectivity. Salomé compares the two primary male characters, Hjalmar, the artist, who has abandoned all ideals in favor of the commonplace, and Gregers, the idealist, who "descends" into a human community with the intention of bringing the "gift" of a relentless and unforgiving skepticism. She draws out their differences from the consummate idealist Brendel:

These two types of people intersect in [Brendel] with wonderful subtlety and significance. One can still follow the fine lines in which all three characters become one and seem to melt into a single, tragic human manifestation. Hjalmar and Brendel step down, so to speak, from both sides of the temple of pure ideality, where Gregers reigns as priest, onto human ground. On the one side, we see an idealism that lacks the courage to raise itself to its full power and height; it does not dare risk the dangers or freedoms of a life of truth, and it seeks to build a protective, sheltering hut of illusions around itself instead of the temple, a decorative, artificial, empty world, in the half darkness of which no harsh light of day can fall, no cold draught can blow, and fantasy can indulge itself in unrestrained dreaming. On the other side, the protest against prejudices, boundaries, and limits to the drive to freedom becomes vagabondage. Gregers's idealism, though it was conceived in complete freedom, roams about purposelessly from one idea to another, one adventure to another, without being able to bring itself to enter the strict consistency of the temple, whose priest he claims to be. (105)

The child Hedwig, whose paternal origins are ambiguous, believes herself to be the daughter of Hjalmar, the father she loves and adores. When Hjalmar discovers the uncertainty of his paternity, he rejects his daughter, the one person who had taken his idealistic pretenses seriously. Her suicide, her sacrifice to truth, is situated at the center of the text and its treatment of emancipation. Rather than dismiss Hedwig's faith in Hjalmar as childish illusion, Salomé sees in her suicide the elements for a reconciliation of freedom and convention, of truth and illusion, for her sacrifice restores meaning to what had come to be Gregers's empty idealism and contemptuousness. Her faith in Hjalmar illuminates his actual desire for liberation, expressed in distorted and crippled form in his "comfortable crutches and artificial inspirations," for the child Hedwig represents the border between the two types of "woman" in Ibsen's work. On the one hand, she shares Nora's and Helene Alving's origins in the confines of the attic, and she externalizes her will by projecting it onto an idealized father figure. She, too, dreams of another place, and were she not a child, according to Salomé, she would tear herself away from that attic world in conscious emancipation, rather than suicide, when she is faced with her father's weakness. On the other hand, because she *is* still a child and experiences herself only in submissive love of the father, she points to the other type of woman, who loses herself in passion and love, to the Rebeccas and Heddas, whose problems derive from the complete absence of boundaries and from their excessively free will. Like the transitional figure Brendel, these women need some way to move in the direction of freely chosen responsibilities and human community, not toward liberation from themselves.

Salomé introduces Rebecca's story immediately upon this announcement of a transition from one kind of woman to the other. Rebecca does not need to escape from the fetters of convention or to be freed from the ravages of congenital theory; she needs some way to give meaning to her "wildness" and lack of restraint, to make them purposeful. Rebecca is an illegitimate child, eventually adopted by her father, who then "sinks to the level of her lover" (113). The father's death pushes Rebecca into the outside world, to Rosmerholm, where she is to care for the sickly wife of Pastor Rosmer. But Rebecca falls into a wild, passionate love for Rosmer. After orchestrating his wife's suicide, Rebecca turns herself into a ghost of his former wife, takes on ideas that are alien to her, represses her wildness, and inevitably fails to live "the strength of her own being":

This new mental flowering, the refinement that Rebecca achieves, has the disastrous disadvantage that it did not grow on her own base and soil. It consists in the arbitrary assimilation of an alien ideal. Rebecca does not take it up in the service of a necessary development of her own being; rather, it overtakes her after she, finished and matured, has put her development and her past behind her. (128–29)

Rosmer and Rebecca both suffer from the transformations they undergo under each other's influence. "For Rosmer, all the strength intended to be his liberation remains only a dream image, which does not even live inside him, but next to him, in Rebecca" (129). Both Rebecca and Rosmer have to die because they no longer have their own lives or selves but can only be each other's inversion.

Rebecca's part in Beate's suicide and her subsequent inability to be happy in Beate's place have been interpreted variously. Mandel notes the differences between Salomé's prepsychoanalytic and Freud's later psychoanalytic reading of the Rebecca tragedy. He quotes from Freud's essay "Some Character Types," in which Freud suggests that Rebecca's behavior

is susceptible of only one solution. The news that Dr. West was her father is the heaviest blow that could strike her, for she was not only his adopted daughter but had been his mistress. . . . She cannot have had anything else on her mind but this love affair when she accounted for her final rejection of Rosmer on the ground that she had a past which made her unworthy to be his wife. . . . this past must seem to her the most serious obstacle to their union—the more serious crime (when compared with the responsibility for driving Beate to suicide).[7]

On Mandel's reading, Salomé "ascribed Rebecca's rejection of Rosmer's marriage proposal to the impact of Beate's 'ghost,' the revenge of Beate."[8]

Even though Salomé's readings predate her familiarity with psychoanalysis and despite her emphasis on Beate's revenge, she does not ignore a more analytic interest in the effects of incest. Incest figures centrally in a great deal of Salomé's work on the psychology of religion, femininity, and sexuality. An unconsummated, unliteralized love of the symbolic father lies at the core of her conceptions of subjectivity itself. But she is emphatic, in her explicitly autobiographical writings, her fiction, and her essays about the dangers of

[7] Quoted in Mandel, Introduction to *Ibsen's Heroines*, p. 33.
[8] Ibid., p. 34.

confusing the symbolic or ideal father with an actual human father or man. In the case of Nora, Salomé shows that the childlike dynamic of idealization introduces her to something just short of adulthood, just short, too, of the necessary divestment of her own desire from the idealized father figure. In Rebecca's case, actual incest represents the costly violation of a psychically necessary love of the idealized father, a violation that interferes with the development of self.

Salomé connects the dissolution of self, from which Rebecca suffers after acceding to Beate's position as wife, "to the tragic fate to which she was born," a fate that results in Rebecca's inability to resist the "attraction to alien ideals" (129). Salomé writes of Rebecca's childhood:

> In both Mrs. Alving's and Nora's emancipation, freedom and truth constitute the highest goal, a peak; in Rebecca's youth, on the other hand, they are nothing more than a flat, luxuriant land on which all the drives are allowed to tumble around in unrestrained caprice. In her inner being, all qualities still coexist, all with equal rights and value. They express themselves in that still-wild innocence of a naïve egoism, which is as unashamed of its own nakedness as the first human being was in the paradise where human and animal could still rest together peacefully because the human power of domination remained alien and unknown. That alone explains Rebecca, that already then, the most incompatible things were naïvely united in her soul, an instinctive, pious thankfulness with a sensual precocity, the lamb with the lion. It explains how she could have stayed with her sick father, tolerated his moods, and lessened his suffering, all with the daughter's friendly patience, even though she had been prematurely released into her complete self-seeking strength. (114)

Salomé sustains her analysis of the effects of incest by focusing on the sudden, "wild, unrestrained sexual passion" for Rosmer that overtakes Rebecca. "The fate under which she was born, the way in which she grew up, the sensual, sultry atmosphere that surrounded her youth—her entire existence up to that point, in all its subtle preconditions and consequences, erupts in [that passion]" (118), according to Salomé. "In the storm of passion, the peacefulness of that still-wild innocence of paradise . . . transforms itself into the horror and perils of the wilderness" (119). Meanwhile, "the human being in the midst of all this, that helpless, abandoned human being, who is not yet sure of herself and not yet aware, simply has no control over the forces that are released" (119).

Salomé argues that Rebecca is incapable of feeling remorse. "Her entire mental orientation does not develop out of remorse but out of habituation and the weakening of will" (119). Rebecca has not been transformed into a new self, even though her old self has been diminished, weakened, and alienated from her "through the ghostly power of an alien spirit," for as Salomé notes, "she experiences a 'horror of the ghost,' a horror of seeing herself die. That is a symptom not of change but of dissolution" (132). If we follow Salomé's analysis carefully, we see that "the ghost" refers to Rebecca's childhood and to the incest that made her unable to "resist attraction to alien ideas" (118), as well as to Beate's ghost, a ghost, after all, that is symptomatic of Rebecca's lack of self, symptomatic of her earlier ghosts. For Salomé, however, unlike Freud, Rebecca's demise is a consequence not of guilt but of the dissolution of a personality that was never integrated. Had she written on Rebecca after her psychoanalytic training, she might very well have analyzed those effects in much the same way as she did in the late nineties.

The "Woman of the Sea," Ellida, negotiates the conflict between self-assertion and boundless passion in ways that obviously captivated Salomé. Like Rebecca, Ellida is an unconstrained, wild being who came into the attic by mistake, without knowing that her mistake would mean irrevocable imprisonment. In the parable that foreshadows Ellida's story, the wild duck is granted her freedom by her captors when they see what pain her accidental captivity has caused her. The captor's act, and the wild duck's ability to take responsibility for herself, then transforms the direction of the bird's desire. Once again, Salomé stresses the dangers for women of love and of those idealizations through which Ellida comes into the world and her own strength, but which also stymie and contain her as long as the culture and the family reduce her to a childlike naïveté.

Ellida is the woman of the sea, who lives through her desire and is trapped within it, unlike Nora and Helene, who are denied access to their own desire for so long. Ellida, according to Salomé, "comes from the place where lust still streams unabated and freedom in nature still reigns—there, where the elemental ebb and flow are still not ossified or bound to the unchanging conventions and habits that constrain free impulses, as the mountains and rocks constrain the fjord dwellers" (148).

An unknown man, a nameless stranger, comes from the sea and, thus, from the place where she, too, originated, and he becomes the occasion for the emergence of Ellida's passion. He has the effect of a symbol, according to Salomé, one that evokes the unknown and the unbounded passion of life. Ellida's relation to him exceeds the bounds of love or personal passion. "It has nothing to do with any single emotion or passion; it is an ethical problem involving the development of the will. In her controlling imagination, Ellida's half-understood, half-conscious drives toward life are pulled together and personified for her in the demonic force of the unknown man" (153). "That man is like the sea," according to Ellida, and Salomé quotes her in order to underline Ellida's mistaken confusion of her own passion and her own origins with "him." Here again, Salomé emphasizes the difference between symbolic and overly real objects of emerging feminine desire:

> [This personification in him], this floating symbol, this mirroring of plea-sure, stands in sharp contrast to Rebecca's passion for Rosmer, which was so completely rooted in the real and in the senses. Now we under-stand why Rebecca's love could only be diminished and killed, could only end in the weakening and death of the entire strength of her being, in the complete dissolution of it, whereas Ellida can outgrow her com-pulsive attraction to the unknown through her own development and experience. The difference that exists between them is akin to the dif-ference between dream and life, symbol and person. (153)

In her reaction to her own passion, Ellida begins to feel both attraction and repulsion toward the alien man; later, her husband, Wangel, experiences a similar convergence of attraction and repul-sion for her. Because of his desire and his anxiety, he insists on protecting and containing her. According to Salomé, Ellida needs to break free of her desire for the stranger in order to be free of a desire that makes her deaf to the reality around her and intensifies the increasingly dangerous one-sidedness of fantasy and passive ex-pectation. To overcome her containment in fantasy without sup-pressing the strength of her passion requires a fragile alliance. Ellida attempts to escape her passion for the stranger by marrying a man whose reality has no meaning for her; the result is the return of the stranger or, perhaps, of the repressed. It so happens, according to Salomé, that Ellida takes a turn that could be titled "The Return of the Unknown [*Unbekannten*]" or "The Revenge of the Strange Man." Salomé emphasizes that Ellida feels superfluous in her husband's world. It is impossible for her to integrate desire and will with "reality," and Wangel contributes to her alienation by "protecting" her from social realities and by excluding her even further from the world in which she lives. Salomé explores the significance of education in comparisons of Nora and Ellida: "In both cases, the catastrophes in their lives are caused by this lack of education and development, and if we look at the situations in which they find themselves in the decisive moments at the end of the plays, we notice a similarity in the conflicts themselves; both cases deal with the tension between marital obligation and personal freedom" (185).

Salomé continues to emphasize the importance of responsibility and its relation to the freedom Ellida needs. Freedom, in and of itself, is meaningless; it acquires meaning only in the context of commitment and purposefulness. Wangel ultimately gives Ellida her freedom out of love for her, but emancipation, according to Salomé, is only part of what Ellida needs to learn to deal with reality. More important is the capacity to assume responsibility for herself, and that involves becoming a self by finding a meaningful engagement in reality, and that by way of the desire for the Other: "This is the urgency and longing of a person whom no one has educated about life or given a place or a task within it. Wangel could have diminished her longing for the unknown only by acquainting her with a small piece of life, a more contained area in which to work, only by opening up the possibility for her to understand how much one can love and accomplish therein" (163). Salomé points to the power of men to block women's access to life in the social. She also suggests, or perhaps acknowledges, that women gain access to their own strength and desires only by way of their idealizations of the symbolic father, and to the social only by way of their connection with men.

Salomé then turns her attention, once again, to the changes required of the male character. In order to participate in Ellida's change, Wangel also must undergo a transformation. "He moves

step-by-step from what is external and given, from the surface of
life, into its interior and depth and, thereby, gains the strength to
change it, even outwardly, in a new, free way" (172). Ellida, on the
other hand, "who has remained too far away from everything that
limits her and could draw her toward the outside in a healthy way,
becomes ill from the depth of her inwardness and is almost to the
point of being able to live life only in the realm of fantasy" (172).
"Slowly, however, a changing situation brings about a positive sub-
stitution of the outer for the inner life" (172). They finally achieve
a transformation that does not diminish their individualities, a "narcissistic love relation" in which both acknowledge the differences
within themselves which were once divided between them, and they
kneel before a shared goal, ideal, or God. The process through which
they become themselves repeats not only one of Salomé's favorite
figures for feminine development but also the situations in which
she has told us she found herself. In the successful exchange between doctor and patient, teacher and student, men and women,
both are changed by their recognition of the (sexual) differences
within each of them, a recognition that is mediated by a third term.
Salomé reproduces the hierarchical assumptions and the social reality that define man as teacher, guide, and doctor. For example, she
describes Wangel's problems with Ellida:

> He was not capable of really guiding the healthy person that she was at
> the outset or of showing her how she might have escaped the dangers
> of her development. For that he would have had to be not only the loyal
> doctor but a leader and her minister, in the highest sense of the word,
> a minister who is not locked in the service of tradition but knows how
> to interpret the secrets of the soul and who dispels all the horror and
> the enigmatic allure of the unknown and the boundless by teaching a
> person how to accept the limited and definite tasks of a real life. (170–
> 71)

Only a minister, or perhaps an analyst. Salomé's suggestion that
the husband play the role of interpreter reflects her conception of
the object of love as the occasion for emergence of self. Salomé
attributes Ellida's recovery not only to her freedom to leave, but also
to her capacity to reclaim responsibility for herself, to reclaim her

right to create her own boundaries. When Ellida begins to orient herself toward reality, she shows the first real signs of recovery.

The sixth and final chapter, like the corresponding parable, suggests that there is one kind of creature that would remain outside forever, excluded from even the most ideal "home" and the most open community. This bird has been damned to homelessness among its own kind because it lacks the will of the "freeborn," yet feels only hostility toward the protectiveness and peacefulness offered by friends. For Hedda Gabler, neither escape nor integration is possible. What remains for her, to paraphrase Salomé, is a life of self-indulgence and ultimate conformity because she lacks the courage to defy convention openly and live according to her own desires. She remains dependent on but deeply resentful of the forms of conventional security that she cannot give up. Her inability either to find peace within that security or to live her own passions brings about inevitable exploitation and destruction of others. Hedda Gabler, with her destructive seductions and machinations under cover and protection of convention, makes a mockery of the other women's struggles, according to Salomé.

At the end of her discussion of Ellida, Salomé suggests that "secondary motifs that would weaken the one integrated, consistent theme [in the plays] are dismissed." She continues: "What is this one thing that is the necessary basis of 'the true marriage'? It is truth and freedom" (188). But Hedda Gabler mocks this central, organic idea, according to Salomé. Rudolph Binion suggests that her "mighty animus against Hedda was meant to dissociate Lou from the Lou-like-monster-wife who would destroy a great work of scholarship in which her husband was involved,"[9] blaming Salomé for Andreas's inability to write and publish. He goes so far as to claim that Hedda Gabler, "that general's daughter and professor's wife," might have been based on stories Ibsen had heard about Salomé. Here Binion's animus against Salomé is on full display. Salomé's polemic against Hedda Gabler does depart from her treatment of the other characters, and it takes on a biting tone that relies on Nietzschean distinctions:

[9] Binion, *Frau Lou*, p. 145.

She resembles a ravenous wolf on which a sheep's skin has been growing for a very long time and who has forfeited its predatory strength only to keep its predatory soul. Damned to the most domesticated and ordinary existence, such a creature protects itself fearfully from every risk—it only plays impotently with its own thirst for freedom, its own wildness, the way a timid hand plays with weapons. . . .

For her there is no goal, and she would not know how to meet it anyway; and so she is forced to content herself with toys that at least help her through the boredom of such a total lack of activity. . . .

Even the average person, in all his ordinariness, is more substantial, is superior to this kind of character. Because he is still able to participate in a development toward a freer life and, therefore, in a reconciliation of the world of freedom with the world of the attic—or at least, to take part in the battle that is waged between them. The only being who is excluded from both worlds is one that takes on the mutually contradictory opposites, in their crass incongruity, in a comical side-light to the genuine overcoming and uniting of those opposites that we see expressed in the words that saved Ellida: "freely and responsibly." (209–10)

In the text itself, Salomé's animus against Hedda Gabler makes the important distinction between the kind of sublime egoism she envisions and the self-serving egotism of those who defy convention simply for the sake of defiance. The Hedda chapter also allows Salomé to distinguish her erotic and independent woman from the pervasive figure of the femme fatale, the Lulus and Salomés that dominated male artists' imaginations and served as the conduit for their fears.

5.

Femininity, Modernity, and Feminism

The so-called woman question was at the heart of the development and legitimation of a range of knowledge and social practice in Wilhelminian Germany. It was posed in many diverse discursive and institutional fields and answered legally, politically, aesthetically, and medically by antifeminist politicians, scholars, and doctors in ways that situated the identity of woman at the center of political struggles over sexuality, economics, governance, and national identity. As the social, economic, and cultural situation of women changed in the second half of the nineteenth century, discursive and institutional interventions in the definition and regulation of sexual difference proliferated.

Until recently, the large and active women's movements in Germany were relegated to the margins of historical and literary historical study. Feminist researchers have now provided ample evidence of the significance of feminist interventions in the struggles over gender and sexuality in Wilhelmine Germany. As Elke Frederiksen notes, "The woman question" and feminism were not marginal phenomena for those who lived between the 1860s and 1914. She quotes one of the best-known researchers of the nineteenth-century German women's movements, Richard Evans, who has steadily maintained that "women's emancipation was one of the great social issues of the day; the woman's movement was bracketed with the youth movement and the labor movement as one of the greatest and most dangerous threats to the civilisation and social order of their time."[1] Evans takes his characterization of the women's movement as one of "the most dangerous threats" from a speech made by Kaiser Wilhelm in 1910.

Feminist research has emphasized the pronounced split in Germany between the proletarian and the bourgeois women's movements, both of them large and active. In her rich collection of texts and documents on the "woman question" in Germany, Frederiksen gives voice to the proletarian movement through the written tracts of Clara Zetkin, Lily Braun, Adelheid Popp, Ottilie Baader, and August Bebel. Frederiksen chooses documents from the bourgeois women's movement(s) which present the range of positions, from the conservatism and ultimate nationalism of a Gertrud Bäumer, for example, through the "moderate" proponents of women's particular cultural mission as mothers, to the more consistently liberal voices of a Helene Lange or Marie Stritt, and, finally, to the more radical positions on equality and sexuality presented by Hedwig Dohm, Helene Stöcker, Minna Cauer, Anita Augspurg, and Lida Gustava Heymann. Researchers such as Frederiksen have stressed the division between the more consistent, rationalist, liberal bourgeois feminists, with their demands for equality and rights, and those who argued strenuously for the specificities of femininity, for women's particular contributions to culture. Of course, the more feminists discover about nineteenth-century German women's movements, the more difficult it becomes to categorize feminists with labels such as radical, moderate, and conservative, since it becomes increasingly clear that the positions held by individual women and even specific groups were internally contradictory and dependent on how specific issues were defined. Nevertheless, it is true that claims for political rights based on arguments of women's equal rationality with men were rejected by political conservatives within the women's movement and by those who believed that the suppression of difference amounted to a repression of woman and the body. Feminists who struggled for concrete so-

[1] Elke Frederiksen, *Die Frauenfrage in Deutschland, 1865–1915* (Stuttgart: Reclam, 1981), pp. 5–43, 6.

cial, legal, and economic changes on the rationalist grounds of equal rights attacked proponents of what they considered to be romantic conceptions of difference for their complicity with reigning misogynist discourses.

In the second half of the nineteenth century, scientific research in anthropology, physiology, and the brain underwrote misogynist attacks on feminism as deviant or unnatural by presenting "evidence" of women's inborn weakness, their natural role as mother, and their natural place in the home. Darwin's work took on major importance in late nineteenth-century Germany, and the natural scientists (Ernst Haeckel, Wilhelm Bölsche), the sexologists (Richard von Krafft-Ebing, Havelock Ellis), the doctors, and the criminal anthropologists (Cesare Lombroso, Paul J. Möbius) constructed biological bases of sexual difference which profoundly influenced the discursive and institutional contests. The biological determinists posited developmental inferiority and greater primitivism for woman and declared that her function for the race required woman to live within the constraints of traditional definitions of her place (in the home). Many of the natural scientists, sexologists, and their popularizers were obsessed with the categorization of "contrary sexual types," of which the feminist was always suspect. Misogynists left no doubt about the perceived threat of female homosexuality and its supposed manifestations in women's political opposition.

Salomé articulated a double-edged critique of what she considered to be the views of both rationalist and romantic feminists, but she also challenged misogynist views of woman's natural inferiority and domesticity and idealist views of her complementarity to man, and she did so from a position outside of what she called "women's emancipation." At least one of her feminist contemporaries dubbed her antifeminist, and many present-day feminist critics have echoed the charge, but Ursula Welsch and Michaela Wiesner have seen her refusal of the "feminist" label as an instance of her rejection of all dogmas. Salomé was well acquainted with many of the best-known bourgeois feminists in Germany. The well-known and influential Swedish feminist Ellen Key, and the Germans Helene Stöcker, Helene Lange, Anita Augspurg, and Gertrud Bäumer, counted themselves among her friends. She was widely read and discussed among feminists, and she engaged with feminist ideas and writings in her own work. And she served as a sort of ideal for many women, including feminists.

Even her most outspoken feminist critic, Hedwig Dohm, acknowledged her own fascination with what she took to be Salomé's contradictions. Dohm objected in print to Salomé's seductive, far-too-long name, which converged with those of two of the most intriguing fin-de-siècle figures, Lulu and Salomé, femmes fatales who both fascinated and horrified by exploding women's supposed passivity and domesticity. Lou Andreas-Salomé and her writings could not then and cannot now be completely separated from those figures, and Salomé herself, whether intentionally or not, played with their evocative power. Her women friends and feminist acquaintances were no less fascinated with that power than were the men who celebrated and feared her.

Her friend Helene Klingenberg describes the kind of controversy Salomé provoked:

> For many, she has become a rare kind of provocation, a spur to higher and higher development, and this by virtue of her suggestive power and her fullness of being, which "enriches everything" and "gives itself over to things." For others, she has become a scandal, because her resistance is as great as her power, her defense against anything that touches her sphere of being in an unproductive way. A complete egoist, in the sense of a "holy self-seeking, with the drive toward obedience to that which is highest" (Nietzsche), completely free of "second-rate doubts."[2]

In Salomé, writes Klingenberg, all human traits combine:

> A tremendous readiness toward life, a humble and courageous ability to hold herself open to it, its delights, its knowledge, but also its deepest pains—all this characterizes her as a person who combines—with unimaginable appeal—the seriousness, the almost terrible seriousness of the man, with the gay lightheartedness of the child, and the devout surrender of the woman.[3]

---

[2] Helene Klingenberg, "Lou Andreas-Salomé," *Deutsche Monatsschrift für Russland*, March 15, 1912, p. 252.
[3] Ibid., p. 237.

What Helene Stöcker found most valuable in Salomé was the consistency of her self-representations, her theories, and other people's views of her. "This is what is characteristic about Lou Andreas-Salomé: neither her philosophical nor her artistic or psychoanalytic work is separable from her personality, in the way that it is for other apparently 'objective' creative artists."[4] Stöcker was one of the few leading German feminists who tried to make Nietzsche a philosopher for feminism or, as Heide Schlüpmann suggests, who made feminism the inevitable outgrowth of Nietzsche's ideas.[5] Salomé was one of Stöcker's most important connections, and though they worked in relative isolation from each other, they shared an interest in Nietzsche's critiques of church, state, and Christian morality in the interests of a new individuality that defied the split between sex and intellect enforced by all three institutions.

Stöcker studied Nietzsche's work when she was a student in Berlin, and in 1906 she published *Die Liebe und die Frauen* (Love and women), a collection of essays on Nietzsche's work. These had originated in a lecture series she had presented as she traveled for the Verein Frauenbildung-Frauenstudien (Association for Women's Education and Women's Studies).[6] In 1905 Stöcker founded the Bund für Mutterschutz und Sexual Reform (League for the Protection of Mothers and for Sexual Reform) and began publication of *Die Neue Generation* (The new generation). Stöcker's support for unwed mothers, for reform in the relations between the sexes, and in favor of women's sexual pleasure made her so unpopular with more moderate middle-class feminists that the *bund* was banned from the General Association of Women's Groups.[7] Increasingly she turned to

---

[4] Helene Stöcker, "Lou Andreas-Salomé: Dichterin und Denkerin," *Neue Generation* (Jan.–March 1931): 53.

[5] Heide Schlüpmann, "Zur Frage der Nietzsche-Rezeption in der Frauenbewegung gestern und heute," in *Nietzsche heute: Die Rezeption seines Werkes nach 1968*, ed. Sigrid Bauschinger, Susan Cocalis, and Sara Lennox (Bern: Francke, 1988), pp. 177–94.

[6] Schlüpmann documents Stöcker's work more fully in "Radikalisierung der Philosophie: Nietzsche-Rezeption und die sexualpolitische Publizistik Helene Stöckers," in *Feministische Studien* 1 (1984): 10–34.

[7] In *The Homosexual Emancipation Movement in Germany* (New York: Arno Press, 1975), James Steakley emphasizes Stöcker's uniqueness. Stöcker became a director of the Scientific Humanitarian Committee, founded by Magnus Hirschfeld. Steakley notes that "on February 10, 1911, the League held a meeting at which Hirschfeld and Stöcker spoke on homosexuality and the Committee's petition campaign. The League

eugenics and social Darwinism, and today her ideas seem politically contradictory.

Stöcker believed that women had the most to gain from Nietzsche's celebration of the fullest development of the individual, free now from "dependence on empirical conditions."[8] Nietzsche's conception of the new individual made it possible for women to define themselves as autonomous, sexual beings, rather than men's inferiors, or imitators. Those who understood the crisis in bourgeois humanist thought and society would, according to Stöcker, see Nietzsche, not Marx, as the "philosopher of the crisis." For Salomé, however, it would not have been consistent with her self-representation and her figuration of woman to have used Nietzsche's (or anyone else's) work as a battle cry in an overt political struggle. Salomé, as we have seen, represented herself as the enactment, not the political advocate, of radical individualism. Stöcker and Salomé parted ways over politics, most pointedly, as Schlüpmann suggests, over Stöcker's pacifism during World War I.

Conservative "feminist" Gertrud Bäumer devotes a chapter to Salomé in *Gestalt und Wandel*, a text that in fact reproduces age-old stereotypes of femininity. She presents an exaggerated stylization of an already inflated perception of Salomé as the "in sich ruhende Frau" (the contentedly self-sufficient woman).

Fearless and shy at the same time, shy, from her youth on, of anything that comes too close, possessed of a hunger for knowledge without being completely bound by it, in all her enthusiasm still fundamentally ungovernable, completely incorruptible. Never a "submissive" woman, even when she admired and loved, independent in every fiber, and in a certain sense unapproachable.... An unassailable piece of nature appears to reside within her. The shape of her head, the beautiful, proud line of the neck always reminded us of the picture of a young girl.[9]

Clearly, Salomé held a fascination for women as well as men. Bäumer's account emphasizes what she stressed in her autobio-

adopted a resolution which may well stand as the first statement by any women's group on homosexuality" (p. 42).
   [8] Schlüpmann, "Zur Frage der Nietzsche-Rezeption," p. 178.
   [9] Gertrud Bäumer, *Gestalt und Wandel: Frauenbildnisse* (Berlin: F. A. Herbig, 1950), pp. 469–70.

graphical constructions and in her own stylizations of femininity, which offer a sense of distance from unwanted intrusion, governance, and the forms of accessibility to women virtually guaranteed by the institutions within which they lived. Salomé resisted possession by another, whether in her marriage or elsewhere, because of the importance to her of an inner sense of the inviolable and a sense of conceptual space within which positions other than the mutually exclusive ones of daughter and son might be imagined. Her mobility within those terms challenges the usual complementarity of the sexes and the imperative that woman must necessarily live through man and his institutional mediations of her potentialities. As Dohm suggests in the 1899 essay "Reaktion in der Frauenbewegung" (Reaction in the women's movement), however, the forms of mobility carved out by Salomé's conceptual and aesthetic work had little immediate social impact beyond the personal spheres in which a woman such as Salomé could exercise it.

In 1899 Salomé published one of her most interesting prepsychoanalytic essays on femininity, "Der Mensch als Weib" (The human being as woman).[10] The essay works within and against the terms of biological and evolutionary thought. For that reason, Salomé's contemporaries and modern-day feminists have rejected the essay as an effort to ontologize a biologistic conception of the specifically feminine. Salomé's consistent antipositivism suggests other possible readings, although, as we will see, Dohm was quite right to suggest that "we find sentences that make an emancipated woman's hair stand on end, and still other sentences that could be taken for the strongest arguments for women's emancipation."[11] The text works against assumptions of woman's inferiority and against rationalistic demands for equality; it argues for woman's self-sufficiency in order to challenge an order of the human within which woman becomes merely the other of man's truths. Salomé figures

[10] This piece was retitled "Die in sich ruhende Frau" when it was published in *Zur Psychologie der Frau*, ed. Gisela Brinker-Gabler (Frankfurt am Main: Fischer Taschenbuch, 1978). The title suggests a less-critical reading of Salomé's representation of "woman," for it loses the antihumanist reversal of the conventional, though hidden, equation of male with "man" or "human." Subsequent page references, from the Brinker-Gabler edition, will be cited in the text.

[11] Hedwig Dohm, "Reaktion in der Frauenbewegung," *Die Zukunft*, Nov. 18, 1899, p. 280.

woman as the better example of "the human" not out of regressive atavism but because of her different trajectory from the old to the new, from the body to the intellect.

This essay, like her Ibsen study, begins with parables—in this case with her appropriation of the fairy tales told by her contemporary, Wilhelm Bölsche, a novelist and popularizer of natural science. Bölsche, as we remember, had introduced Salomé to Naturalist circles in Berlin, where he was well known for both his fiction and his popular scientific theory, which grounded the possibility of social change in his faith in evolution. In her memoirs, Salomé wrote that she appreciated the theater world of the Naturalist Movement for its spirit of youth and renewal, but she strenuously objected to the excessive realism of Naturalist art. By this point, Salomé had developed a strong critique of positivism, rationalism, and biological reductionism, and she clearly preferred what she considered Ibsen's psychological subtlety to the Berlin Naturalists' excessive realism.

In 1898 she had published a positive review of the first volume of *Das Liebesleben in der Natur* (Love life in nature), Bölsche's three-volume analysis of human behavior according to natural law and, most specifically, the laws of evolution.[12] Salomé objected to his strict adherence to natural law and argued explicitly and implicitly for the relative autonomy of human psychic life from its basis in biology. As Rudolph Binion suggests, Salomé proposed a discontinuity in the development of body and mind, arguing that in the sphere of the erotic at least, mental functions lag way behind biological differentiation and specialization. Binion credits her with seeing "through the value judgment latent in the phrase 'higher forms of life.' "[13] "Der Mensch als Weib" is but one example of her resistance to those value judgments and to forms of sterile faith among scientists.[14] Salomé's later psychoanalytical critiques of

---

[12] Wilhelm Bölsche, *Das Liebesleben in der Natur: Eine Entwicklungsgeschichte der Liebe* (Leipzig: Eugen Diederichs, 1898–1903).

[13] See Rudolph Binion, *Frau Lou: Nietzsche's Wayward Disciple* (Princeton: Princeton University Press, 1968), p. 231.

[14] In her Introduction to *Zur Psychologie der Frau*, p. 20, Brinker-Gabler argues that Salomé uses parody in her deployment of biological analogies.

Bölsche and Haeckel draw on these earlier critical appropriations and reworkings of Bölsche's "tales."

Bölsche had used fairy tales to explain the derivation of human life from earlier forms. Salomé draws on a combination of science and fable to develop her version of the significance of our "primal infancy" (*Urkindheit*), our derivation from nature, and its determinations. Salomé eschews a simple referential model of representation in favor of the performative value of proliferation. In explaining the roots of culture, she acknowledges the paradox of a consciousness that conceives its own conditions of possibility. As Daniel Purdy has argued in an unpublished essay, "Salomé links these two levels (consciousness and its base) by weakening the claims to certainty that biology and consciousness . . . maintained. Both spheres are softened up through romantic metaphor." Purdy cites an important passage from Salomé's essay, in which she reverses the expected relationship between subject and object:

> There is something about this process, however much we might transliterate it into fairy-tale style, that works in such a way, as if out of some sort of primal depth, gray with age, a mirror glimmered darkly up to the light of day, a mirror on whose secret-filled ground the sexual physiognomy of human beings is already recognizable in outline form. (285–86)

Purdy notes:

> While this passage does not summarize the whole of Salomé's method it does reveal her reversal of the traditional epistemological relationship between subject and object. Rather than having the viewer look out onto the object, Salomé here has the object, the mirror, shine up towards the viewer. The movement from the mirror to the viewer obviously suggests the reflection of light from the viewer to the mirror and then back to the viewer. She thereby retains the awareness that any understanding of the nonconscious, physical basis of knowledge can be gained only through consciousness itself. However, Salomé also suppresses the gaze from the viewer to the mirror by leaving it out of her description, thereby suggesting that the mirror generates its own gaze. . . . Salomé indicates that her reading of the basis of consciousness is inspired by a flickering vision from its sexual fundament, yet does not eliminate the idealist notion that

we can understand objects only through our own categories of thought—
Salomé uses the fairy tale as the category of thought through which she
interprets the origins of consciousness.[15]

As we have seen, all Salomé's work on the psychology of religion
articulates just such a view of consciousness. We are not all that far
removed, she argues, in apparent agreement with Bölsche, from a
primal state of nature, from "organisms that have not yet differentiated themselves into plants or animals, and in which we can
observe all of the various kinds of multiplication and reproduction
right up to the final development of sexual differences" (285). In the
account that follows, Salomé resists an appeal to scientific accuracy.
Her account of femininity is based not on scientific truth but on a
reading strategy that corresponds to her own idealization of "the
feminine" as an expansion outward in all directions, rather than the
linear movement of "scientific" argumentation, which proceeds
neatly from point to point. The following passage demonstrates the
particular ways in which Salomé inhabits the determinist assumptions in her contemporaries' invocations of anatomy and its
analogues:

These sexual differences arise out of the smallness and mobility of some
one-celled bodies and out of the largeness and indolence of the others
and, indeed, in such a way that the former characteristic always derives
from the latter: such little cells that become too small—for example,
because their parent cells had split themselves into all-too-many or all-
too-unequal child-cells in order to remain capable of life—are especially
dependent on attachment and are therefore forced into searching and
swarming outward. The larger cells, on the other hand, who, relatively
speaking, lack less on their way to slowly achieving the maturity of the
parent cells, have less need for such striving forward and therefore simply
rest in their place or nearby. (285)

In other words, the one-celled organism does not split into two
complementary halves that then find themselves again in love. Different cells make the passage toward maturity differently. The larger
cells are less irreparably split from their origins, and, hence, less in

[15] Daniel Purdy, "Lou Andreas-Salomé's Reactionary Feminine Style," unpublished essay, pp. 14–15.

need of coupling. For all its playfulness, this account anticipates what Salomé will make of Freud's theory of narcissism twenty years later.

We read on to find that the smaller, more frenetic, and forward-striving *Vorwärtsstrebende* cells are the masculine; the larger, more complete, and more serene, the feminine. The narrator emphasizes that this interpretation flies in the face of traditional conceptions of the masculine and feminine, and of the assumptions of the women's emancipation movement. Salomé's fairy tale and its implications enact a double-sided polemic, on the one hand, against the traditional equation of the more fully "human" with "masculinity" and, on the other hand, against the formulations and apparent ambitions of the liberal bourgeois women's movement and what she perceived to be its overly rationalistic insistence on equating women with men, on flattening out psychic life. She uses the relation between nobility and parvenu as an analogy for the relation between femininity and masculinity:

> There is a self-sufficiency and repose in [the feminine], in accordance with the deepest intentionality of being, which cannot be reconciled with the restlessness and disquiet of that which pushes itself forward with such passion to the outermost limits and splinters all its forces more and more intensively and pointedly in the service of specialized activities. In this the feminine behaves in relation to masculinity as a piece of age-old aristocracy, in its own castle and land, relates to the future-rich parvenu with his secure future, the parvenu who might make it much farther but who also sees the ideals of an ultimate beauty and completeness constantly disappear before his very eyes. (286)

Or as Binion has paraphrased, "Feminine is to masculine as the bluest-blooded aristocracy entrenched in its castle is to the most enterprising upstart who, venturing farther and farther afield, sees his ideal of fulfillment, like the horizon, recede indefinitely."[16] Femininity operates as the symbol of what the parvenu has lost in the linear movement of historical progress, as the object of his envy. Salomé proposes that the feminine is the more unified, the more similar to the structure of being. Neither femininity nor being, how-

[16] Binion, *Frau Lou*, p. 234.

ever, has absolute or absolutely knowable referents or origins in Salomé's essay. Femininity serves as the strategic base for the pro-liferation of enabling stories or utopian projections; it works to ex-pose the meaning of woman for man and to refigure her meanings for woman.

In her reading of Salomé's essay, Rose-Maria Gropp stresses that "woman" operates as signifier of lack, and hence desire, throughout the text and in that sense motivates the text's own movements.[17] On her reading, Weib, or woman, that "signifier of ubiquitous de-sire," is the subject of Salomé's writing, and Gropp credits Salomé with having carefully distinguished between woman as symbol and empirical women, between Weib and Frau. In her defense of Salomé's careful distinctions, however, Gropp avoids what is most provoc-ative about Salomé's work, namely, the very confusion of "woman" and women. Even when she distinguishes, "woman" nonetheless leans on women, and in those moments, "woman" appears to be-come prescriptive for women. Moreover, as we shall see, Salomé does not always distinguish between Weib and Frau.

Still, for now, let us stay with what Salomé's "woman" does to challenge conventional definitions of sexual difference. Salomé states the challenge unequivocally: "These two worlds become so wonderfully complex in themselves the more they develop; they ought not to be conceived as mere halves of one another, as so often happens, unfortunately, out of misunderstanding, for example, in the popular turn of phrase about the feminine being the passively receptive container, and the masculine being the actively creative contents" (288). With recourse to biological metaphor once again, and in anticipation of some of Freud's analogies relating the active to masculinity and the passive to femininity, Salomé asserts that the female egg is as active and as significant to the act of creation as the sperm and, further, reminds her readers that the egg is developed from that original "cellular construction" that was once capable of unsexed reproduction. She then proceeds to quote contemporary scientists on the possibilities of female parthenogenesis. Implicitly, she once again questions the value judgments inherent in misogynist

[17] Rose-Maria Gropp, "Das Weib existiert nicht," in Lou Andreas-Salomé, ed. Rilke Gesellschaft (Karlsruhe: Von Loeper, 1986), p. 49.

evolutionary views and treats science as a set of stories she can use to her own ends.

She reemphasizes the possibility of other than popular readings:

> I quote a passage from Johannes Ranke's well-known *Characteristic Features of Human Physiology* with only minimal abbreviation only in order to point out how dramatically the accepted physiological view contradicts the phrase mentioned above about the feminine element as the passive appendage to the creative man. With the same, or indeed much greater appearance of legitimacy, we could, instead of speaking in those terms, have spoken of the masculine element as generally the more dependent, the needier—as the more submissive, so to speak, that which is used up by the self-seeking feminine as a welcome contribution to her development. (290)

Salomé's grammatical qualifications have significant implications. With equal, or even greater, "appearance of legitimacy," she writes, one could speak of the greater need and dependence of the masculine. One could, but it is just a matter of appearances, not essence or truths but effects. We could say, with apparently more legitimacy that the masculine is "more submissive, so to speak." Salomé does not present man's dependence in the form of a counterscientific argument; she presents it as a fiction with the same legitimacy as the particular fiction that is usually derived from a supposedly scientific base, if not more. The greater neediness of the masculine derives from the sacrifices demanded of it, not from a natural relation between biology and its division of the sexes.

Again, I distinguish Salomé's readings and her writing from then-popular conceptions of the feminine which simply affirmed, even glorified, woman's role as a complement to man's. Though Salomé works within the metaphorical language of some of the most romantically misogynist contemporary theories of sex differences, she is concerned with other possible stories, with the symbolic significance of "woman" in the psychic lives of men and women, not with biological limits. In the next passage, Salomé comments on the distortions in all idealizations of woman's passive other-directedness, even in its supposedly most glorious forms, in motherhood and love of a man:

> The upside-down conception of the feminine basically commits one and the same mistake in its view of the passive dependence of woman, whether it emphasizes woman as an appendage of man or whether it emphasizes the maternal in woman, because even the maternal, when it is conceived in terms of passive receptivity and bearing, leads to the same false conclusions; we see both representatives of this direction everywhere within the so-called "woman question." Just like all the others, they overlook that woman is first and foremost something completely for herself, just like the man, and all further relations follow from that. (290–91)

In this passage, Salomé exposes the ways in which even feminist participants in the debates over the "woman question" repeat conventional definitions of woman as "for others." "Woman," for women, must primarily be for herself, symbol of self-absorption rather than dependence and other-directedness.

Salomé proceeds with her case for woman's self-sufficiency by writing a story of the process of reproduction in which she can show the greater unity in woman of what she calls "doing" and "being," a unity of apparently contradictory drives that have been less isolated from one another in woman than in man. Salomé suggests that fathering, from a purely biological point of view, consists of a momentary, temporary participation in creation, isolated from a man's other activities and from his body. The woman is more fully, more materially involved in the act of creation, and this pattern defines a fundamental difference between the masculine and the feminine. In the passages that follow, Salomé rewrites the meanings of female eroticism in ways that point back toward her interest in Nietzsche and forward to Freud. Woman lives in a much more immediate and involved relation to her body, with the result that it is much more obvious in woman than in man that intellectual life is a "flowering, a transformation of the great sexually determined root of all existence into the absolutely finest form" (292). This explains woman's privileged status as the object of philosophical and psychological investigation, according to Salomé.

We recall Salomé's challenges to men's supposedly greater objectivity in their work. For Salomé, the difference between masculine and feminine approaches is "real," but not necessarily absolute. What she regrets in the male scholar and his objectivity is the masculine amnesia that erases the feminine itself by projecting it outward, by separating object from subject, knowledge from sex. For this reason, the feminine comes to serve as both the externalized source of his knowledge and symbol of his own forgotten past. In figuring femininity as that which man has suppressed, forgotten, and projected outward onto women, Salomé avoids a complete confusion of femininity with biological essence.

Out of the distinction between the relative unity of contradictory drives in woman and the isolation and renunciation of difference in man, Salomé develops a rather involved interpretation of sexuality. She is interested in the apparent paradox that conventional wisdom can consider woman "the less sexual sex, in the narrow sense of the word" (292), by virtue of what Salomé calls her greater eroticism. The problem arises from the *Wortbegriff* (conception of the word) and all that it occludes, according to Salomé, for woman both is and is not more sexual than man; in effect, she is different. Salomé challenges traditional notions of woman's chastity, her purity, her asexual being, without denying the difference that those very categories have both expressed and veiled. Her form of transvaluation does not simply reverse the values associated with those labels but challenges the meaning of sexuality as such and the legitimacy of the comparison of man and woman. Salomé attempts to avoid both the conservative bourgeois feminist negation of women's sexuality and "equality arguments" at the same time. In her critique of one form of male sexuality, Salomé wrests sexuality from the acts in which it is meant to reside:

> The man, who is capable of a raw momentary satisfaction of his sexuality without any particular involvement of his other feelings, uses or misuses, if we have to put it that way, his more highly differentiated physical constitution. . . . This mechanistic, almost automated, character gives the process its ugliness. . . . The more undifferentiated being of woman, the not-yet-divided drives toward intimacy, and the intensive reciprocity of all the drives, ensures to feminine eroticism the deeper beauty. (292–93)

Paradoxically, perhaps, this less differentiated, more dispersed eroticism accounts for the greater freedom enjoyed by woman in relation to all that lies outside her. The revaluation of purity and chastity contests even as it reproduces conventional assumptions; it does not challenge the difference between masculine and feminine economies, nor does it uphold feminine chastity as a moral virtue but challenges once again "the sexual relation" between man and woman as a hierarchical complementarity in which woman's sexuality is defined as less than man's. Like a number of present-day feminists, Salomé works with fantasies of the body, its drives, its pleasures, and its rootedness in the materiality of life itself; she uses difference to announce that that which is most taken away by phallocentric orders of renunciation can be defined as that which is most woman's own, the basis of her difference. In an argument that prefigures contemporary feminist uses of psychoanalysis against phallogocentrism, Salomé attacks the tyranny of the specular and its centrality to those conceptual terms that efface woman: "In woman, with regard to sexuality, it is as it is psychically: the positive moment in her life in its internal workings cannot be perceived with any precision, whereas the workings and achievements of the man, as they press themselves outward, permit convincing conclusions about underlying and corresponding needs. And the sexual phenomenon itself was not even understood physiologically until recently except in a one-sided way, only in its external functioning" (294). In other words, woman becomes the source of knowledge at the point at which the object recedes from visibility, recedes from a verifiable, empirical place to the realm of the internal workings of the psyche, from the merely physiological to the psychic.

Salomé goes on to lament that women artists are not creating the conditions of visibility for woman, not even, or perhaps especially not, those writers and artists whose attempts to represent woman present mere defenses of or attacks against male representations. Salomé's critique is aimed at representation, at what she calls documentation, and the sexual division on which it depends. In a provocative polemic (which Hedwig Dohm would answer head-on in an essay to which I shall return), Salomé argues that women "have to listen to *his* works of art, if we want to be moved by the deepest and loveliest, the simplest and strongest of what lives in woman" (295). We should listen not just to any "he," but, for example, to a Peter Altenberg, whose originality, according to Salomé, has less to do with his being a man than with his *Pikanterie*, "piquancy," "which I cannot characterize here without taking too great a detour" (295).

In her memoirs Salomé writes that "when you were with him, you did not think of man or woman but of a being from a rich, third realm." About his writing, she notes, "What was new and exciting about his little creations is the curious way in which he prevented both sexes equally from maturing to adults and made their 'staying infantile' a poetic specialty that also found complete expression in his most personal individuality."[18] The concept of inhibited development (of his characters) emerges only after her work with psychoanalysis, but her emphasis on the artist's fundamental psychic bisexuality and on the creativity of internal sexual differences was consistent. Salomé characterizes Altenberg's relation to femininity: "because [his relation to the feminine in writing] takes a great deal of that sharp, accentuated consciousness from him, the objective and the active qualities of the male sex, it allows him to appear more unified, more organic, merged with that which he creates, and it keeps him, to some extent, in the happiness of intellectual pregnancy" (295–96).

Salomé conceives of the artist or the stylist as giving life to the conceptual, and this notion appears over and over in her explanation of the appeal of specific men and specific texts, of Nietzsche, for example, or Altenberg. Nevertheless, she argues that the male stylist is not "woman," nor is woman an artist in the terms in which "artist" is conventionally understood. Although his femininity may be the source of style, the male artist necessarily sacrifices the feminine in his worship of the product and its exchange value. Woman, according to this story, resides in her femininity and resists putting a part, an objectified piece, of herself into circulation, or at least resists the overvaluation of that object of exchange. Her creative drives are less focused on production and more integrated into her experience: "Perhaps it has become the lot of woman, according to ancient laws, to resemble a tree whose fruits are not supposed to be picked, separated, individually packed, shipped, and put to the most diverse purposes, but which wants instead simply to be a tree in the totality of its flowering, ripening, shade-giving beauty" (297).

Salomé does not suggest that woman, or women, should not

---

[18] Lou Andreas-Salomé, *Lebensrückblick: Grundriß einiger Lebenserinnerungen*, ed. Ernst Pfeiffer (Frankfurt am Main: Insel, 1968), p. 106.

produce anything either artistically or in any other sphere, but she does suggest that woman cannot enter the competitive world of the market without suffering a distortion of her femininity. Though she is clearly invested in guarding against integration into an order of competition and achievement which privileges isolated acts and products over diversity and excess, she also reproduces the equation of artistic creativity and achievement with masculinity. When Salomé argues that woman has less need for the forms of proof and approval that underwrite male achievement, she also suggests that "her lack" of his need constitutes woman's "natural greatness" (297). Woman's lack of need is distinguished from actual women's needs in order to avoid the conceptual collapse of reality and possibility, in order to avoid empiricism. Still, there is more than a hint of disapproval and hence prescriptiveness in Salomé's views of what women lack of "woman." Salomé's woman works to create the conditions of visibility for values that are opposed to the sacrificial, renunciatory order of the masculine or masculine humanism:

> The feminine tendency simply to bring itself to ever broader and richer self-unfolding, even with every conceivable effort toward intellectual development, instead of giving one's self over in objective commitment to a single goal, has often brought women up against the charge of dilettantism, of inconsistency and superficiality. In fact, it is difficult for a woman to follow a line that simply leads straight ahead, difficult not to digress, not to validate a sudden impulse, not to take pleasure in change. . . . Hence, the understanding in woman for things that cannot be made plausible to the intellect as such; she is able to harbor many more contradictions, whereas man first has to reject the very same things theoretically in order to come to clarity with himself. (298)

In this passage, Salomé makes a connection between masculinity and a particular epistemological and stylistic linearity that requires "casting off" and denial. What characterizes the masculine theorist is the repression of differences, of contradiction, of sudden impulses and detours, of things that are implausible because "illogical." Clarity requires the theoretical eradication of contradictions and differences. And from this critique of clarity, we are brought to the question of truth, to two different orders in relation to truth, orders that once again bear the name of the masculine and feminine:

Truth represents itself to man most forcefully as that with which we have to come to terms logically and that which, for that very reason, a majority of brains of normal intellectual development would affirm; a compelling truth for woman is always only that which is life enhancing, that to which she can say yes with her entire, her deepest and most undivided being, even though in some cases only she can say yes. Woman has particular resonance for the fact that the essence of things is, in the end, not simple and logical but plural and alogical—woman, by instinct, thinks individually from case to case, even when she has been logically trained. (298–99)

What "man" concedes only with difficulty—the intrusion of feeling, of psychic life into the abstract and logical—woman claims as the basis of her knowledge. Salomé's interest in the work of Nietzsche and Freud takes on an important dimension as the figure "woman" comes to serve as a critique of logical positivism. Indeed, in this, as in the preceding quotation, Salomé's woman certainly recalls the woman of Nietzsche's philosophy and seems to anticipate the woman of Freud's psychoanalysis. This is the affirmative woman that "Nietzsche loves," or at least envies. But here she is also more, for she is not only the object of the male intellectual's envy or the objectification of what he has repressed in himself but the motor of woman's subjectivity and intellectuality.

The text then moves to the level of the social and the empirical, and here Salomé uses the German word *Frau* instead of *Weib* to designate actual women as opposed to woman as a figure, a symbol, or a utopian possibility. At the outset of this section of the text, Salomé distinguishes the argument for a feminine difference—one that cannot be circumscribed or defined as the complement to man— from the reality of women's lives and aspirations. Salomé argues that *women* no longer feel the need to imitate men, to use male pseudonyms in either the literal or the figurative sense, but are still far from exploring feminine difference as something positive. She argues against the political fight for women's equality with man which she sees as sameness and advocates difference, conceived as the multiplicity and unbounded possibility within woman:

Until [women] cease doing that and try to conceive themselves in their *difference* from man and, for the moment, *exclusively in terms of that dif-*

ference, with as much surrender and depth as possible—honestly using all the most subtle physical and psychical hints—until then, they will not know how broad and powerful they could prove to be in the structure of their own being and how wide the boundaries of their worlds are in reality. Woman still has not been sufficiently with herself and, for that reason (and to that very extent), has not become sufficiently "woman." (300)

Woman, then, as the name of multiplicity and possibility, exceeds the order of the masculine, the logical, the linear, and exceeds as well the conventional divisions drawn between male and female. Woman, if she can be said to be "anything," is that difference without content or borders, the difference that women have hardly begun to explore for themselves. Here Salomé appears to suggest that women will discover themselves only when they cease needing and aspiring to masculine (subject) positions. Her own privilege, and her conceptual and psychological focus, allow her to downplay the extent to which taking up those positions was essential to creating the social and economic conditions under which woman's multiplicities could become meaningful.

Salomé does concede that convention, prejudice, and lack of opportunity stand in the way of women's exploration of "woman," but so too do the purely reactive and oppositional modes within the feminist struggle itself. She also concedes that work is a matter of social necessity for women which "words alone cannot change." In the face of social necessity, she suggests, the best we can hope for is that in her struggle for survival woman "might put her feminine stamp on things, instead of losing herself in them" (301). Salomé's resistance to feminism and her efforts to refigure and revalue the space of femininity also include a homophobic reaction to women who appear to usurp the place of men, of mannish women. We can also credit her, however, with anticipating the objections of anti-feminist critics of women's increasingly unconventional choices; she cleverly answers them by figuring those choices in ways that make them compatible with the most idealist conceptions of woman's harmonious nature:

Young women who appear to be pursuing unfeminine goals may, in fact, simply be trying to expand themselves, their woman-souls. . . . If one denies them their efforts, their strongest abilities shrivel up, and they are damned to eternal disharmony, awkward and unproportioned. In this sense, one can only preach freedom, and again and again freedom, even if one has to destroy every artificial barrier and limit, because there is more reason to trust the voices of desire in people, even when they express themselves falsely, than to trust preconceived and ready-made theories. (301)

In Salomé's responses to German bourgeois feminists, we find astute philosophical, psychological, and aesthetic critiques, as well as politically naïve objections to necessary forms of struggle, arising, it is true, from her privilege, but also from her insular focus on aesthetics and psychology and her tendency to assimilate the complexities of the social to the structural terms in which she makes her philosophical critiques of feminism. In the passage just quoted, Salomé argues that all forms of resistance by women, no matter how distorted they may seem, evidence a profound underlying desire for a different process of growth and change. The freedom to move in any direction, to try any of the multiple ways of realizing the potential for change, for transformation and growth, is ultimately the most important thing. Here of course, in a curious way, Salomé could be said to rejoin Nietzsche, for whom feminism was tolerable as long as it could be viewed as just another step toward the ends of "man."

In the ensuing passages, Salomé cleverly redefines domesticity and the separation of home (read: woman) and work (read: man). Against those who object that the freedom she advocates flies in the face of woman's domesticity, that it threatens to make her "undomestic," *unheimisch*, Salomé offers the metaphor of the snail, who "crawls contentedly on its way carrying its little home on its back. The little home is her own, but on the way, all kinds of things grow, things that she desires and needs in order to grow into a true, vigorous snail" (302). Salomé treats stereotypes to expose the stakes in their production and use, namely, the fear of difference and the attempt to contain it. Woman remains at home while under way, she is in no danger of slipping out of her femininity, which is rewritten as an unlocatable, unfixed domesticity. Woman's defense against subordination to his terms is a nomadic narcissism.

Salomé uses the figure of the snail and woman's mobile domesticity to highlight man's need for woman's domesticity. He is the one, she writes, who needs the house, the constraints on woman, the boundaries of home, and the familial law as a rest from the exhaustion he suffers from spending his strength and productivity in pursuit of external goals to which he brings himself as a sacrifice. Woman's law, her truth, and her ethics, unlike those of man, are a question of style, according to Salomé, rather than loyalty to civilization, to goals assumed to be outside and above. Here the similarities between Nietzsche's and Salomé's affirmative woman emerge quite clearly, as does the difference Salomé saw between herself, as woman, and him: "That's where we sometimes get the impression of a singular combination of opposites in woman: the impression at one and the same time of the wilder, more impulsive, more filled with contradiction, and the more harmonious, more at peace, more balanced; of the instinctive protest against law, order, responsibility, obligation, and at the same time, of a higher ethics that never violates itself" (303).

The text follows up with an "unappealing comparison." One could, if one wanted, compare woman to a band of thieves who live in total disrespect for the law and without any relation or connection to other classes of people, who act out of strict and binding rules that have grown out of their own "way of being." Woman, writes Salomé, as if once again in discussion with Nietzsche or Freud, is less "civilized" and less capable of acculturation and domestication. Man is "overly civilized," on the other hand, "in that he partly drills and partly actually sublimates his willingly sacrificial nature for the most varied tasks, until it can no longer operate as a unified, harmonious organization" (303). Although "he" emphasizes her weaknesses, he needs "woman," for she is still what he no longer is, the projection of what he has sacrificed in order to be a man. Woman, for man, is both more primitive and more complete, necessarily the object of his phantasmal projections and his need. For that reason, a man's love for a woman is always caught up in what she symbolizes of "woman." Drawing on prevailing conceptions of man's greater variability, Salomé suggests that an individual woman is always more woman than an individual man is man. Woman, Salomé continues, lacks the anxiety over loss out of which he produces and attempts to control both himself and her. She is less likely to confuse her own inner goals with those imposed from outside and, hence, less prone to conformity and blind obedience. Man's overcivilization makes him dangerously susceptible to the external, the father's law.

Sexual difference and questions of desire become central to conceptions of subjectivity and sociality. Individuation within a masculine economy requires sacrifice and renunciation, ensures "progress," and is conflated with the male as such. There is no need to be envious, Salomé assures women readers: "Just as woman appears to man as the less individualized being, so she also appears as that being that still participates in a more unmediated way in life itself and can operate as its personalized mouthpiece, in a goodness and wisdom beyond all reason" (306). The issue of loss has further implications; the order of the masculine—the linear, the bounded, and the apparently coherent—requires the denial of death, which is, for Salomé, a question of form: "Just as a drop of water that falls into the sea loses its form but in the process merely returns home to its element, so too, the demise of the single individual in death or its implication in the supreme powers of life makes more sense to woman than to man's sensibilities" (306).

The essay continues by interpreting "the tragic" and the heroic as specifically masculine orders. For woman, self-assertion, subjectivity, and the giving up of self "are nourished out of the same endless source, and therefore she snuggles up with instinctive faith to the final secrets of demise and ascent" (307). The order of the masculine requires division, which is a consequence of human life, and also the denial of what are called the *Naturboden*, the "foundations" out of which he emerges as subject. The male hero's struggles against death, dissolution, the abject give the tragic and the heroic their significance:

> We have only to imagine the bodies of the two sexes—from a purely aesthetic perspective, as if it required us to fix upon only the most significant lines of each—in their destruction through elemental powers, and we will be amazed at the instinctiveness of the emerging image: immediately we see the naked male body with strained muscles, unwilling and defiant, as if he proved his ultimate beauty only in such dissension from what is happening—woman, on the other hand, with the soft curves of her body appears to need to lean and bow, to give in to the forces, so that beauty might find itself in beauty. (307)

Salomé then ends by exploring the meanings of women's piety, establishing the difference between a feminine relation to belief and an atheistic one. Again Salomé uses the stereotype of female piety and argues the impossibility of "her" atheism in order to point to the possibility of woman's objectless love. She returns to her project of assimilating all apparent forms of women's emancipation into woman's self-becoming. Salomé suggests that "a lot of the conflicts from which women today suffer, in marriage, in society, and in their struggle for survival, have this meaning [of woman's self-becoming], even though it may seem as though woman were struggling her way out of femininity rather than into it" (308). Part of the reason women find it so hard to articulate what is really at stake for them, according to Salomé, is the demise of religion, which once provided a language in which woman could articulate her own destiny and her relation to something "beyond all human relations, conflicts, and obligations. Today she can barely express what she means when she speaks of an obedience to herself that is higher and more intimately destined than obedience to a world outside" (308). Precisely because of this impoverishment of language, which psychoanalysis will later solve, "woman's need to expand in a way that is harmonious with herself gets confused beyond all distinction for those outside of her with some sort of ambitious or manly [*mannweiblichen*] drives that want to free themselves at the cost of the rest of her being" (308–9). For Salomé, the greatest danger lies in woman's own tendency to believe those outsiders and to define herself in terms of a partial career development or to resign herself to being the appendage to some man, thereby "turning herself voluntarily into a mere vehicle for his high-handedness" (308). Salomé notes

the entirely too loud and too conscious cry for the man and only for the man . . . the feverish overstimulation and greed that drive hundreds of unfulfilled women into a myriad of individual occupational activities. . . . Both currents have this in common, that they externalize woman's inner center of gravity and transfer it out of her into another person or thing, thereby dislocating her natural balance. They produce a kind of idolatry that drains her deepest human productivity. (309)

These are precisely the terms Salomé uses to discuss Ibsen's heroines of course. Of Ellida's ultimate internalization of "the alien man" and the consequent end to her obsession with him, she suggests that "freedom ceases to lure her because it no longer seduces from the distance; Ellida resides in freedom."[19] But Salomé's dread of the masculine woman, or the woman who succumbs to the ugliness and vulgarities of modern work life, too easily rejoins the most conservative late nineteenth-century arguments *against* women's work and *for* the conservation of her natural balance. Here is a clear instance in which the limits of Salomé's internal critique of her male compatriots emerge. In complicity with her friends and colleagues among bourgeois artists and thinkers, Salomé idealizes a femininity that can appear to delegitimate woman's political struggles, even as it authorizes her agency on aesthetic and intellectual fronts. In a sense, Salomé's "woman" expresses the desire to "have it both ways"; she advocates absolute freedom from within the terms of gender polarity. The contradictions become amply clear in the closing pages of the essay when Salomé frames woman's self-sufficiency in terms of its appeal for truly manly modern men, who are "as horrified of women who seek salvation in men as of those who seek it in emancipation" (310).

The essay ends with a turn to the importance to man of woman's piety, distinguishing between masculine and feminine economies once again:

And when the man then slowly descends from these heights into daily life and the loud workday and sees *woman:* then it must appear to him as though he saw eternity itself in the form of a young, kneeling being, of whom it is impossible to know whether it kneels in order to be closer to earth or more open to heaven. Indeed, the two are so unified in their expression, as if there were something embodied in the expression that exalts all humanness out of the old biblical words, like a symbol: Everything is yours! You, however, are God's. (311)

The allusion to "The Women and Their Effects at a Distance" in *The Gay Science* is unmistakable. The passage also recalls Salomé's attributions of envy to the male philosopher and his need for "woman." Such an ending emphasizes once again the symbolic function of

[19] Lou Andreas-Salomé, *Henrik Ibsens Frauengestalten nach seinen sechs Familiendramen* (Berlin: H. Bloch, 1892), p. 175.

woman as his lack, but perhaps also as her possibility. Woman's mediation of man's subjectivity takes an interesting turn in this conception of a new heterosexuality. What woman does for man is return him to his own relation to that which exceeds the individual and his consciousness. She no longer offers him a passive or blank screen for his projects or projections. Woman represents something that he only rarely experiences, "never in the valleys of life, but on its mountain peaks," in those moments when he, too, experiences himself as a mere tool in the hands of something that exceeds him, when he, too, experiences himself "in a secret union with all that exists" (311). Salomé's heterosexuality unites man and woman in their orientation to something larger than either of them, something to which she has as unmediated a relation as he and which frees her from social convention and dependence on him.

There are other possible readings of Salomé's essay. One such is Hedwig Dohm's highly critical response in "Reaktion in der Frauen-bewegung" (Reaction in the women's movement) to what she per-ceived as Salomé's appropriation of the "woman" of German idealism. Dohm, who was born in 1833, was eighteen years Salomé's senior. She had experienced the radicalism associated with the 1848 revolution in Berlin and had become a leading figure in the more radical arm of the German bourgeois feminist movement. Her views went way beyond bourgeois arguments for better education for women based on notions of feminine moral superiority and mater-nalism. The emphasis on women's difference, which tended to be grounded in women's capacity to reproduce and nurture, dominated the more moderate wing of the movement. Dohm, however, with stunning polemics, argued the self-evidence of women's equality with men and their consequent claim on equal rights. She advocated female suffrage long before other bourgeois feminists and advanced a goal of full political participation for women. Dohm believed that women's differences from men were the consequence of historical and social environment, not nature. With considerable wit and a gift for satire, she pointed out how arguments for women's differ-ence facilitated women's oppression, and she sought to expose the structures of privilege and blindness which implicity obfuscated the issues. Dohm's particular demystifications drew on rational argument and scientific truth to contest the profoundly illogical and contradictory arguments of the German antifeminists. Yet, although she strategically countered ideological mystifications with fact, she deployed orientalist oppositions between the "sultry mysteries" of the East and the rational clarities of the West in the process.

Dohm's response to Salomé's 1899 essay highlights her frustration at Salomé's contradictions and her seductive language and style, a style that participates in intentional obfuscation, according to Dohm. In her critique, Dohm also avails herself of many of the stereotypes through which others approached Salomé. "Frau Lou," as she calls her, is one of those "serpentine ladies with their colors and sinuous lines."[20] With Salomé she links two other such serpentine ladies, Ellen Key and Laura Marholm, exposing inconsistencies in the work of all three. In resisting rationalist equality arguments in the belief that their intent was to erase difference, according to Dohm, they erected man once again as the single norm.

Salomé is neither consistent nor loyal, but Dohm is at first seduced by style. She comes to her senses in her second reading of the essay, "and then I found in Frau Lou's ideal woman something of a sublimated high-intellectual harem, without the sultan, of course, but the narcissism is there. . . . she leads us into a fairy-tale land of pure spirits and hearts" (282). When Dohm equates the East, fantasy, sexuality, and narcissism, she reproduces a very common stylization of Salomé. Her critics, and even Salomé herself (though her valuation was different), often depicted her as the *harem Frau*. Having perceived Salomé's seductiveness, Dohm finds her betrayal all the harder to bear: " 'Even you, my son Brutus,' I thought in distress, after I had read her piece 'Der Mensch als Weib.' Frau Lou (her entire far-too-long name eats up too much paper) antifeminist!" (280). Dohm has no problem taking up "the masculine position." She positions herself here in the place of the father, she resists being consumed by Salomé's name, she consigns Salomé to the ranks of the antifeminists—all as introduction to a much more sustained preoccupation with her. In fact, Dohm's resistance to "Frau Lou"

[20] Dohm, "Reaktion in der Frauenbewegung," p. 280, hereafter cited in the text.

takes up much of the rest of the article, ostensibly a polemic against Marholm and Key as well as Salomé. Salomé creates the biggest problems for the critic intent on dismissing all three as antifeminists.

Dohm begins her discussion of Salomé's essay with long quotations from some of what Dohm takes to be the most poetic passages, noting their seductiveness: "She speaks to us out of this essay as if through a delicate veil, or as if out of a certain distance; and the more dubious her writing becomes, the more subtly she feels around in it" (280). The distance and the veil disturb Dohm the activist because she believes they obscure social realities. Inevitably, she counters seduction and aesthetic mystification with the possibility of truth, derived from rationality and "science." Modern man no longer believes, according to Dohm; he demands proof. In her plea for reason and sobriety, Dohm succumbs to stereotypes of the East, the veil, seduction, and deception. She literalizes the philosophical implications of Nietzsche's or Salomé's veiled untruths, locates them in the "East," and opposes them with Western science and truth.

For feminists such as Dohm, rationality and science, not poetics or erotics, carried the promise of equality for women. On the basis of her belief in science, Dohm condemns the son Lou and saves herself from temptation by asserting: "We want to be convinced. We demand proof. And she owes us that with her vision of woman. . . . with her magical melodies . . . Lou half drew me in, I half collapsed. Then I read the piece again; and the magic was broken. And my sober intellect reacted strongly and clearly against my deep sympathies" (281–82). Dohm accuses Salomé of failing to be straightforward, of speaking from behind the veil, from a distance, perhaps from as far away as the East, and she accuses her of telling lies about "woman" that seduced her almost to the point of collapse. For Dohm, style and its veiling effects are the culprit. Beautiful metaphors cannot tell the truth. The rest of Dohm's reading and critique of Salomé's essay alternates between dismissing its arguments as mysticism and subjecting individual points and metaphors to the test of reality. For Dohm, it is a question not simply of truth and science but of politics.

Dohm juxtaposes Salomé's metaphors to realities to make important points about the material conditions of women's lives. She successfully exposes the problems, even the dangers, of any literal reading of Salomé's essay, outlining Salomé's ignorance and obfuscation of how women actually live and noting the insularity of the philosophical, aesthetic, and even religious terms within which Salomé works. But for all the importance of Dohm's critiques, the perceived split between rationalism and romanticism, which Salomé sought to displace, remains.

Dohm accuses all three "antifeminists" of prescribing what women should be, of opposing women's work outside the home, of holding feminists in contempt, of overvaluing men. "The three are united," she wrote, "in thinking that we could dispense with the works of women in art and science. Frau Lou calls what a woman produces: 'fallen fruit.' . . . Even Frau Lou's works, fallen fruit? If I thought they were, I would never pick them up, and I always do" (284–85). Dohm reduces the ambiguities and the differences among these three women in order to contest their loyalty to the terms of what I have called an insistent oedipalization or heterosexualization. She complains:

> By God, if these dear and highly talented writers are so passionately opposed to women's professional activity and their competition with the man, why don't they stay within the sphere of femininity, far away from any vocation or work? And why don't these women make their arguments simple and clear—yes, particularly clear? Why do they disguise their thoughts? There are so many other realms more appropriate than the woman question for poetic effusions. (290–91)

In spite of her polemic, Dohm remains frustrated by contradictions right to the end; her claims are punctuated with questions. Salomé escaped the confines of conventional femininity, its frames, its borders, its representations, not simply because she made an exception of herself but because she wrote precisely against representation, against constraint, against "truth," and in favor of style, of radical individualism, of living. In her critique of representation, however, Salomé also exposed her loyalty to the aesthetic and philosophical values of the male-dominated cultural elites in which she moved, for some of whom feminism constituted yet another intrusion of a vulgar and ugly modernity.

Salomé's response to an article written by her friend Frieda von Bülow about men's assessments of women's writing serves as a case in point. Salomé finds her friend's views too indignant, too filled, in other words, with *ressentiment*.[21] Von Bülow asserts that women should not shun male critics' use of the category *Frauendichtung*, "women's writing," but should embrace that label as the highest form of praise. Nothing could be emptier or more distorted than the conventional term of approval: "If the title did not say so, one would never believe that a woman had written this work."[22] Von Bülow claims that women should write as women, rather than imitate male art.

Salomé acknowledges the seeming self-evidence of von Bülow's views, then makes their shortcomings plain through an ironic parable of an artistically gifted fox. It seems obvious that the fox should write as a fox, she notes, from his experience as a fox and about foxiness, rather than imitate the human. But to represent oneself as a fox, she concludes, is "journalism, not art." Art for the fox would consist in unfoxlike similarities with, say, a Goethe. "What the fox should develop, should he want to produce art, is his anomalous status with respect to the human, even if his fox essence comes up short." Again, Salomé refuses consignment to an identity and its representation. She applies the implications of the fox story to women: "Now, of course, women are not foxes, at least not in this sense. But it isn't impossible to imagine that their unintended devaluation according to male standards in the area of art had as deep and secret a justification as if they really were foxes" (237).

Salomé points to the writings of Gabriele Reuter as evidence to support her claim that the "documents" produced by women about women are not artistic. Men write about issues and problems that transcend their sex. It is more difficult for women to do so, Salomé writes, because they are not as capable of such transcendence:

Women, too, possess the basic prerequisite for all kinds of creativity, the intense absorption with all the material of one's own life and being. They do not possess the second condition, in which the actual capacity for art resides, in the same measure as men: that characteristic selfless willing-

[21] Lou Andreas-Salomé, "Ketzereien gegen die moderne Frau," *Die Zukunft* 26 (1899): 237–40, hereafter cited in the text.
[22] Salomé quotes from Frieda von Bülow, "Männerurtheil über Frauendichtung," *Die Zukunft* 26 (1899): 26–29.

ness to be used up by the artistic creation as our lord and master, for the success of which alone one trembles, becomes feverish, and is deeply indifferent to oneself. The major reason for this is related to the fact that in woman all individual activities of the being as a whole stand in a closer and more lively reciprocity with one another than is necessary for man with his capacity for specialized display of strength. (238)

Rather than react to male evaluations, as von Bülow does in her article, women should simply refuse comparisons, both those that condemn and those that praise. If publishers would allow it, it would be better, according to Salomé, for women to publish anonymously so as to undo the conflation of ego and product: "Precisely the more personal quality of their material, its less artistically formed quality, should, as recompense, make them indifferent to that most personal vanity of becoming famous" (239).

Salomé questions conventions of authorship and suggests other forms of subjectivity, forms that do not merely repeat or reverse the terms of the male canon. Her particular use of difference here remains mired in the homage to the canon and its fathers, however, even as it works to protect women from the pitfalls of male ego investments and the effects of a commercialization of art that relies on fame and glamour, rather than the intrinsic quality of a work. Such forms of protection also "protect" women from the world and can only come, of course, from a position of relative privilege and independence. She ends with a loving portrait of Marie von Ebner-Eschenbach, who was not a "woman writer" or the "equivalent of the male" but someone whose works "transcended" the sex of the author without sacrificing the person behind them. This ending makes it possible to read Salomé's parable and its application to women as the search for a speaking position that neither effaces nor remains caught within sexual difference.

In her review of Ellen Key's *Mißbrauchte Frauenkraft* (Women's misused energy), Salomé differentiates herself from both Key and Marholm, though from within an underlying unity with Key.[23] Ellen Key, eventually a close friend of Salomé's, introduced the concept of "women's misused energy," which substantially influenced de-

[23] Lou Andreas-Salomé, review of *Mißbrauchte Frauenkraft*, in *Die Frau* 5 (1898): 513–16, hereafter cited in the text.

bates over the "woman question" in Germany. Key wrote and spoke against the tendency among feminists to focus on legal, social, economic, and occupational equality with men. Drawing on a perceived dissatisfaction and apparent lack of fulfillment among working women, Key made her plea for locating the essence of femininity in maternity. In this, she seemed to reproduce then-popular sentiments and pseudoscientific arguments against the education of women and the "misuse" of their reproductive and nurturing natures. In her account of Key's effects on German feminists, both bourgeois and proletarian, Kay Goodman notes Key's emphasis on "the power of motherliness," which translated into woman's difference, her natural talents, and the importance of her values for the harmonious working of society as a whole.[24] As Goodman shows, Key also advocated the vote and expanded career choices for women, but on the basis of woman's specific contribution of feminine (read: maternal) values. Key also became active in the Bund für Mutterschutz, which advocated social reforms that would acknowledge and support unwed mothers and women's sexual agency.

According to Goodman, Key's focus on women's specific cultural role and their particular contributions to the "race" and "nation" found fertile ground in Germany among conservative bourgeois feminists who continued to identify woman with mother and to celebrate her cultural mission in society as a whole; but Key's focus also found a positive reception among such proletarian leaders as Clara Zetkin, who also fought for the recognition of difference. And women such as Lily Braun, too, who straddled the line between the proletarian and bourgeois movements, shared Key's definition of femininity and sexual relations, over against what they perceived to be the rationalist direction in "the classical land of the women's movement, England." Goodman points to what she calls the "rather traditional homophobia" in Key's or Braun's horror of so-called mannish intellectuals, a tendency that appears to be inherent in so many of the

---

[24] Kay Goodman, "Motherhood and Work: The Concept of the Misuse of Women's Energy, 1895–1905," in *German Women in the Eighteenth and Nineteenth Centuries: A Social and Literary History*, ed. Ruth Ellen Joeres and Mary Jo Maynes (Bloomington: Indiana University Press, 1986), pp. 110–27.

involutions, as opposed to revolutions, of conventional definitions of sexual difference.[25] It recalls a tendency I see in Salomé's work as well.

Salomé reviewed Key's book soon after it was published in Germany in 1898. In the first paragraph she acknowledges Key's importance and notes her own identification with Key, situating the Swedish feminist between the radical feminists and the antifeminists. Salomé's focus is Key's insistence on the "sexual nature of woman" and her attendant insistence on woman's freedom. She stresses Key's arguments in favor of equality without identity and sameness, without requiring women to become like men. She goes on to criticize the rationalist argument that sexual difference exists only on the level of the "lower instincts," which should be transcended through reason, for both she and Key read this transcendence as a repression through which man and woman become the same, equally disembodied and stripped of particularity. This form of equality or the identically human is predicated on denying, on "overcoming," sex, "instinct," body. It is this challenge of the rationalist position as repressive and somatophobic, however, which brought many feminists to condemn Key as reactionary and biologistic for the inevitable ways in which her arguments appeared to line up with the antifeminist arguments of notorious male misogynists.

Salomé outlines what she sees as a growing split within the women's movement, between those who insist upon the development of the specificity and multiplicities of woman and those who aspire to what she calls the victory of the male over the female in woman. Salomé attacks the political and conceptual failures of abstract humanism, which "build on the idea that the woman, through her efforts, will in time slip out of her feminine nature, like the butterfly out of a tight cocoon, in order to become 'a human being' in a certain sexless, abstract sense of the word" (514). Key believes that women's strength is misused not only in the sacrifices exacted by the conventional order of sexual difference but also in some previously male professions that are predicated on the renunciation of femininity, of

[25] Ibid., p. 123.

difference from and within the masculine. Though women must work, Key believes, they must not sacrifice femininity. Salomé quotes from Key's essay to highlight their agreement:

> The next step forward—by no means backward—is to emphasize the justification of freedom on the basis of nonequality. For just as surely as it was a great cultural loss that only 'the sex' and not feminine individuality was realized, it is surely just as great a cultural loss when we overlook and underestimate the infinitely rich sexual moment in individual differentiation with a uniformity that levels individuality all over again. (515)

From this point of obvious agreement, Salomé builds a polemic against both Marholm and Key for their efforts to define woman's essential difference, Marholm for her conception of woman's erotic *Grundtrieb*, "fundamental drive," toward man, and Key for her conception of woman's fundamental maternal drive. Both reduce woman to some original, primal, and determining drive. From the concept of "the mother" or "the maternal," for example, Key constructs what Salomé calls an entire schematic philosophy in which woman once again is reduced to passivity. She finds problems too in the ways both Key and Marholm externalize woman's essence onto either man or child in the erotic or the maternal relation and its instinctual determinations. Salomé deftly uses Key's words against her when she professes agreement with Key's following claim, a claim that locates both Key and Marholm in the midst of the various *lebensphilosophical* or life-reform movements at the turn of the century. "The return to one's own I, to primal nature, to the great, mysterious ground that is our life source—this return is the most significant trend at the end of the century," she agrees, "but it is precisely for that reason that there is for me still too much of the schematic in her book, which leaves the 'mysterious great' too little room to move, to document itself without constraint" (515). The mystery cannot be represented or systematized or made into the basis of a philosophy with claims to nature, nor should it be.

Salomé ends by developing her position with respect to theory, to system, and to truth. Her trajectory can be followed through all her engagements with the discursive terrain of her period:

I consider it very improbable that any theoretical analysis, no matter how sophisticated, will be able to tell us anything essential or enlightening about woman anytime soon: the best thing will always be the subjective flavoring through which the personality of the author offers an unintended self-display along with her logical conclusions and thereby contributes to the psychology of women. In the meantime women should try to blossom, each in her own way and each under that sun that burns brightest for her. We can then leave the categorizations and classifications of those flowering individual examples, without any envy, to another, later time. (515–16)

Rather than propose prescriptions, Salomé refuses any conceptual and behavioral constraints on that which is just coming into being. She targets the tyranny of the conceptual and systematic, and the zeal with which her contemporaries categorized, named, and regulated femininity. The systems that represent the essence of "woman" require exclusion, the exclusion, Salomé tells us, of what woman could be. For Salomé, the differences "woman" signifies create a space within which masculine and feminine cannot be equated with literal men and women. But as Dohm shows, Salomé locates her unprohibited, unprescribed woman exclusively in the realm of fantasy and aesthetics, or perhaps Salomé locates the realms of fantasy and aesthetics as the only register in which femininity can become more than its hegemonic social definition allows. For all the value of her interventions and her efforts to open up what is socially intelligible to differences, Salomé's constructions exclude the social, its contingencies, and the limits on the positions it allows and requires, even or especially for those who oppose its constraints.

6.

Femininity in Salomé's Fiction

"Fenitschka" is one of Salomé's most interesting explicitly fictional works. Published in 1898 but written perhaps as much as a dozen years earlier, in 1886, it demonstrates the particular ways in which Salomé both appropriates and undercuts stereotypical turn-of-the-century representations of woman.[1] Like much of Salomé's prose, this narrative, too, provides the occasion for an exploration of philosophical, social, and primarily psychic dilemmas. Despite the popularity of her fiction at the time of its publication, critics have subsequently dismissed it for its tendency to dramatize philosophical or psychological debates, for its overly cerebral character. Salomé claimed that she wrote fiction only for pragmatic reasons, in order to sustain the financial independence that allowed her to stay in Germany. In that claim, she instantiates her conception of a femininity concerned only with the process, not with the product of writing. As we remember, in her memoirs she claimed to dislike her fictional texts because they were written in a sort of masculine protest against Gillot's efforts to cure her of her obsessional fantasizing. She criticized her fiction's consequently "male" point of view, which sees the female characters through the eyes of the man.

Precisely because the texts are narrated from a man's point of view, however, Salomé's stories succeed in exploring and even di-

[1] Ute Treder makes a similar argument about the significance of this text in *Von der Hexe zur Hysterikerin: Zur Verfestigungsgeschichte des "Ewig Weiblichen"* (Bonn: Bouvier, 1984).

agnosing masculine projections of femininity. Salomé puts some of her own reflections on the social and cultural constituents of woman's supposed "mysteriousness" into the thoughts of self-critical male figures, through whom we read the enigma that woman is, for them. Writing from the perspective of her male characters, Salomé also succeeds in engaging what she might have called the oscillation within herself over questions of femininity and feminism.

In "Fenitschka," the reader is introduced to the character Fenitschka, a Russian intellectual visiting Paris, through the eyes of Max Werner, whom many have read as a transparent depiction of Nietzsche. Werner becomes the mouthpiece for masculine reflections on typically male expectations and needs. Right from the outset, both on the level of plot and on the structural level, Fenitschka unsettles Werner's point of view. Her explosion of social expectations and her return of Werner's "look" lead to Werner's reflections on the cultural construction of woman's mystery. Constantly surprised and consequently angry, Werner learns that the enigmatic and therefore seductive power of a woman like Fenitschka has nothing to do with her essence as woman. It results from his needs and the inadequacy of conventional views and expectations to account for her multiplicity, her pluralities, for they demand that she be one thing or the other, that she be sex or mind, "free" or studious, a grisette or a nun. The story displaces these polarities by refusing to fix Fenitschka within such categories. She presents no truthful representation of woman to counter Werner's mystifications. As always, Salomé is more interested in grounding "woman" in a lack of boundaries and categorizations, more interested, too, in the psyche and its complex struggles than in social realities, more interested in analysis than in referentiality.

As Werner and Fenitschka draw closer at the level of the plot, their identities and differences diminish at the level of structure as well. In the last scene, Werner becomes a sort of enabling presence, a third term; at Fenitschka's bidding, he hides in her bedroom while she breaks up with her lover in the next room. His presence in her bedroom makes it possible for her to separate from a lover who had wanted to "possess her." Werner leaves the apartment in silence after her lover has left and returns to Germany without seeing Fenitschka again. In some sense, Fenitschka could be said to have interiorized Werner's masculine, protective, and self-reflective presence. The very lack of narrative resolution makes "Fenitschka" provocative, although it has been criticized for lacking form. Fenitschka's refusal of her lover's marriage proposal is figured neither as ultimate freedom nor as tragedy. The narrative ends with a curious configuration of separations. The lack of closure reminds us how deeply and completely conventional closure relies on literal or figurative marriages for resolution.

Because the story line and the details are so close to (auto)-biographical, "Fentischka," like so much of Salomé's fiction, has been read as autobiography and used to substantiate some biographers' analyses of Salomé. The text is all the richer for its resonance with the stories of her encounters with Frank Wedekind and Friedrich Nietzsche. Here, Salomé places so many of the accusations leveled at her into the mouths of Fenitschka's critics and incisively responds to them. As in much of her fiction, she integrates anecdotes from her more explicitly autobiographical writings as well as her essays. These characteristic intertextual references challenge interpretive claims to biographical referentiality by virtue of their appearance in so many different forms and genres.

Particular anecdotes do seem to take on a certain centrality for her conception of self and for others' perceptions of her. "Fenitschka" begins with an account of an incident in a Parisian cafe which cannot help but remind us of the descriptions of her first encounter with Frank Wedekind. Werner misreads Fenitschka's behavior in that café, and his consequent attempt to "take advantage of her" in his hotel room echoes Salomé's description in the memoirs of her night in Paris with Wedekind. It is simply not clear where the original version is, which version is a copy, and even less clear whether the story in the memoirs comments on an actual incident.[2] What matters is Salomé's proliferation of such stories and her particular reflections on them.

The story line is relatively straightforward. Max Werner meets Fenitschka in a cafe in Paris where they have been brought together

---

[2] Treder and others have suggested that Wedekind's character Lulu was named for Lou Andreas-Salomé as a subtle form of revenge. Literary historians, however, have traced the character through many figurations and have found no evidence that he based her on Salomé.

as part of a larger group of friends and acquaintances. The narrative emphasizes the relation between his "look" and her apparent mysteriousness from the beginning. Max Werner sees an intellectual woman dressed in "black, nunlike clothes," typical of "that kind of woman," of any intellectual woman, from his point of view. But she makes a slightly different impression as well. The narrator tells us that Fenitschka was invisible to Werner: "The only thing that made an impression on him were her eyes, which looked at every object—and every person with such openness and clarity."[3] Her open look disturbs the apparent monopoly of Werner's point of view. Fenitschka turns out to be more than the passive object of his gaze. The narrator compensates for the impression left by Fenitschka's intelligent eyes by emphasizing Werner's subsequent perception of her "short nose, which left enough room for kissing" (8). What then transpires heightens the confusion of looks and points of view. Everyone in the crowded cafe tries either to ignore or to take the point of view of a man who is harassing the grisette with whom he is sitting. Only Fenitschka, of all the women and men, refuses the easy complicity with the abusive man by standing up and looking straight into the eyes of the grisette, establishing a strong identification as well as a form of solidarity.

In her reading of "Fenitschka," Ute Treder stresses that the identification establishes both women's defiance of social norms, and she suggests that such an identification emerges out of Salomé's insistence that intellectuality and sexuality have the same roots, in eros. Nevertheless, Fenitschka's identification at the level of plot and perspective with the "scorned woman" confuses Werner and leads to some fatal conclusions on his part about the "true nature" of this Russian woman. Having dismissed all the warnings about the social censure that her support for the grisette will potentially bring, Fenitschka is open to Werner's suspicion that her intellectual interests are mere guises.

Werner and Fenitschka leave the cafe with their group for a walk through Paris, and then the two extend the walk to a predawn exploration that cannot help but remind us of Salomé's walks with

---

[3] *Fenitschka. Eine Ausschweifung. Zwei Erzählungen*, ed. Ernst Pfeiffer (Frankfurt am Main: Ullstein Taschenbuch, 1982), cited hereafter in the text.

Rée through Rome. Werner appears to control the narrative just as he appears to control the direction of the walk. But, Fenitschka's "simple readiness" annoys Werner as he struggles to pin her down, to draw his all-too-typical conclusions about the relationship between what he sees as her mask and her essence:

> Wasn't there something behind this little nun's dress, something that attracted notice underneath the clothing, something only loosely girded—behind this open, spiritualized face, something hot with sensuality that could only fool a complete idiot?—Was his own fantasy playing a trick on him or did Fenia remind him of the leanness, the spirituality, and the stylized simplicity of a modern Pre-Raphaelite figure, who wants to appear so chaste but is secretly surrounded by strangely intoxicating flowers whose hot colors betray her. (13)

Here, the narrative highlights its play with the then-common representation of woman as precisely such a deceiving Pre-Raphaelite figure. Werner's efforts to establish the order between surface and depths leads him to an embarrassing but typical reduction of Fenitschka to sex. When he lures her into his hotel room and accosts her, he finds her shocked and repulsed by his assumptions. She becomes critical of her own stubborn naïveté, which she calls her "stupidity," but explains it by telling Werner he is the first to take advantage of her assumption of "brotherly" relations with men. At this point in the text, narrative voice and narrative control shift at least momentarily to Fenitschka.

Things are more complicated than a simple misperception of reality; the opening scene promises, and the second part of the story ensures that it is never a matter of misunderstood innocence or discovered guilt. Fenitschka is neither the asexual student, assuredly chaste, nor the loose woman whose availability is guaranteed. Man's efforts to apply dichotomous identifications in his own interests are undercut, and his belief in a simple relation between surface and depth is denied. The text does not counter the reduction to sex with claims of sexual purity or innocence or with exaggerated claims of rationality. Instead, it attempts to confuse those divisions, to insist on the basis of rationality and knowledge in sexuality, without reducing any one term to the others. It attempts, in other words, to represent women's "humanity" as more than man's, as affirmative.

Lou Salomé

Werner and Fenitschka meet again in Russia a year later on the occasion of Werner's sister's wedding. Werner now sees Fenitschka differently. She has shed her nun's clothing for what he perceives to be a more womanly look, and he interprets the change as a sign of her growth into mature womanhood. Again, he wonders whether he has now met the real Fenitschka, whether the real woman has finally emerged. The wedding is an ideal location for the clash between his views and hers. It invokes distinctions between the sexes, between the West and Russia, between the modern and the traditional. Werner suggests that Fenitschka is falsely romanticizing the rhythms and traditions of Russia; he provokes the following exchange:

> These long marriage ceremonies have really been stripped of any deeper meaning.
> Fenia shook her head.
> Not at all! On the contrary! If you strip away the external form, what is the deeper meaning? It goes something like this: there are two people who want to join themselves together for ever—presumably because they love each other—but not just for the sake of their personal being-in-love but in the service of something higher, a third thing in which they can then connect indissolubly. Otherwise, the entire indivisible bond has no purpose. No, they want to get beyond the purely personal, the purely emotional—whether they name it God or the holiness of the family or the eternity of marriage vows or something similar. In any case, there is something else in it—other than just love between the sexes. (22)

In Fenitschka's rebuttal, we find Salomé's own view of the importance of a removed third term in the relationship between man and woman. As the exchange continues, Fenitschka emphasizes the distinction between Russia and Europe, tracing Werner's cynicism about tradition and ritual to the irreconcilable gap in Europe between the forms and the essence of life. The evils of that particular modernity, she says, have not invaded Russia, where there is still an indivisible, if conflictual, relationship between belief and knowledge, religion and science, love and worship. Of course, in Fenitschka's, as in Salomé's own case, the overdrawn distinctions between male and female, between tradition and modernity, between Russia and Europe are refigured. Woman is not relegated to the space of tradition and undifferentiation, but her movement in and through modernity is imagined to be different.

Werner discovers that Fenitschka is having a secret affair, and he becomes her confidant. Fenitschka describes her love affair as her recovery and her peace, but the relationship becomes increasingly conflictual and problematic when outside pressures and censure threaten its privacy. Once people in St. Petersburg have *seen* Fenitschka with her lover, Werner's willingness to listen and observe without seeing becomes increasingly important, the catalyst for Fenitschka's eventual decision to give up the affair in favor of her independence. The significance and the pain of her imposed silence, and Werner's consequent importance to her, resonate with Salomé's stories of Gillot and later of Freud. When Werner first hears about Fenitschka's grandfather's suspicions that she may be having an illicit affair, he experiences renewed doubts about his "grasp" of Fenitschka, who had proven herself to him in Paris to be the asexual intellectual that her appearance had first suggested to him. The onslaught of new confusions demonstrates his continued difficulty in seeing anything other than limiting opposites. He reflects on his own confusions:

> Why? Why in both cases had he perceived her in such typical ways, fixed her in such crass terms? It was strange that he found it so difficult to imagine women in their simply human multiplicity and not just on the basis of their sexual nature, not just half-schematically. Whether one idealized them or satanized them, they were always reduced by being isolated in a relation back to the man. Perhaps the so-called sphinxlike character of woman emerged out of woman's full humanness, which was in no way inferior to man's, out of the fact that this violent simplification could not grasp their humanness. (36)

Werner's meditation takes on an almost programmatic quality when he begins to question the simplicity and reductiveness of his own perceptions and consequent categorizations.

Meanwhile, both Werner and Fenitschka are forced to deal with the rumors that have begun to circulate about her in St. Petersburg. One incident in particular refers back to the Parisian cafe and forward to Fenitschka's later fear that she is one of the grisettes. Werner suggests to Fenitschka's worried grandfather that women in St. Petersburg are easily confused with one another "because they are all darkly disguised in the same way," and he adds, "Every lady therefore has to count on having at least a couple of doubles" (33). Werner's remarks suggest that women's lack of individuality (for man) and their consequent interchangeability derive from socially imposed disguises. But they also suggest an actual lack of difference between "good" women and "bad."

The question of visibility and the problem of doubles gain in urgency until they become the key to understanding women's experience of love and men's experience of women. The text introduces "the demonic" quality of love in a scene in which Werner and Fenitschka pause in front of an art store window to look at a popular illustration of Mikhail Lermontov's *Dämon*, woman's seduction by the demon, her submission to him, and her death at his hands. Fenitschka finds these representations of love utterly familiar and recalls how prevalent they were in Russian households. Werner and Fenitschka then start to discuss the "nature of love," and Fenitschka contests the demonic view with her ideal of a love characterized by serenity and health. Werner attempts to explain Fenitschka's surprising ideal by emphasizing her integrity and her self-reliance in the face of external sanctions. He compares his own fiancée's experience of the contradiction between desire and legitimacy to Fenitschka's:

> Max Werner's thoughts inevitably put Irmgard into the same situation, and he saw how she suffered and bled just at the thought of the destruction of a girl's reputation. Did she really possess so much more human fear, so much less psychic strength than Fenia? No! He knew her too well for that. But she condemned and praised the same things, and to the same degree, that public morality condemned or praised. When she came into conflict with the prescribed way of life, then she also came into conflict with herself. Hence, she trembled with secret fear in the midst of the rush of a kiss, as if the walls had ears—hence, too, the feeling that love was both the genius of her life and the all-powerful demon and tempter, which has the power to drive away the angel. Irmgard did not expect Fenia's "peacefulness" from love. (33–34)

In a subsequent discussion of the effects of secrecy, Fenitschka argues that the veil and the secret, which Werner finds so attractive, are sources of suffering for the women who are forced to hide. In an exchange over the merits of fighting for the right to live their desires openly, Fenitschka challenges Werner's romanticizations of secrecy and intimacy in a way that seems to invert the positions they took at the Russian wedding. At times, Max Werner's perspective on women's political struggle for self-determination seems closer than Fenitschka's to Salomé's own. It is interesting, for that very reason, that Werner imagines that Fenitschka would like to be proven wrong:

> "We inevitably measure the worth of a thing according to whether we would make it a matter of principle, whether we could fight for its legitimacy."
>
> "My God! women have suddenly become so ready to fight!" he observed laughing, "so horribly positive and aggressive, that they are hardly tolerable. You see, that comes from all the women's emancipation, all the studying, and all these ideals of struggle. Women are the real upstarts! Excuse me, there is something quite youthful and powerful about it all, but it has absolutely no refined taste. To put everything up for discussion, even the most undiscussable things, to throw everything into the public, even the most intimate things—do you find that somehow beautiful? I don't. It makes everything horribly crass, it distorts everything into the nationalistic, it wipes away all gentle nuances, and holds everything up to dreadful, harsh glaring lights."
>
> Although Fenia fought against him, it seemed to him quite unmistakably as though she would like to be disproved. (39)

We could read this exchange as one of many instances of Salomé's own ambivalence toward feminism. It is as if she wishes her own utopian ideals, like Fenitschka's, to be achieved without political struggle, without the harsh light of day, without ugliness or *ressentiment*. Though her criticisms of some feminist positions, particularly nationalism, were important, she remains caught at times in the elitism of her insular aesthetic and psychological focus, as Werner does here.

Fenitschka's ultimate separation from her lover shows that things are more complicated than either Fenitschka's or Werner's positions on love. In an essay from the late 1890s, whose title translates as "Thoughts on the problem of love," Salomé develops her theoretical conception of the erotic as that which defies the everyday and the institutional, as the unrepresentable and uncontainable.[4] The narrative "Fenitschka" politicizes this theory more directly. Fenitschka faces a conflict born, in part, of the historical and social constraints within which women love. In her accounts of her own life, in her essays on the problems of love and sex, and in her fiction, Salomé emphasizes the danger of women's investment in a passion for a man which organizes her desire masochistically as a desire to submit to the power she has projected onto and idealized in the man. Without denying the strength of such desires, Salomé actually makes a historical argument in "Fenitschka," when she suggests that women have to struggle not only against convention and social constraint but also against the long historical formation and organization of their subjectivity in a masochistic all-consuming passion for the man. Her characters' triumphs result from their ability to reclaim their own desire, to refuse "emasculation," to recognize the strength and plenitude as their own, and to elaborate their erotic powers in work and social life. Salomé's woman was indeed beyond castration and, at this historical moment, beyond man. As Ute Treder maintains,

For Lou Andreas-Salomé, the particular historicity of woman is given by her exclusion from the process of the rational mastery of nature, and for that very reason, she is not implicated in the alienation of man. Therefore, she is still more closely connected with the sexual roots of existence. But for Salomé, what followed from that was not what followed for her male colleagues—namely, the fixation of femininity in a plantlike naturalness—but rather a transformation of unalienated life experience into life's erotic fullness. . . . This "self-seeking" that "radiates life" is the basis on which the exclusion of woman from reality can be turned into the demand for inclusion in reality on equal grounds, an inclusion that rested not on masculine rules and patterns but on the historicity of her own existence.[5]

These are no simple triumphs, because Salomé is never satisfied with the option of renunciation.

Fenitschka's dilemma leads to a critique of the social constituents of the experience of love and the expression of desire. Werner ob-

---

[4] Lou Andreas-Salomé, "Gedanken über das Liebesproblem," in Neue Deutsche Rundschau 11 (1900): 1009–27, reprinted in Die Erotik: Vier Aufsätze, ed. Ernst Pfeiffer (Munich: Ullstein Materialien, 1979).
[5] Treder, Von der Hexe, pp. 127–28.

serves that Fenitschka's reaction to her lover's marriage proposal resembles the reaction a man would have to the suggestion that he marry another man. Even as he works toward an analysis of the similarity between men and women, Werner also points to the threat posed by social, psychological, and erotic changes in the relations between the sexes, the threat posed by the other within oneself, by suggesting the difficulty for any man not only of the position of woman but also of homosexuality. Werner reflects on the relationship between social changes and changes in the organization and place of desire:

> If a man sometimes loves a woman less deeply and less absolutely than she loves him, it may very well have to do with the fact that she has usually possessed less significance for his entire intellectual existence than he for her. He recovers with her, more than he needs her outside of the love. So Fenia, perhaps, is recovering from her own intellectual struggles and exertions with the man she loves—after years of concentrated study and asceticism, a reaction that she assumes unconsciously, quite naïvely. The marriage proposal suddenly disrupted her peaceful, restful thoughts about it; it allowed her to wake up, and to become clear.
>
> Naturally that never occurred to the other, the notion that she did not love him enough to bind herself to him forever. About inferior women we assume that their inclinations will ultimately be bereft of depth and fidelity—but it seems like a sacrilege in women of high standing. And yet, Max Werner asked himself, could it be that the decisive reasons might be the same that so easily tempt the man to open only a part of his inner self to his love, to set it limits, to put it *next to* and not *above* his other life interests? The woman who organizes her life, and takes it into her own hands as the man does, will naturally come into very similar situations, conflicts, and temptations as he, and will suffer much more for it because of her long, very differently organized woman's history. (59)

Here the movement of the text emphasizes Fenitschka's suffering and her struggles. She does not make her decision to leave her lover easily or without a sense of horror at what she suddenly fears is her similarity to the grisettes. Fenitschka is caught between the conventional alternatives of virgin and whore, between the false alternatives of a fidelity that costs her her own identity and an independence defined as the infidelity of the inferior woman. She struggles to escape the dangers of her own potential for submission to an erotics of dependence, even as she avoids social conventions. She merely negotiates, she does not resolve the contradictions or completely escape the constraints. Part of her negotiation involves the evacuation, at the end of the story, of both Werner and her lover, and a return to that which cannot be narrated.

Leonie Müller-Loreck finds evidence in this text that Salomé shared her contemporaries' views of woman as primitive, elemental, and simple in an overrationalized, instrumentalized, and mechanized world. She isolates particular statements of the main character to support this view. According to Müller-Loreck, "Fenitschka's description of her feeling for life as cosmic experience contains her self-characterization as woman, the way that she lived in the imagination of artists around 1900."[6] Müller-Loreck fails, however, to attend to the ways in which Salomé problematizes this cosmic experience in her fiction and in her accounts of her own struggles against submission to such a "cosmic" or "erotic" pull.[7] The contrast between what Fenitschka imagines love to be and her actual experience of it provides one of the most important moments in this text. Müller-Loreck does agree that Salomé should be differentiated from such writers as Franziska von Reventlow, whose views of women conformed much more readily to the popular reduction of woman to sexuality and "life." Nothing demonstrates Salomé's distance from such reductions more clearly than her exploration in "Fenitschka" of women's supposed enigma.

In both her essays and her fiction, Salomé deploys a remarkably rational approach to her own and other women's enigmatic force, their supposedly "sphinxlike" quality for men, by identifying it with women's "intellectual-sensual double construction," which is mysterious only in the context of traditional conceptions of sexual difference and of modern man's lack. "Fenitschka," however, does not simply expose masculine investments, idealizations, or demoniza-

---

[6] Leonie Müller-Loreck, *Die erzählende Dichtung Lou Andreas-Salomé: Ihr Zusammenhaug mit der Literatur um 1900* (Stuttgart: Hans Dieter Heinz, 1976), pp. 6, 86.

[7] Treder notes Müller-Loreck's legitimate association of Salomé's conception of love with dominant *Jugendstil* representations, but as Treder argues, the interpretation of Salomé's writings on love is not exhausted by such identifications of her work with the *Zeitgeist* (128). Treder, too, suggests that Salomé consciously subverts the very stereotypes on which she leans.

tions of woman, it also works to ground women's agency. In her discussion of Salomé's relation to dominant stereotypes and representations, Treder, too, suggests that a narrative such as "Fenitschka" subverts, even explodes, the *Zeitgeist* from within: "Fenitschka is the symbol of the realization of the human being as woman, independent of masculine thought, and the reversal of those signifiers of masculine conceptions of the feminine." Treder credits Salomé with the insight "that women not only have to demand complete equality within historical reality but also have to insist upon the particular historicity of their existence, which can only be freed from its ahistorical *ur*-mythical categories and inserted concretely into history in opposition to existing forms of normalization." Treder further suggests that "Der Mensch als Weib" signals the possibility of living that which no longer is and cannot yet be. The task, according to Treder's reading of Salomé, is to write the concrete history of woman between past and future.[8] I part ways with Treder only when she seems to assume that Salomé believed in the ultimate realization of such a concrete utopia. For Salomé, there would be no end to a sense of "the no longer" and the "yet to be," and it is only in that space, that gap, she felt, that one can speak of "woman" as such.

The title of her study, which can be translated "From the witch to the hysteric," announces the developmental and, indeed, emancipatory model that Treder employs. Treder sees Salomé's "Fenitschka" as a sort of end and high point, an instance of the subversion of male projections, and the *Subjektwerdung*, the "becoming a subject," of women. Because of the way "Fenitschka" works with problems of idealization and convention, it is a fitting choice for a discussion of male fantasy. I also think, however, that Treder's emancipatory model and the situation of "Fenitschka" within it obscure the contradictions, conflicts, and open-endedness of the story by reading it in overly optimistic tones.

Treder's reading of "Eine Ausschweifung," published together with "Fenitschka" in 1898, also shows the problems with such an emancipatory model. "Eine Ausschweifung," which describes "feminine masochism" and explores its causes, is one of Salomé's most

[8] Treder, *Von der Hexe*, pp. 128, 131.

interesting pieces of fiction. Salomé makes the character Adine a site for the struggle between submission and self-assertion; in her we see the erotic pull for women in subordination and even pain. According to Treder, Salomé sees "the representation of voluntary submission as standing in the 'service of a transition from the old to the new' in which the weakness of the subordinate shows itself to be the potential strength of a superior."[9] I agree with Treder that Salomé sees women's voluntary subordination as a historical problem, but I cannot agree that Adine is a transitional figure from the unemancipated to the emancipated and autonomous. Salomé never suggests that the oscillation between self-loss and self-assertion would cease to exist in a "new" world. Clearly, Salomé did not perceive psychic realities as perfectly continuous with social changes, or with feminist ideals.

[9] Ibid., p. 81.

7.

Salomé, Narcissus, and Freud

In her memoirs, Salomé reports that she first met Freud in 1911 at the Psychoanalytic Congress in Weimar. She attended the congress with her friend Dr. Paul Bjerre, a Swedish analyst, rumored to be her lover, whom she met on one of her visits to her friend Ellen Key.[1] At least one of her biographers has suggested that Salomé could have met Freud in the 1890s in Vienna, where she frequently visited Arthur Schnitzler, Richard Beer-Hofmann, and Hugo von Hofmannsthal, her lover Friedrich Pinneles, his sister Broncia, and Marie von Ebner-Eschenbach. Salomé certainly participated in a discursive universe that prepared the way for Freud's psychoanalysis, and as I have argued, her work had long since anticipated an analytic account of unconscious psychic life. By the time the Weimar congress began, she had studied and discussed psychoanalytic thought adequately enough to disagree with Bjerre's understanding of psychoanalysis in favor of a "truly Freudian one." She would continue to part ways with those thinkers who, like Bjerre, insisted on jettisoning Freud's location of the development of psychic life in sexuality.

Just after the Weimar congress, on September 27, 1912, Salomé wrote Freud:

[1] For the most complete information on Salomé's study of psychoanalysis prior to the Weimar congress, see Ursula Welsch and Michaela Wiesner, *Lou Andreas-Salomé: Vom "Lebensurgrund" zur Psychoanalyse* (Munich: Verlag Internationale Psychoanalyse, 1988).

Dear Professor,
    Since attending the Weimar Congress last autumn, the study of psycho-analysis has continued to preoccupy me, and the further I penetrate into it the more absorbed I become. And now my wish to spend some months in Vienna is about to be realized. And you will allow me to approach you, and attend your lectures, and also to be admitted to your Wednesday evenings, won't you? The sole aim of my visit to Vienna is to devote myself further to every aspect of this matter. Yours faithfully, Lou Andreas-Salomé.[2]

As Wendy Deutelbaum has suggested, "Though Lou requests in so forward a way as to make almost impolite a negative reply, she also appears to know to express, at the outset, her exclusive allegiance." Salomé, says Deutelbaum, is "both assertive and deferent, tenacious and agile," and "she would become, as no one else would, what Freud would call his 'point of fixation' " during the last twenty-five years of his life.[3] Their correspondence, which began in 1911 and continued through old age, demonstrates mutual respect, love, and need—need understood not in terms of that romantic dream of two necessary and complementary halves but as Jane Gallop has characterized the need of psychoanalysis and feminism for each other:

I do not consider this need of each for the other as a sign of some weakness. Rather that in order to exercise the strength of flexibility they must encounter each other, for in mutual exclusions they are liable to seek the strength of rigid defense. The radical potential in their marriage is not a mystical fusion obliterating all difference and conflict, but a provocative contact which opens each to what is not encompassed by the limits of identity.[4]

When Salomé met Freud in 1911, she was fifty years old. She was well known as a writer and essayist, both famous and infamous for her liaison with and her subsequent work on Nietzsche. She had already written ten novels and over five times that many essays and

---

[2] *Sigmund Freud and Lou Andreas-Salomé: Letters*, ed. Ernst Pfeiffer, trans. William Robson-Scott and Elaine Robson-Scott (New York: Norton, 1985), p. 7, cited hereafter in the text as *SF*.
[3] Wendy Deutelbaum, "Disputes and Truces: The Correspondence of Lou Andreas-Salomé and Sigmund Freud," paper delivered in New York at the 1983 meeting of the Modern Language Association, p. 3.
[4] Jane Gallop, *The Daughter's Seduction* (Ithaca: Cornell University Press, 1982), p. 7.

reviews on the psychology of religion, art, "woman," and eroticism. By that time Alfred Adler had left Freud's circle, C. G. Jung's departure was imminent, and internal conflict was pronounced. Yet interest in psychoanalysis was expanding outside the narrow circles to which it had been confined. There is no doubt that Salomé was perceived to be an important, prestigious outsider.[5] But Salomé did not remain the outsider that "the brothers," most notably Ernest Jones, would have her be. In his response to Salomé's initial request, on October 1, 1912, Freud expresses what Deutelbaum has interpreted as his need for her and her "magic":

> Dear Frau Andreas,
>   When you come to Vienna we shall all do our best to introduce you to what little of psycho-analysis can be demonstrated and imparted. I have already interpreted your attendance at the Weimar Congress as a favourable omen. Yours faithfully, Freud. (SF 7)

Salomé represents herself during her stay in Vienna as part of the brotherhood, but with a difference, a difference that allowed her to move freely in and out of their circles. The "sons" have found various ways of diminishing her importance to Freud and her contributions to him and to psychoanalysis. In his biography of Freud, Ernest Jones turns Salomé into an ornament, one of the many women who fascinated Freud, but nothing more.

> There was often some intellectual woman, usually a patient or student, in Freud's life whose company he specially enjoyed. At this time it was Lou Andreas-Salomé, who had studied with him before the war. She was a woman with a remarkable flair for great men, and she counted a large number among her friends. . . . It was said of her that she attached herself to the greatest men of the nineteenth and twentieth century: Nietzsche and Freud respectively. Freud greatly admired her lofty and serene character as something far above his own, and she had a full appreciation of Freud's achievements.[6]

---

[5] See Welsch and Wiesner, *Lou Andreas-Salomé*, on Freud's discussions of Salomé with Jung in the section titled "In der Schule bei Freud," especially the subsection "Vaterfigur und Brüdergemeinschaft," pp. 232–37.

[6] Ernest Jones, *The Life and Work of Sigmund Freud*, 3 vols. (New York: Basic Books, 1953–57), 2:176–77.

Jones makes Salomé safe for the brotherhood by locating her outside of the Freudian circle, in the position occupied by "some intellectual woman." Her character, his achievement, her lack (of knowledge), his teachings, her designs, his judgments, her seductions, his identity—those "old dreams of symmetry" in which difference is erased.[7]

More recently, François Roustang dismisses Salomé's importance by reducing the possible positions in relation to Freud to either total conformity or rebellion and independence. Within such a scheme, it would not be possible to conceive of the relationship between Salomé and Freud as anything other than a relationship between the adoring daughter and the law, or a repetition of the son's choices between discipleship and rebellion. Roustang dismisses Salomé's importance to Freud and her ability to find a degree of freedom in her personal and working relationship with him in the same breath as he dismisses Anna Freud. He suggests that neither woman threatened either Freud the man or his theories. Because they represented lifeless reproductions or total disciples, it was possible for them to "transform psychoanalysis into a Russian novel or a school textbook" with Freud's blessings.[8] When he relegates Salomé to the margins of what he defines as "the Freudian way of thinking" and "what is necessary to the analysis," Roustang permits himself to contend that it was not possible to be in Freud's inner circle and to think independently as a psychoanalyst at the same time. When Roustang drives such a wedge between love, transference, and identification, on the one hand, and sociality and the negativity of analysis, on the other, he effaces Salomé's efforts to imagine and negotiate those apparent oppositions by working "in love" with a removed other. She both understood and exploited one of the few available options for women within an institution like psychoanalysis, but she also diagnosed the masculine inability to think opposites differently.[9]

---

[7] For the most suggestive and provocative theoretical treatment of figurative scenes of father-daughter seductions, specifically in the encounter between feminism and psychoanalysis, see Gallop, *The Daughter's Seduction.*

[8] François Roustang, *Dire Mastery: Discipleship from Freud to Lacan,* trans. Ned Lukacher (Baltimore: Johns Hopkins University Press, 1982), p. 11.

[9] For Binion, of course, Salomé's relation to Freud constitutes a reemergence of penis envy and castration wishes, a desire not only to meet Freud but to usurp his authority and position on the grounds of narcissism. Here, as elsewhere, any assertion

Though still others have trivialized her differences from Freud or dismissed her work as "outside the Freudian way of thinking," Karl M. Abenheimer credits Salomé with a fundamental and successful methodological critique of psychoanalysis. Abenheimer asserts "that on Freud's side, it was amazing that the friendship remained undisturbed, for Lou was a frank critic of many of his basic theoretical ideas." He notes Freud's profound appreciation of Salomé as "the understanding psychologist par excellence," then goes on to examine the nature of Salomé's critiques,[10] making what I consider to be several important arguments about Salomé's relation to psychology and psychoanalysis. As he notes, Salomé did not consider psychoanalysis to be a natural science, and she resisted technical, scientific language throughout her career as analyst and writer. Stanley Leavy writes that "to the psychoanalyst the writings of Lou Andreas-Salomé are a strange world, where familiar words appear in the most unexpected connections and where familiar concepts have undergone a transformation that is often delightful, often perplexing, and always surprising."[11] Freud commented many times on his own inability to follow aspects of Salomé's work, specifically what he saw as the poetic, philosophic, and synthetic transformations and elaborations of psychoanalytic concepts and, most of all, her indomitable optimism. Salomé thanked Freud for providing "a long lead," for extending within the sense of a common project the freedom to stray from the letter of the law. She also confronted him in her correspondence, her essays, and her book *Mein Dank an Freud*, with the philosophical, literary, and synthetic moments in his own work and with the instabilities of the boundary between science and poetry.

Abenheimer suggests that for Salomé, psychoanalysis belonged

---

of difference or independence on Salomé's part becomes threat and destruction, and Salomé's psychoanalytic work mere rationalization for her destructive designs. For an interesting discussion of the implications of Binion's analysis, using Salomé's accounts of her relationship with Freud, see Mary Jacobus, "Judith and Holofernes and the Phallic Woman," in *Reading Woman: Essays in Feminist Criticism* (New York: Columbia University Press, 1986), pp. 110–36.

[10] Karl M. Abenheimer, "Lou Andreas-Salomé's Main Contribution to Psychoanalysis," *Spring* (1971): 24.

[11] Stanley Leavy, Introduction to *The Freud Journal of Lou Andreas-Salomé* (New York: Basic Books, 1964), p. 2.

to the "human sciences," and he traces her conception of the distinction between natural and human science to Wilhelm Dilthey, the well-known and influential philosopher in Berlin to whom *Lebensphilosophie* is often traced. As Abenheimer shows, Salomé follows Dilthey's descriptions of an " 'understanding psychology', [one that] deals with qualities of subjective experiences irrespective of whatever objective factors a scientist may discover as causing them." He noted that "Dilthey describes the same dualism [as Salomé] by pointing out that only the psychological data and their interconnections are actually experienced and thus are open to our inner understanding, whilst the causal and other connections of objective nature are only hypothetically postulated but not experienced." And Abenheimer adds, the basic concepts of psychological understanding "have their origin not in scientific reasoning but in the totality of emotional experience." Accordingly, Salomé saw scientific concepts and ideas as "mere analogies" in psychology. Yet, Abenheimer argues correctly that Freud's success in developing a "systematic, empirical study of how man understands himself," and his efforts to locate the basis of human psychology in sex, or what Salomé will understand as the larger term eros, ensured her loyalty to him, despite her resistance to the claims to natural science.[12]

Salomé stressed over and over that psychoanalysis and Freud allowed her the only pedagogical relation that displaced the hierarchical gender divide and inevitable appropriation that had characterized other pedagogical exchanges, other all-too-conventional scenes of seduction. They allowed her a relationship to a "father" which granted her her own desires, her own name, and her own ability to think without requiring the renunciation or the murder of the father.[13] It is significant that Freud and Salomé's relationship was sustained at a distance, primarily through their correspondence, which lasted over twenty years, until Salomé's death. These letters are rich with the interplay of intimacy and distance between them, with what Deutelbaum has called their rhetorical strategies for balancing asymmetrical positions. Salomé was the only woman with

---

[12] Abenheimer, "Salomé's Main Contribution," pp. 25, 26, 28.
[13] Roustang's definition of a successful dissolution of the transference in *Dire Mastery*.

whom Freud sustained such a long correspondence. She did not remain in the position of student in relation to the person Freud or to psychoanalysis. On the basis of her association with Freud and her pursuit of psychoanalysis, Salomé took up her own position as colleague, teacher, and lay analyst with Freud's encouragement and his referrals. In addition to her analytic work, Salomé wrote several psychoanalytic essays for *Imago* on precisely those topics that had preoccupied her throughout her intellectual life: femininity, eroticism, religion, artistic creativity, and narcissism.

Moreover, despite her promises, Salomé's allegiance to Freud was not her only allegiance at the age of fifty, and her multiple connections and investments also provided an antidote to the sons' transferential tragedies. After all, Salomé announced to Freud her intention to visit Adler's seminar, and she gave up her contact with Adler only when the tensions threatened to interfere in her work with Freud. She spent much of her time in Vienna with Viktor Tausk and at his lectures, despite Freud's increasingly negative feelings about him. Her diary entries from her year in Vienna make it evident that she preferred Tausk's concept of elaboration to Freud's exclusive focus on repression and sublimation. Although many have assumed that Tausk was her lover, Welsch and Wiesner stick to Salomé's own contention that he was not. Nevertheless, Salomé spent a significant amount of time in Vienna with Tausk and his family, and the two shared not only psychoanalytic work but the new entertainment of the cinema. Salomé helped Tausk prepare his lectures and later helped him with his publications. Both in conversation and as a reader, Salomé does indeed seem to have been a remarkably gifted interlocutor, able to understand what the author wanted to share and to draw out its implications. As Welsch and Wiesner point out, Tausk's name appears in Salomé's *Freud Journal* more often than Freud's. In his discussion of Freud's relationship with Tausk, Roustang characterizes Salomé's role in terms that highlight her independence:

Andreas-Salomé used Tausk in order to gain access to Freud, while still keeping her distance. What circulated between the three was love, with all its illusions, but also with all its games, which is why death was held at bay. When Andreas-Salomé separated from Tausk, the break was not catastrophic for him, for she had never been his support nor his "subject who is supposed to know," nor had Freud been the support for either of them, except perhaps at a considerable distance. Andreas-Salomé genuinely defended Tausk in front of Freud, fully aware of the irritation this caused him; but she never played into Freud's hands in such a way that he could have used her against Tausk. Freud was later to acknowledge this, almost in the form of a reproach to Andreas-Salomé: "I would long since have dropped him had you not so boosted him in my esteem." This was as good as admitting that Andreas-Salomé had used Freud's love for her in order to force him to respect Tausk and leave him room to survive. Although Andreas-Salomé had chosen Freud for a master, she had not allowed this mastery to lose all sense of proportion, nor had she permitted the enslavement to allow itself to be stifled by death.[14]

From her studies with Freud in 1911–1912 until her death, Salomé worked with, visited, and corresponded with the major psychoanalytic figures in Berlin, Munich, Vienna, Budapest. She valued the sense of a shared intellectual and practical project enormously, as she did the ongoing exchanges with colleagues that such work entailed. In their biography of Salomé, Welsch and Wiesner emphasize Salomé's comparisons of her involvement in psychoanalysis to the time she and Rée had spent in Berlin, surrounded by scores of philosophers, biologists, and social scientists. She managed to pursue her own intellectual and professional work without having to choose between total conformity and total rejection. She attributed her freedom to span these poles to the daughter's advantage in relation to the father as ideal. In the process, she destabilized strict boundaries between definitions of masculinity and femininity, but she did not, nor could she, completely escape the discursive constraints of phallic law.

The correspondence between Salomé and Freud operated on the ground of an assumed and strategic unity. They sometimes communicated by mail even during Salomé's stay in Vienna. In her study of the epistolary rules employed by Freud and Salomé, Deutelbaum shows that they negotiated their relationship by avoiding both too much hierarchy and too much familiarity. Once Salomé joined Freud's circle in Vienna, Deutelbaum suggests that "her specific problem had now become one of manipulating her outsiderness,

[14] Roustang, *Dire Mastery*, pp. 73–75.

Freud's source of consolation and the emblem of his power, into insiderness, a place for herself, sanctioned by the master, within the psychoanalytic society." Freud's task, on the other hand, was to refuse the role of pedantic professor and maintain an equitable exchange. "The negotiation of the boundaries between inside and out operated on a number of levels," according to Deutelbaum, "and results in no conclusive division. Salomé refers to a 'we,' to 'our movement' quite unabashedly even as she maintains enough distance to make psychoanalysis her idiosyncratic own." Deutelbaum also exposes the centrality of conventional conceptions of sexual difference to the negotiations, and she demonstrates the extent to which Salomé figures for Freud as the "understander *par excellence*" of "our" theories, as an embellisher and a synthesizer whose literary, philosophical, and synthetic excesses properly belonged outside his psychoanalysis. Even as Freud warns her against her excesses, Salomé thanks him for curing her of her tendency toward *Schönfarberei*, "excessive optimism," for showing her the importance of careful observation and analysis. But as Deutelbaum argues, "if Freud is the guardian of his ego, that part of himself that separates and dissects, Lou is the apologist for her undifferentiation." Salomé claims analytic strengths for herself even as she exploits the role of appreciative daughter. And she argues over and over that Freud's own contribution was based on his willingness and ability to work against his own resistance to the irrational and the romantic with a consequently rational approach to an undenied and undeniable irrational. She lost no opportunity to remind or to show Freud the literary and philosophical, even romantic, aspects of his own work. Deutelbaum concludes that Salomé and Freud's negotiations exceeded any simple complementarity and avoided any absolute division: "To dissect in such a way as not to leave life fragmented, a mere collection of parts and pieces, to depict nuance as well as hard outline, to endow something of the artist's brush to the analyst's knife: this is the scientific synthesis Lou and Freud created, the oxymoron their epistolary accommodations struggled so persistently to invent.[15]

The relationship and correspondence between Salomé and Anna

---

[15] Deutelbaum, "Disputes and Truces," pp. 8–9, 16.

Freud adds to the picture of Salomé's relationship to Freud. In 1912 when Salomé was in Vienna, Anna Freud was seventeen years old, about to finish lyceum, and in the process of recovering from a serious bout of appendicitis. The two women met for the first time in 1921, when Freud invited Salomé to visit him and his family in Vienna. According to Salomé's own accounts of her visit, she spent the bulk of her time with twenty-six-year-old Anna, who had dedicated herself to her father and to psychoanalysis. During Salomé's visit to Vienna, the two women worked together on some of the issues that intrigued them both, including the psychoanalytic implications of beating fantasies and anal eroticism. They continued to think and work together for many years, through Anna Freud's visits to Göttingen, a shared vacation, and a regular correspondence that lasted until Salomé's death.

In her biography of Anna Freud, Elisabeth Young-Bruehl accords Salomé a significant, indeed, an irreplaceable role in Anna Freud's life. She was not the first "older, childless woman" to become the younger woman's confidante—what Freud called her "good mother"—but she was to become "the most loyal and constant friend of her early adulthood," and Young-Bruehl continues, "although Marie Bonaparte later took up parts of the large role Frau Lou had played, there was no true successor."[16]

What made Salomé so important to Anna Freud also consolidated her importance to Sigmund Freud as well. She was the nonjudgmental confidante to whom each could confide concerns about the other and about the father-daughter relationship itself. Salomé, unlike other analyst friends, never challenged either Sigmund's analysis of his daughter or Anna's decision to devote her life to taking care of her father and his science. Young-Bruehl cites a letter that Anna Freud wrote to Salomé in 1932, in which she muses: "I cannot tell you how often I think of a sentence you spoke to me once, that it does not matter what fate one has if one only really lives it."[17]

In approving of Anna Freud's devotion to her father, Salomé endorsed both the masculinity complex expressed in her career decision and in her identification with her father and the underlying

---

[16] Elisabeth Young-Bruehl, *Anna Freud* (New York: Summit Books, 1988), p. 223.
[17] Ibid., p. 230.

feminine capacity for surrender and for sublimation of the love for the father. That sublimation allowed the daughter to sustain her love (at a distance) and thus to sustain her femininity. "As an exemplary figure," Young-Bruehl contends, "Lou represented an important synthetic possibility: she was a 'purely feminine' type, but also an intellectual, a thinker and a writer with a 'masculine' (in her own terms) bent for sweeping syntheses, bold conjectures, poetic leaps."[18] In this context, Salomé's own claims for femininity as the more human, by virtue of its integration of conflictual impulses, appears to be both resistant to and complicit with Freud's ideal.

In her account of Salomé's relationship with Anna Freud, Ursula Welsch emphasizes the intensity of their friendship in its independence from Sigmund Freud and the importance to both women of their shared intellectual work. Anna Freud's work on beating fantasies and daydreams, which won her membership in the Vienna Psychoanalytic Society in 1922, was, to a great extent, the product of her collaboration with Salomé, as Anna Freud herself acknowledged. In 1921 Salomé brought her own interest in daydreams, fantasies, and anal eroticism to her discussions with Anna Freud. She had already published an essay on anal eroticism in *Imago* (1916), and in 1921 she was about to publish "Narziβmus als Doppelrichtung" (Narcissism as double directionality) in the same psychoanalytic journal. Recall as well Salomé's representations of her own childhood as locked in a world of daydreams, freed only by the introduction of rational thought in the form of the father-teacher Hendrik Gillot. Though Salomé never diagnosed that child in terms of unresolved incest wishes, it is not coincidental that she structured her life story along the lines of this available narrative. The correspondence between the two shows the degree to which Anna Freud shared not only her theoretical and analytic work with Salomé but also her concerns about the psychoanalytic movement. Welsch provides evidence that both Sigmund and Anna Freud credited Salomé with enormous contributions to Anna's growing confidence in her intellectual and practical analytic strengths, and Anna Freud derived great pleasure from Salomé's fiction, of which she was an ardent fan. Both Young-Bruehl's and Welsch's accounts of Salomé's rela-

[18] Ibid., p. 113.

tionship with Anna Freud demonstrate how integral a part of the Freud circle, indeed of the family, Salomé was.

Still, Salomé's exchange with Sigmund Freud was more important to her intellectually. Salomé's unity and her differences with Freud were played out on the ground of narcissism. Writing to her in the summer of 1917, Freud wonders whether his development of the concept of narcissism ensured Salomé's loyalty to him, and allowed her to "unite [his] fragments into a structural whole" without joining the ranks of those who would impose false, premature philosophical syntheses: "Without this, I feel, you too might have slipped away from me to the system-builders, to Jung or even more to Adler. But by way of the ego-libido you have observed how I work. . . . It seems that in this way I have gained your confidence" (*SF* 61). Salomé had said as much to Freud in a letter of 1915 when she emphasized, as she so often did, the distinction she felt he had made in his essay "On Narcissism" between narcissism as a developmental stage, characterized by the libidinal hypercathexis of the ego, and a prior, good narcissism, which constituted that limit or border designating a preobject, presubject state of undifferentiation. "It was on this crux," she wrote, "that my parting from A[lfred] Adler really took place. In that which makes him blind to the actuality of the sexual a main role is played by a confusion of power instinct with sexual instinct; his power instinct is simply narcissism of the second type" (*SF* 24).

From the beginning of her stay in Vienna in 1912, Salomé had explored her differences with Adler en route to consolidating her agreements with Freud.[19] "I have become more and more absorbed in *Beyond the Pleasure Principle*," she wrote to Freud in December 1920, "[and] you can easily imagine what pleasure this book has given me, since I was plagued by the worry that you were not in agreement with me on the matter of the 'passive instinct'; and yet it is only from this standpoint that Adler can be conclusively disproved, as I told him in Vienna" (*SF*, 105). Salomé fought for the significance of "passive instincts" as a support for the unconscious, in the face of what she considered to be Adler's overvaluation of

---

[19] See Welsch and Wiesner, *Lou Andreas-Salomé*, pp. 224–32, for more information on Salomé's contact with Adler before and after she arrived in Vienna.

the ego and consequent denigration of the unconscious and passivity. She defined passivity as openness and receptivity to the life that lives through but is neither encompassed by nor accessible to the conscious subject—as a yielding to that which exceeds and, from a certain point of view, may seem to threaten the ego and its demands for control and coherence.

Salomé takes aspects of her challenge to Adler over to her exchanges with Freud about narcissism. Here we see the connections between Salomé's work on femininity and her particular appropriations of psychoanalysis. Once again, she locates femininity and the feminine psyche as the source of psychoanalytic as well as philosophical reflection by constructing a narrative of the development of the feminine ego which makes it difficult to draw sharp distinctions between conscious and unconscious, self and other, ego and sexuality, masculine and feminine.

In his 1914 essay "On Narcissism," Freud did, in fact, posit a "normal" or "good" narcissism that differentiated his unconscious quite clearly from Adler's. Freud conceived of a primary narcissism that precedes secondary narcissism, or egotism, and remains operative throughout life in all object love:

> Thus we form a conception of an original libidinal cathexis of the ego, part of which cathexis is later yielded up to objects, but which fundamentally persists and is related to the object-cathexes much as the body of a protoplasmic animalcule is related to the pseudopodia which it puts out. In our researches, taking, as they did, neurotic symptoms for their starting-point, this part of the disposition of the libido necessarily remained hidden from us at the outset. We were struck only by the emanations from this libido—the object-cathexes, which can be put forth and drawn back again.[20]

In this passage, Freud notes that this new conception of narcissism constitutes a change from his earlier views, when "this part of the disposition of the libido necessarily remained hidden from us" (ON 58). Salomé found the change most important; it may even have seemed to her a capitulation of sorts. What distinguished Freud's

[20] Sigmund Freud, "On Narcissism: An Introduction," *General Psychological Theory* (New York: Macmillan, Collier Books, 1963), p. 58, hereafter cited in the text as ON.

unconscious for her was what she claimed (against Freud's protests) to be its basis in an inaccessible but nonetheless actual material undifferentation, a presymbolic narcissism from within which the ego sets itself apart but from which it never fully departs. She would remind Freud that his image of the "protoplasmic animalcule," with the pseudopodia that it puts out and then withdraws, affirmed her view of an autotelic narcissism, of which object libido was secondary and derivative. Salomé advocated an unconscious that originated in something other than repressions or inhibitions, an unconscious with a positive dimension which offered the possibility of "regression" to a primal undifferentiation without pathology, to "woman," whom she defined as "a regressive without a neurosis."

Freud's primary narcissism was not necessarily Salomé's. Freud considered undifferentiation to be beyond the scope of psychoanalysis, and his primary narcissism actually described a side-by-side relation of "the energies [ego and sexual] operating in the mind" (ON 59), rather than a state of undifferentiation. He suggested that "in the narcissistic state they exist side by side and that our analysis is not a fine enough instrument to distinguish them; only where there is object-cathexis is it possible to discriminate a sexual energy—the libido—from an energy pertaining to the ego-instincts" (ON 59). Though we cannot distinguish them, analysis ought nevertheless to assume an original distinction. In order to explain the importance of such a distinction, Freud refers to his work on the transference neuroses and to the original hypothesis that followed from that work, which posited an original discrimination between ego instincts and sexual instincts; from that original hypothesis, Freud continues, the "differentiation of the libido into that which is proper to the ego and that which attaches itself to objects" becomes a "necessary extension." The theory of two different energies in the mind proves useful, according to Freud, and moreover, "there are biological considerations in its favor" (ON 60). In Freud's new scheme, autoeroticism remained an early libidinal stage, which was followed by primary narcissism and then by a secondary narcissism that involved egoism. Primary narcissism was visible only in later efforts to recover it. And what was recovered in adult life was material that had been repressed, not, as for Salomé, the sustained effects of an original, still fantasized connection with All.

In the third section of his essay, Freud discusses the formation of the ego ideal as one important example of the adult's recovery of primary narcissism. "The development of the ego consists in a departure from the primary narcissism and results in a vigorous attempt to recover it," he writes. "This departure is brought about by means of the displacement of libido to an ego-ideal imposed from without, while gratification is derived from the attainment of this ideal" (ON 80). According to Freud, this ideal ego becomes the target of "the self-love which the real ego enjoyed in childhood" (ON 74). This ego-ideal, however, is "imposed from without," as we learn when Freud turns to the instance of "the conscience" as that "institution in the mind which performs the task of seeing that narcissistic gratification is secured from the ego-ideal and that, with this end in view, constantly watches the real ego and measures it by that ideal" (ON 75). Because of this imposition from the outside, object relations are again privileged over the autotelic narcissism that Salomé associates with femininity.[21]

For Salomé, the ego-ideal was produced from within an undifferentiated psyche, and it authorized rather than punished. By positing such an unpunitive, loved ego-ideal, Salomé sustained her claims for the autotelic development of the (at least) feminine psyche and for a fundamental indifference to objects. Still, Salomé stressed over and over, in keeping with Freud's own formulations, that narcissism was that border beyond which analysis could not go, that it must therefore be seen as a reservoir of unsolved and, according to Freud, unsolvable problems, not as a key to their solution. Salomé explains the epistemological importance of Freud's narcissism concept in the following terms: "To hold fast to Freud's present concept of narcissism means in effect to hold fast to psychology's right to its own media and methods no matter what. And that means to be allowed to write, with appropriate obscurity, its personal mark of X, even there where the psychic organization eludes it, instead of defecting into the alien clarity belonging to another side of existence called the 'physical'."[22] Salomé held consistently to Freud's view of the inaccessibility of primary narcissism to analysis. Nevertheless,

[21] For a fascinating reading of Freud's tendency to make narcissistic pleasure "a derivative of object relations," see Leo Bersani, *The Culture of Redemption* (Cambridge: Harvard University Press, 1990).

[22] *The Freud Journal of Lou Andreas-Salomé*, trans. Stanley Leavy (New York: Basic Books, 1964), pp. 33–34, hereafter cited in the text as *FJ*.

as Freud warned her, she did not let her commitments to him prevent her from identifying sites of the recovery in adult life of just such undifferentiation. She remained interested in the moments when that narcissistic undifferentiation was recovered in artistic creativity or sexual love, to name two examples.

Freud, we remember, believed that undifferentiation was inaccessible to observation not only originally but throughout life. In moments of creativity or sexual love, Freud pointed to what was accessible to analysis, namely, the pleasurable opening up of the repressed. Salomé remained dissatisfied with Freud's limits. In *Mein Dank an Freud*, Salomé explicitly charges that Freud and his followers failed to exploit the rich implications of his own concept of narcissism. "Our authors," she writes, "most of the time confuse narcissism with simple self-love." In this open letter to Freud on his seventy-fifth birthday, Salomé reminds him that he once admitted to her in writing that they had probably not distinguished carefully enough between unconscious and conscious self-love. "And this," she continues, "is precisely the point at which the "self" sees itself turned into its opposite, at the point where love for oneself still inseparably includes the—selfless—original connection with all."[23] She goes on to explain why that point is so hard to grasp, using Freud's language against him:

> The confusion of "self-love" in the usual sense of the word, with such an everything-in-one inclusion, in which the self is not yet separated out and isolated, can occur most easily in the realm of the body, because inside and outside constantly express themselves to us together in contradiction. But this is what led you to use the image of the animalcules for narcissism, animalcules that send out pseudopodia only in order to dissolve them again in their own lumps of protoplasm—just as we take our libido back into ourselves, as into a reservoir of still undivided I-world and outer-world, before every new object investment. (*MD* 19)

Here, of course, Freud's fear that Salomé would slip too far into the realm of philosophy, away from observable phenomena, seems amply justified. It is therefore all the more remarkable that Salomé

[23] Lou Andreas-Salomé, *Mein Dank an Freud: Offener Brief an Professor Sigmund Freud zu seinem 75. Geburtstag* (Vienna: Internationaler Psychoanalytischer Verlag, 1931), pp. 18–19, hereafter cited in the text as *MD*.

should continue her discussion by accusing him of moving from the psychoanalytic possibilities of his concept to philosophy in his later work. She introduces what she calls "a blasphemous insertion," the notion that "a fully developed narcissism concept would have made your later 'id,' to which I am not positively disposed in any case, superfluous. After all, the 'id' no longer reflects the limit of our competence but extends beyond it into philosophical conceptualizations, so that soon there are as many ids as there are philosophers. Psychoanalytically, that remains confusing, as if we had sat down at an overfull table" (MD 19).

In 1913 Salomé published an essay on religion and "early God worship" in Imago.[24] There she seems to vacillate somewhat ambivalently between rhetorical concessions to Freud and her own derivation of the "Father-God" from desires that precede and exceed oedipal wishes and complexes. In her notes to Freud about artistic expression and the relationship in it between fantasy and reality, she argues against deriving pleasure and creativity solely from the pleasurable opening up of the repressed, claiming that they are present "still more perhaps on account of the objective element in the primal experiences which is regained in this manner: those experiences which were not at least indirectly reanimated through object-libido, but which are made accessible only under the powerful touch of phantasy to all reaches of the conscious intellect—and in this way extend our personality, hemmed in as it is by object libido, to spheres which were once its province and which it now regains."[25] Once again, Salomé challenges any concept of the unconscious which completely subordinates it to the demands or strategies of the ego, and she defies the privilege Freud seems to accord to object-libido over narcissism.

In the very same letters in which she criticizes Adler, Salomé objects to Freud's own tendency to conceive of the unconscious as contingent upon or even derivative of the ego and its repressions. She opposes those tendencies for their erasure of a positive form of desire. In the letter already quoted in which she attacks Adler's "masculine protest," Salomé also cautions Freud against his own

[24] Salomé, "Von frühem Gottesdienst," Imago 2.5 (1913): 457–67.
[25] Pfeiffer's notes, SF 227.

overvaluation of civilization, rationality, and development. She chooses to focus on Freud's tendency to confuse pathologically withdrawn individuals with "primitive man," so that the "primitive," the irrational, and the infantile take on the status of immature versions of normal, rational adulthood, which necessarily must be renounced. In opposing what she calls Freud's "confusions," she does not celebrate the unconscious or the infantile for its own sake but attempts to demonstrate the fundamental inseparability of apparently oppositional terms, their systemic relation and mutual implication. Thus, she can present her concerns as reminders of Freud's own fundamental project. When Salomé insists on the folding back of opposites into each other, she does not collapse differences into what Freud feared as the "inchoate mass." Instead, she works to destabilize oppositions on the basis of their *Aus-ein-ander-setzung*, "differentiation," from within what may have been and is now fantasized as an undifferentiation. Samuel Weber provides the suggestive definition of Freud's own use of the term *Auseinandersetzung*:

> In current use it signifies both the act of addressing, dealing with an issue, a problem, or person . . . and the kind of polemics Freud practiced in regard to Adler and Jung. . . . Between these different meanings a highly complex configuration begins to emerge, in which the postulation (*Setzung*) of identity—be it that of the subject, the object, or of meaning itself—appears increasingly to be the effect of a process of reduplication or of reciprocal separation (*aus-ein-ander*).[26]

Salomé expresses her differences with Freud, or with his emphases, when she writes to him about questions of religion, artistic creativity, homosexuality, and ethics. In each case, she objects to Freud's derivation of those phenomena from inhibitions in development, his definition of them as compensatory or reparatory. Her fascination with Tausk's concept of elaboration becomes evident here. For Salomé, "primitive religion," infantile preoccupations, artistic creativity, even neuroses were not so much compensatory formations as elaborations of a primary narcissism, even a primary

[26] Samuel Weber, *The Legend of Freud* (Minneapolis: University of Minnesota Press, 1982), p. 24.

masochism, again, inaccessible except to fantasy, but evident nonetheless.

In a letter responding to Freud's *Future of an Illusion*, for example, Salomé presents her disagreements with Freud as "attitudinal differences" from within their fundamental agreement. She suggests that Freud found it difficult to "forgive the 'common man' his religion, whereas to me this remains a subject of great interest in all its various forms" (*SF* 183). And she notes that "if we are going to find it 'humiliating' when anyone enters into a pact with these religious infantilisms, then we must treat a person's culture and intelligence in precisely the same way—just as we now know how to assess moral indignation at its true worth" (*SF* 183). As we might expect from Salomé's earlier work, she refuses to reduce the not-yet-intellectualized religion of the common man to the status of a compensation and continues to view it as the effort to represent something of the fullness of life, something of the human subject's conflictual sense of omnipotence and vulnerability. In a letter to Freud written in 1915, Salomé asserts that she "also believe[s] that the most primitive ideas of immortality derive less from anxiety than from the wish to symbolize such a sense of security: *originally*" (*SF* 31).

In a journal entry from 1913, she blames developmental theory for the suppression of the creative, if regressive, direction of narcissism. If philosophical speculation needs to be excluded from psychoanalysis, she argues, then the developmental theories of a Haeckel ought to be excluded as well. She questions the boundaries drawn between philosophy and science by drawing out the implications of developmental logic:

> Since therapy and morbid complexes are involved, the conscious state is forthwith denominated the "higher," in contrast to the "primitive" or "atavistic." These practical considerations irreparably acquire philosophic status and a fixed overemphasis on consciousness, as though everything infantile were pathological because of immaturity. It ought instead to be the task of psychoanalysis by means of its radical mode of thought to direct developmental theory beyond itself. (*FJ* 115)

Salomé was not advocating obscurity or undecidability for its own sake; she was challenging the hypostasization of apparent opposites which had set up rigid and antagonistic boundaries between the primitive and the civilized, between nature and culture, and perhaps most significantly, between sexuality and ego.

In a journal entry from 1913 titled "Inversion" (*FJ* 102), Salomé worked again on the relationship Freud had set up between sexuality and ego. In response to Freud's reference to civilized man as the homosexually repressed savage, she challenges the assumed superiority of "the civilized," "the heterosexual," and "the ego," and the consequent warding off of the primitive, homosexual, and the sexual itself. If sexuality and ego develop through reciprocal separation and cannot be said to exist as such except in relation to each other, she argues, then they ought not to be considered inevitable threats to each other. Sexuality presents a threat to the ego only according to the "orientation of the boundary" drawn between them. (*FJ* 102) Heterosexuality need not be a threat at all, she continues, and homosexuality only insofar as it draws the subject back into a form of sexuality dominant at a moment when the ego was in its early formative stages and, hence, still weak. Even as she adopts a great deal of developmental logic, she goes on to contest what she sees as the argument that the repression of homosexuality is required to make civilization possible. The narcissism that persists in "inverts," according to Salomé, is the very ground of sublimation in civilized man; that persistent narcissism, not the repression of homosexuality, is what makes sociality possible, that which the so-called savage has in far greater proportion than civilized man. Kindness and sociality, far from being defenses against repressed homosexuality, are actually elaborations of homosexuality into a general benevolence toward one's own kind. In *Mein Dank an Freud* she challenges psychoanalytic prejudices with a characteristic critical gesture:

What I never find emphasized enough among us (alongside the stress on the defects of inversion in both directions) is the positive dimension, the advantage they have over the usual heterosexuality. I mean the advantage in that which prevents the homoerotic person to some extent from taking that final step to unify him/herself as heterosexual. In that hesitation before the final maturity—he carries something of our fundamental erotic character with him, something that otherwise only the early eros has, but is now collected and guarded in a way that those early infantile outlets could not yet accomplish. By holding onto them, they experience another kind of maturity, which he would have to forfeit if he became a unisexual "half." (*MD* 29–30)

Salomé celebrates the not-yet-sundered unity of infantile experience that she sees in the homosexual. Given the language with which she resists the reduction of both women and men to mere halves of a heterosexual whole in all her work, given her celebration in woman of a less irreparable split, and given her clear preference for people who seemed to her to have succumbed less completely to that split, it seems fair to read this passage as implicit self-identification with at least psychic inversion and as her identification of woman with a fundamental bisexuality. Again and again, Salomé fights what she takes to be Freud's insistence on radical separations and repression as the basis of development and civilization.

Salomé's essay on anal erotism demonstrates again the trajectory of her method and her thought. Although it takes up a critique of Freud, Freud considered the article to be one of the best things she had ever written. In comparison with her earlier psychoanalytic essays, this conformed most closely to psychoanalytic terminology and method. Her analysis of anal eroticism and its fundamental role in the development of subjectivity and sexuality exhibits the same commitment to a nonrenunciatory view of development. Salomé begins by describing the prejudices in the public at large against psychoanalytic interest in anal eroticism. As she suggests, "However strong the resistance has always been [to Freud's emphasis on the sexual factor] and, in particular, to his 'infantile sexuality'—the disgust over all that still seems significantly smaller than that over anal sexuality, specifically."[27]

In her emphasis on the two-sided resolution of anal pleasures in their confrontation with "culture" and socialization, Salomé challenges the primacy of the oedipal complex in the formation of subjectivity. Salomé believed that oedipal desires and their resolution also follow the pattern of earlier confrontations with reality and earlier incorporations of narcissistic desire in their formation of the ego. Again, she stressed the indestructibility of narcissistic desire

[27] Lou Andreas-Salomé, " 'Anal' und 'Sexual,' " *Imago* 4.5 (1915/16): 249–73, cited hereafter in the text as AS.

and pleasure and their compatibility with, rather than exclusive opposition to, ego and sociality. As ever, she insisted on the incorporation into "higher" forms of those "infantile" productive pleasures and desires that are denied only at the risk of eradicating the "fullness of life."

Salomé found much more in the anal phase than the child's education in cleanliness and its effects. According to Salomé, a positive feeling for life also emerges from this stage of development.

> In his time, it was so typical for people to laugh when Freud drew attention to the infant's anal pleasure in relation to its constipation, and yet, it is through this pleasure that the small "I" first shows itself to be master of a situation that began with repression. Because the anal pleasure brings a positive moment (the autoerotic joy in one's own physicality) to the drive-negating coercions from the outside, the human child consolidates itself again as identical with its criticized corporeality. (AS 250)

Salomé goes on to distinguish between earlier instances of refusal—the refusal of the mother's breast, for example—and the renunciations required in the anal phase, in which the sense of self-world unity is more irreparably split. "The anal libido, given the fundamentally hate-inducing experience of becoming solitary, something that is satanized from the beginning, has to start out from the dogmatic protest: 'I' and Father (the mother) are not one" (AS 251–52). Salomé then makes the arguments that Freud incorporated into his own work:

> In our judgment, with regard to anality, two different things are involved: a reality and a symbol. On the one hand, original living forms of earlier physical pleasure, which are pulled out of this sphere during normal development and taken over into forms of a more mature sexuality, and, on the other hand, a symbolic working-through of what has been shelled or emptied out of the substance of reality in order to become an expression of repudiation. A third disastrous relation between these two is made possible by their imprecise differentiation from each other, by their confusion. Such confusion can occur, either because the original prohibition was too emphatic, too threatening to the child, so that fear and panic stay attached to those activities of the drive that have long since grown out of the anal forms of pleasure, or because, in fact, something

of those infantile pleasures crossed over into later sexual forms, inhibiting them. (AS 255)

Though this third possibility can be disastrous, it also serves to point to the instabilities between infantile (anal) and more mature (genital) sexualities. In the second section of her essay, Salomé reminds her readers that "it is characteristic for animals that anal and genital orientations go together completely" (AS 259). Even in human beings, she continues, "there is such a kinship between anal and genital processes—not just in the beginning, before they have completely developed, but precisely in the realm of sexual maturity, we could find the regressions of the anal erotic to be richly supported by the body" (AS 259). Salomé ends these reflections with the claim that Freud and others have loved to quote: "It is no accident that the genital apparatus remains so closely connected locally to the anus (and in woman is merely rented from it)" (AS 259). She goes on, unsurprisingly, to associate anal sexuality with autoeroticism and genitality with the demand for the partner. The positive dimension of anal sexuality which persists in us, according to Salomé, is its reminder "of that most primary world and self-unity, which expressed itself anal-erotically and which, raised out of its vulgar materiality, still hovers over everything that appeals to us, everything that we hold dear throughout our entire lives, as its ultimate ancient sanction" (AS 262). Finally, Salomé stresses once again that what we take to be our most elevated sublimations are drawn from the same soil as what we take to be our basest impulses. The reciprocal interpenetration of apparent opposites is both fact and ideal for her, is "woman."

In *Mein Dank an Freud*, Salomé summarizes the significance of anal eroticism and urges her readers not to overlook its importance out of overcivilized disgust:

The enormously important, even positive role the experience of anality plays with regard to our intellectual attitude toward the world is often disregarded, even by us. In the struggle for that first cleanliness, the child experiences its bodily excretions, at one and the same time, as a piece of the external world, as foreign objects that it must distance, repudiate, and, still, as itself, as a part of itself that it would like to keep in and around itself; differentiated and self-identified, the infant now experiences, in place of autoerotic confusion, a bridging between inside and outside precisely in their distinction: and precisely this is the prelude to our lifelong intellectual activity—to our learning about how increasing distinctions and the strength of the drives' embrace, which keeps the outside world with us in interpenetration, work together. (*MD* 23–24)

According to Salomé, it is crucial that the child learn the distinction between actual anal processes and their symbolic value, if s/he is to have a normal sexual life. If the symbolic status of the anal as the abject makes its way into further development, then guilt feelings emerge in relation to sexuality, and the adult cannot experience sexuality as the joyous reconnection to one's own roots. Out of the conflict between libidinal and ego drives, the "self" expands and grows, not only because of the renunciation of the repressed drives but also because of the experience of them. They become operative in the formation of subjectivity as well. For Salomé, neither ego nor sexual drives can be allowed to gain the upper hand.

Salomé's emphasis on the greater proximity of and uneasy differentiation between anal erotism and genital sexuality in women contributes to her elevation of femininity. In a journal entry with the provocative title "Commonplace" standing unpunctuated next to "Man and Woman," masculinity and femininity are embedded in a discussion of negativity and pessimism. A commonplace, Salomé argues, is that which can no longer germinate ideas, and simply wears itself out. It follows that "all negative attitudes toward life, however well-founded, however ingeniously got up, lead to platitude," that "the nonintuitive apprehension of life, which is more accessible to our intellect, does give rise to the proposition that culture has caused a decline of life, a culture obtained by a deficit in life, a culture of the weak" (*FJ* 117–18). The echoes of Nietzsche here are quite clear. In fact, Salomé refers directly to Nietzsche in her meditation on the issue of negativity. The weak sex, from the point of view of woman, Salomé writes, is man, the sex that has renounced its (even anal) narcissism too exclusively in favor of culture. "Woman—the fortunate animal: really just as prone to regressive narcissism as the neurotic, not really undifferentiated like animals, but a regressive without a neurosis. For a neurotic, the wish to become a woman would really mean the wish to become healthy. And it is always a wish to be happy. Only in womankind is sexuality no surrender of the ego boundary, no schism; it abides as the homeland of personality, which can still include all the sublimations of the intellect without losing itself" (*FJ* 118). The relation between sexuality and ego is "by nature" conflictual, according to Salomé, who reminds Freud of what she took to be his own argument. Everything depends on the orientation of the boundary drawn between them. In "man" the line is rigid; narcissism's double directionality is clearer in "woman."

Salomé's emphasis on primary narcissism is linked to her writings on fidelity and infidelity, since desire and sexual drive are precisely that which cannot be fulfilled by a supposedly complementary other. "Is it not then the great problem of sex," she asks, "that it not only strives to quench the thirst, but that it also consists in the yearning for the thirst itself, that the physical relief of tension, of satiation, at the same time disappoints, because it diminishes the tension" (*SF* 25). Salomé refers to intellectual and sexual fidelities as fixations, as illusory promises of fulfillment, and she found psychoanalytic language for the moral of her Ibsen studies: the failure or inability to recognize one's own desire in any idealization of the other is a most dangerous trap. In an entry in her *Freud Journal*, Salomé mused that "[leaving] need not be a gesture of abandonment . . . but of reverence . . . [for it] engaged him once more within the infinite context of relationships which close behind him and receive him into their grandeur" (*FJ* 123–24). Woman, according to Salomé, has no choice but to be unfaithful if she is to avoid the dilemma of isolation, on the one hand, or loss of self, on the other.

In the second section of his 1914 essay, Freud introduces the narcissistic, self-sufficient woman as the purest feminine type with regard to questions of object choice. He discusses the evidence of narcissism and its recovery in adult life by focusing on transference neuroses, organic illness, and love. Freud draws a distinction between two different, though overlapping models of object choice, the anaclitic, which he defines as the choice of love object based on the mother or her substitute, and the narcissistic, the choice of love object on the model of the self. Anaclitic object choice, which ultimately becomes the ethical norm for Freud, reinforces the view that "the sexual instincts are at the outset supported upon the ego-instincts; only later do they become independent of these, and even then we have an indication of that original dependence" (ON 68). Freud goes on to propose clear differences between the sexes with regard to types of object choice.

> Complete object-love of the anaclitic type is, properly speaking, characteristic of the man. It displays the marked sexual over-estimation which is doubtless derived from the original narcissism of the child, now transferred to the sexual object. . . . A different course is followed in the type most frequently met with in women, which is probably the purest and truest feminine type. With the development of puberty the maturing of the female sexual organs, which up till then have been in a condition of latency, seems to bring about an intensification of the original narcissism, and this is unfavourable to the development of a true object-love with its accompanying sexual over-estimation; there arises in the woman a certain self-sufficiency (especially when there is a ripening into beauty) which compensates her for the social restrictions upon her object-choice. (ON 69–70)

In this passage we see the difficulties that psychoanalytic narratives of feminine development present for any attempt to explain object choice in women. If the little girl is to be heterosexual, she cannot follow the anaclitic model which at least implicitly suggests an active sexuality and a feminine love object, the mother. Given "the social restrictions upon her object-choice," Freud in this essay sees narcissism, understood as the desire to be loved, as the only "feminine" possibility.

In an essay written in 1928, whose title may be translated "The consequences of the fact that it was not woman who killed the father," Salomé does what critics such as Sarah Kofman will do somewhat differently some fifty years later: she uses Freud's work on narcissism to expose "man's" renunciation of his material connectedness and his mortality. Salomé's 1928 essay demonstrates her frequent rhetorical and intersubjective strategy of setting herself apart from within the terms that she claims unite her with Freud. She and Freud agree, in the words of Sarah Kofman, that "what renders woman enigmatic would no longer be some 'natural deficiency,' a lack of some kind or other, but on the contrary her affirmative narcissistic self-sufficiency and her indifference." "It is no accident," Kofman writes, "that Freud's essay 'On Narcissism' was written in 1914, a time when he was particularly taken with Lou Andreas-Salomé."[28] More than one critic has made a great deal of the "charming account of the 'narcissistic cat' " which Freud shared with Salomé during one of their first, more personal conversations.[29] According to the account in the *Freud Journal* (89), Freud told her of a cat that climbed into his office window. He greeted it ambivalently because he had not been overly fond of animals, and he was particularly wary of this cat when it "climbed down from the sofa on which it had made itself comfortable and began to inspect in passing the antique objects which he had placed for the time being on the floor." He was afraid of what might happen to his objects, his treasures if he tried to chase the cat away, and so he let it stay. The cat "proceeded to make known its archaeological satisfaction by purring, and with its lithe grace did not cause the slightest damage." Despite his affection and attention, the cat paid him no mind and looked at him as she looked at all other objects. He gained only the slightest response when he courted the cat's attention "with the ingenious enticement of his shoe-toe." Freud concludes the story of the "unequal relationship" with the cat's sudden illness and death, which followed "the most painstaking" treatments. "It succumbed to pneumonia," Freud is supposed to have said, "leaving naught of itself behind but a symbolic picture of all the peaceful and playful charm of true egoism." By virtue of her distance and her absences, Salomé could become such a symbolic picture herself. In her reading of the story, and of Salomé's relation to Freud, Mary Jacobus suggests that "for Freud, of course, it was Lou Andreas-Salomé herself who displayed 'all the peaceful and playful charm of true egoism,' and whose beauty made her the type of the narcissistic woman whom he elsewhere compares to a cat. . . . Unscarred by castration anxiety, the narcissistic woman, far from breaking the analyst's '*disjecta membra*,' makes them whole."[30] Like Young-Bruehl, Jacobus links Salomé's "lack of anxiety over castration" to her response to

[28] Sarah Kofman, "The Narcissistic Woman: Freud and Girard," *Diacritics* (Sept. 1980): 37, 36.
[29] For a particularly interesting discussion, see Jacobus, *Reading Woman*, pp. 134–36.
[30] Ibid., p. 135.

Freud's "Taboo of Virginity," in which Freud had stressed the psychic threat to men of women's (envious) hostility toward them. Salomé suggests to Freud that man's fear of woman may have its roots, too, in a possible matriarchal prehistory, in which woman "may have been the dominant partner" and is now "feared as an agent of retribution" (SF 89).

What Salomé and Kofman emphasize, however, is Freud's difficulty sustaining the division he sets up in his narcissism essay between masculine anaclitic (ethical) and feminine narcissistic object choices, since the masculine object choice and overvaluation of the object develop by way of the prior narcissistic cathexis of the self, by way of the feminine. And Freud has even more problems with his ultimate condemnation of woman's narcissism and with his claim that motherhood provides the appropriate ethical redemption. As Kofman seems to suggest, the theorist is subject to the same forms of forgetfulness as the little boy, the same fraud, the forgetting that allows too sharp and self-evident a line between unconscious and conscious, desire and autonomy, pleasure and ethics. "All ethical autonomy," writes Salomé, "doubtless constitutes a compromise between command and desire. . . . while it renders what is desired unattainable—given the ideal strictness of the value demanded, it draws what is commanded from the depths of the dream of all-encompassing, all-sustaining Being."[31] Freud cannot escape narcissism as the ground of ethics or love, nor can he sustain what Salomé sees as the unnecessarily rigid dichotomy in his definition of civilization between narcissism and sociality, between self-sufficiency and ethics.

Salomé's essay on the consequences of the fact that it was not the daughter who killed the father begins by explaining her title. It refers, she reminds her readers, to Freud's proposition that the first human crime (and the advent of culture) was the murder of the father. With this beginning Salomé acknowledges her indebtedness to Freud and her intention to work on woman's difference from within his narrative. The freedom she assumes to work both within

---

[31] Binion's translation of excerpts from Salomé's "Narzißmus als Doppelrichtung," *Imago* 7.4 (1921): 376. See Rudolph Binion, *Frau Lou: Nietzsche's Wayward Disciple* (Princeton: Princeton University Press, 1968), p. 552.

and against Freud's terms determines both the method and the content of the essay. At the beginning of the second paragraph, Salomé ventures a suggestion: if Freud's speculation about the beginnings of culture is true, is "so," then it cannot have been without consequence that the daughter remained free of the son's primal guilt.[32] The "if it is true" marks the hypothetical character of his and, by implication, her arguments, that which she would have called their symbolic rather than their truth value. Our myths, she once wrote to Freud, are that to which we resort when we reach the limit of what we can observe empirically and follow rationally.

Following Freud's lead, Salomé sets out to explain the process through which the son's murder of the father is transformed into a remorseful, deferential deification of him on the part of the then-conformist and obedient son. Salomé appeals to what she sees as the only instance of such deification or idealization accessible in our lived experience, namely, the idealization of the object in erotic love. Again, she takes up Freud's own work on the masculine object choice, the aggressive as opposed to the passive type, characterized by an overvaluation of the love object and a dependence for his sense of self on the reciprocation of that love. Salomé suggests that there is no natural basis for such object choice or for such idealizations. Nothing prepares us for it in advance, since what precedes it is that lack of differentiation that Freud called narcissism. She then goes on to explain the lasting effects of narcissism in the relation between psyche and body. As a consequence of the development of the ego and the separation between subject and object, the body becomes the material limit of our narcissism, because it comes to mark the boundary between self and other, and it is experienced as if it were external to us; the body is also the point of contact and connection through which the narcissistic remains at play, it is both *Grenz* and *Bindestrich*, that to which we can have no unmediated relation but also which we cannot escape. Hence, by analogy, narcissism is inescapable (WDF 26).

The masculine overvaluation of the object, man's ethics, which

[32] Lou Andreas-Salomé, "Was daraus folgt, dass es nicht die Frau gewesen ist, die den Vater totgeschlagen hat," in *Almanach für das Jahr 1928* (Vienna: Internationaler Psychoanalytischer, 1928), p. 25, hereafter cited in the text as WDF.

has no natural basis, according to Salomé, would seem to involve social intervention into a previously narcissistic state. The renunciation and forgetting of narcissism requires guilt over incestuous wishes and murderous fantasies. The son's fantasy of murdering the father involves a deep narcissistic wound, since the father is, after all, the son's future. The son, with his murderous wishes for omnipotence, is transformed into a remorseful and obedient subject who overvalues the love object even as he misrecognizes his suppressed desire for a reunion as ethical ideals. The daughter, Salomé argues, need not suppress incestuous wishes so violently, need not fall out of love, at least if we take Freud's mythical narrative seriously (WDF 27); she is not forced to internalize a prohibitive and punitive law.

Here Salomé subtly insists on the often forgotten distinction in Freud's own 1914 narcissism essay between ego ideal and superego, or conscience; Salomé makes conscience the fate of the male and the unpunitive ego ideal the daughter's difference. Woman is less likely to confuse desire with ethics and, hence, has greater sobriety in relation to the law. The daughter, Salomé writes, resolves her own tendency to idealize the father through a series of ever more subtle, more refined sublimations without having to murder the father or repress her narcissistic sense of connectedness; therefore, desire and self-assertion coexist more peacefully in her (WDF 27). Woman remains more "at home" in her materiality, no matter how sublimated or spiritualized her relation to it might be. The sublimations required of her are articulated in terms of a rounding out, a growing and expanding that is horizontal and spatial and does not depart for a point above or beyond but reabsorbs the traces of a history that is never renounced. The man who has forgotten the desire at the basis of his ethics and his aspirations reacts more sensitively to external law, vacillating between guilt and desire, between a "natural rebelliousness that would destroy anything in its way" and the impulse to achieve his own worth in the approval of that punitive other (WDF 28). This conflict between the desire for total independence from the father and the equally strong desire to submit to the father explains the ambivalent relations of Freud's "sons" to their father, according to Salomé. And the failure to work through this conflict, to recognize its basis in an only apparently paradoxical narcissistic desire for unity makes men blind to their own desires, obliging them to separate mind and body, intellect and eros, rational and irrational, ethics and love.

If there is lack, then, it is the son's lack, for his trajectory involves a linear, teleological, sacrificial verticality and includes the imperative to aspire and achieve with the illusory promise that identification with and obedience to the father will reconstitute the lost whole. "It is no wonder," Salomé wrote elsewhere, "that the male neurotic's desire to be happy is often expressed as a desire to be a woman," to be what she called that "regressive without a neurosis" (FJ 118). In "Zum Typus Weib" (Woman as type) Salomé draws out the paradox that constitutes the daughter's difference and her advantage:

[Woman is able] to experience what is most vital as most sublimated. This mentalizing, idealizing, draws its spontaneity from the fact that, in the transferences of love, their point of departure remains more palpably present for the feminine-unitary nature throughout life. . . . The individual [beloved] person in all his factuality becomes for her so to say transparent in all directions, a diaphane with human contour through which the fullness of the whole gleams, unbroken and unforgotten.[33]

Salomé concludes her essay on the consequences for woman of not having killed the father by folding whatever sexual differences she has established back on themselves. At the point of furthest development of his masculinity, man displays his submissiveness by giving himself over to his ideal and exposing the feminine-passive or narcissistic moment that is always at work, even in what are apparently the greatest separations. Masculine and feminine approach the border of their difference and tend to become each other, according to Salomé (WDF 28). If the masculine opens out onto the feminine in the drive to achieve and become father, motherhood works as the at least metaphorical point at which woman can be said to have opened onto masculinity. Motherhood combines the feminine capacity for giving with the masculine capacity to create, to protect, and to lead. In motherhood, Salomé argues, woman

[33] Binion's translation of an excerpt from Salomé's "Zum Typus Weib," *Imago* 3.1 (1914): 11, in *Frau Lou*, p. 555.

realizes her sublimated homosexuality. Furthermore, that is what has always elicited man's fascination and his envy, both because it transgresses the conventional boundaries of femininity, reaching over into the masculine, and also because man is denied that experience of the body (WDF 29). For that reason, Salomé argues, the mother becomes the essence of that which is inaccessible and figures for man as a symbol more than a real human being, a symbol of the inseparability, perhaps even the ultimate undecidability of all differentiations, the narcissism that must be repressed if masculine identity is to be secured. Woman exists for man somewhere between the *Kreatürlichen* (creature) and the *Überpersonellen* (transcendental) in a position of the indeterminate and the commonplace (WDF 29). This is not Freud's ethical mother, not the redemption of woman's narcissism, but its manifestation, and thus the source of man's fascination and his horror.

This position between the animal and the transcendental, this undecidability, became oppressive, according to Salomé, when the worship of God became the worship of man; at that point, that undecidable figure, that *Mittelding*, was domesticated into the respectable wife. Whereas woman once belonged directly to the "Father God," the worship of man and the domestication of woman cut her off from that world of possibility signified by the father and unfulfillable by any human relation. Penis envy, writes Salomé, is a form of desire for equality based in *ressentiment,* and it emerged along with the possibility of the enslavement of woman by man (WDF 29). At this point, woman must struggle against the human male for access to that which is as naturally hers as it is his in its inaccessibility. In that humanist glorification of the hu-*man* subject, there is no sexual relation; there is only a fraudulent complementarity that makes woman his lack and his completion. As soon as woman's access to her own desire is mediated through the human male, as soon as competition with him is her only hope of escape from domestication, the daughter begins to kill the father herself and, with "him," precious parts of herself (WDF 29).

The essay ends by discussing the implications of these changes for the relations between the sexes. The only viable relation she can see is based on the furthest possible development of the sexual differences within each one, rather than on the projection of difference onto a supposedly complementary and ideal other half—hence, the significance to her of Freud's notion of bisexuality, which she understood as sexual indeterminacy that "can be awakened by the opposite sex, as a consequence of the other's profound approach, his understanding, and his embrace" (*FJ* 60–61). And so it is, Salomé writes later, "that only slightly homosexual men see the universally human qualities in woman and are erotically disposed toward them"; the more exclusively heterosexual, self-repressive man prefers the feminine woman in the most circumscribed sense of the word (*FJ* 188–89).

Salomé's 1928 essay is typical of her excavations of the internal differences of psychoanalysis, excavations formulated as reminders to Freud of the implications of his own work, perhaps of his own slight "homosexuality." Salomé made use of what she characterized as the daughter's good fortune in relation to Freud, maintaining the privilege and pleasure of speaking in his name without giving herself over to his terms and limitations. Salomé avoided "war" with Freud, just as she avoided submission, by sustaining a relationship that she described as beyond fidelity and infidelity, enabled both to acknowledge and to destabilize gender and genre lines, by her agreement and by her refusal to take either exclusive position, insider or outsider. Salomé insisted, as Roustang notes, on turning psychoanalysis into a Russian novel; she contaminated science with the philosophical and aesthetic, even exposed the instabilities of the lines drawn between art and science, fiction and truth. And she continued to the end to thank Freud and psychoanalysis for correcting her tendency toward romantic mystifications and hallucinated syntheses. Working within Freud's master narrative, Salomé has made a place for femininity that is neither pure negativity nor that positive, only because redemptive, mother. She has proposed that Freud's narrative of femininity might go elsewhere, along a route that allows for women's agency without requiring the *ressentiment* of castration and its attendant envy.

In her thanks to Freud, Salomé invokes the distinction she has elsewhere established between Nietzsche and Freud in recounting the effect on her of Freud's method:

After you had shown us a case of neurosis by working backwards a few
times, level by level—the way you then suddenly revealed it to us, in
its inviolate wholeness, with one grasp, in much the same way as someone slips a cake from its mold. What moved me—us—in that moment,
was the unavoidable sensation, the certainty, by no means intended by
you: human life—life itself—is poetry. We live it unconsciously, day by
day, as piece by piece, but in its inviolate wholeness it lives us, it writes
us. Far, far from the old phrases about "making one's life a work of art"
(from the narcissism of which most assuredly psychoanalysis, indeed
only psychoanalysis, has cured us); we are not our own works of art.
(*MD* 14)

Acknowledging Freud's lead, his commitment to careful observation
and rational analysis, Salomé thanks him for giving her access to
those possibilities within herself, for allowing what she might have
called bisexual positions.

Her letters to Freud give us some information about her own work
as a lay analyst. When he chastises her for undercharging her patients, she explains the effects on her analysands of the collapse of
the German currency and assures him that the opportunity to work
is reward enough to enable her to make sacrifices in times of scarcity.
Her work with Frau E. demonstrates her commitment, the dangers
of overinvestment, and something of her relation to Freud.

Frau E. was a patient whom Freud referred to Salomé, assessing
her as an agoraphobic, seemingly "depraved in character," unin-
telligent, wealthy and "probably not worth the effort." In the same
letter, dated January 28, 1925, Freud adds that Frau E. and her
husband, a young, handsome man "who loves his misfortune too
much to give it up," would be accompanied by a perfectly reliable,
intelligent lawyer, Dr. H. (*SF* 148). He closes with the request to
Lou "under the direst of threats" to charge the patient at least twenty
gold marks per hour. Salomé had already arranged for a lower fee
when Freud's letter arrived, or so she told Freud. In her first letter
about Frau E., Salomé confirms the suspicion that the patient may
be difficult and Dr. H. more helpful (*SF* 150). In a second letter,
however, written less than two weeks after the first, she gives a
different account, changing her assessment of Frau E. and meditat-
ing on the emotional "life" that analysis has given her:

In your letter to me back then, you correctly mentioned that the patient's intelligence was not great and that this might get in the way; I sense that, but on the other hand, I sense, too, how much better and better I feel about her in my determination to understand her completely and to help her. I know this small progress in my self and for me it is one of the most heartwarming joys; because alone with myself I am a cold, old animal surrounded by very few. For that reason I am so thankful to be able to flow out with such warmth within psychoanalytic work. (*SF* 151)

Psychoanalytic work provides the boundaries that allow for the free flow of emotional warmth and connection, boundaries that Salomé has sought in all her work and her relationships. As her work with Frau E. progresses, Salomé becomes not only more and more positively disposed toward her client but more confident of her desire and ability to heal; she also becomes more and more suspicious of the husband and the lawyer, who begin to interfere in the analysis with divorce proceedings and threats to take custody of her children, despite their commitment to at least six months of noninterference. In an urgent letter to Freud in May 1925 and followed by an almost identical one in June, Salomé expresses her rage at the husband and the lawyer, her deep involvement in the case, and her request for Freud's approval of a course of action about which she is obviously ambivalent (*SF* 156–57). Salomé plans to demand that the husband and lawyer cease interfering and then to help Frau E. gain access to her children. In response, Freud urges Salomé to consider his advice not cruel but "simply correct" (*SF* 159). Since the husband had committed a breach in the contract, Salomé should break off treatment immediately and cease having anything to do with Frau E.'s affairs. "It is not your business to prepare Frau E. for her divorce. You are neither legal adviser nor universal aunt, but a therapist, who can only do her work if the agreed conditions are adhered to. And that is all" (*SF* 159). In her response, Salomé makes sure she establishes their basic agreement, and even reports that she had come to the same conclusion herself before she received his letter. She then goes on to report, however, that she had since discovered circumstances that would allow her to continue Frau E.'s treatment. She had learned that Frau E.'s father, not her husband, had been financing the analysis; therefore, she could continue the analysis and yet heed Freud's (or her own) advice to disengage from her investment in Frau E.'s personal affairs. Again, she muses on the importance of boundaries to the free flow of her own emotions in analysis: "The fact that this clear line of demarcation has been established I owe to you alone. I began to realize that I was taking the interruption to the treatment too emotionally. I had become too elated at the gradual improvement in face of the difficulties involved. I now, I believe, see the position as it is" (SF 159). Again, Salomé grapples with the "double directionality" of woman's desire, or of analytic work, toward and against clear boundaries.

Salomé's analytic work sometimes did not substantiate Freud's theories, his theories of sexual difference in particular. In the correspondence, for example, she reports a case of a boy who suffered from fear of the male penis in the same way as the girl does (SF 74). Salomé provided this observation, which she based on Rilke's childhood terrors, as part of an ongoing argument with Freud over his explanation of the taboo of virginity, which he had attributed to female penis envy and male castration anxieties. With her analysis of Rilke's fears of the penis, she subtly undercut the neat symmetry in Freud's theories of male castration anxiety and female penis envy. A second "unusual" case concerned Salomé's discovery that little girls feminize their fathers by imagining that it is the father who gives birth, just as boys masculinize their mothers with the fantasy of the phallic mother (SF 203). Once again, she was able to explain her differences with Freud in terms of a fundamental unity when she credited her observations to her use of the Freudian method, which required careful attention to the details that emerged in analysis and allowed the construction of theory only on the basis of such observations.

Salomé described the analytic situation as a relationship that allows for active as well as passive involvement on the part of both analyst and analysand, protected as they are by the rules that demarcate those two positions. That demarcation makes play, excess, emotional release, and identification possible. In Mein Dank an Freud, Salomé emphasizes how important it is for the analyst to take a passive role, in keeping with Freudian doctrine, but she also points to the ways in which that passivity is necessarily an activity. Analysis requires identification on the grounds of the humanness that analyst and analysand share, if the analyst's impenetrability is not to become a defense against his or her own unconscious. Again, Salomé conceives of an unconscious and a possible identification that cannot be reduced to the status of mere repository for repressed material but are, instead, a shared implication in a totality that exceeds, even as it includes, both analyst and analysand. To be restored through the practice of analysis to a sense of humility as well as a sense of "All-Being" requires such selfless identification, and that, for Salomé, was the constant gift of psychoanalysis and psychoanalytic technique not only to the analysand but also to the analyst who was open enough to allow it. The kind of identification Salomé had in mind did not involve pedagogical, moral, religious, or any other kind of direction or advice from the analyst. For Salomé, narcissistic identification, like the unconscious, was without content. She distanced herself explicitly from those analysts and social reformers who sought direct applications of psychoanalysis in the service of normalization: "Instead of the arrogant trust that they grant themselves, they should instead trust the unconscious *Besserwissen* [superior knowledge] of one who has truly healed and who is like a fish who has been returned to its element, and doesn't need any directions in the water, a fish that we, with our directives, then only delay on foreign soil" (*MD* 13).

Salomé carefully defined the double phenomenon of giving and taking, of active and passive, of separation and identification, by opposing it to the compulsion to make analysands in the analyst's own image. She worked against an overly hierarchical relation between a supposedly knowing analyst and an unknowing analysand:

It involves a doubled phenomenon of giving and taking, since the goals of the research can be reached only on the basis of the experience of one human being of another, and this experience, on the other hand, only as the result of scientific objectivity. At the end of the work, if it was really successful, when the analyst sees the departing analysand at the open door that leads back into everyday life, he probably quietly asks himself the question: "Would you also have been able to overcome and to accomplish that?" All the more since it had to occur to him how often a sudden slip into neurosis presupposes the subtlest, most spiritual ambitions and overexertions. At the point of separation there is, for that very reason, something of the most serious respect that any human being can owe another. (*MD* 13–14)

Salomé carefully distinguished between a commonsense definition of health as adaptation and a psychoanalytic definition of health. In teaching analyses, for example, she suggests that the question is often whether the analysand "isn't staying too healthy," not "what makes you sick" (*MD* 15–16). She adds a third form to the two usual forms of resistance to analysis. "In place of a clinging to repression and an adherence to the symptoms of repression, we also experience a third resistance," she writes, "the unwillingness to accept intrusions into one's pleasantly framed, blameless little house, into the unity of one's person. . . . Illness means a disturbance in functioning, but health can also be falsely defined as short on substance, within which one is nonetheless intact" (*MD* 16). For Salomé, becoming healthy involved

access to one's primal ground, to that which flows up in us in a life-creating way from the unconscious. The return home to oneself takes place in [the analysand] as a return to something that he indeed is, but which is also more than he [is]. . . . Recovery is an action of love. The coming to oneself is first a return home in the feeling of being welcomed and celebrated in the All-Together. (*MD* 17)

Salomé concludes her *Freud Journal* with a discussion of her relation to Freud and to psychoanalysis:

The way in which one beholds a person in psychoanalysis is something that goes beyond all affect toward him; somewhere in the depths both aversion and love become only differences of degree.

A relationship is achieved beyond one's own fidelity or infidelity.

Approximately this way: if, before, we had entered into the partner so swiftly and forcefully that he was too quickly left behind, to our own disappointment, now we would turn quietly, strangely, and see him following, and be close to him. And yet not close to him, but to all. Close anew to all, and in it, to ourselves. And all the vanished people of the past arise anew, against whom we have sinned by letting them go; there they are, as from all eternity, marked by eternity—

peaceful, monumental, and one with being itself, as the rock figures of Abu Simbel are one with the Egyptian rock and yet sit enthroned, in the form of men, over the water and the landscape. (*FJ* 191–93, translation modified)

Conclusion

Salomé could be said to have structured her relationship to Freud, as she structured her relationships to other important (male) figures, in such a way as to return them and herself to a fundamental bisexuality. In an entry in her *Freud Journal*, Salomé makes a clear distinction between positive and negative manifestations of bisexuality:

> The presence of masculinity in woman, of femininity in man, which we all have, operates differently in individual cases, with respect to the effect of bisexuality on the whole person. In some cases, it completely emancipates the person from his / her own sex, creating thereby a disturbance in the harmony of his / her being. In these cases, it erases the stamp of femininity from woman and feminizes man. Others, on the contrary, are only the more deeply tinged in the spiritual hue of their own sex, as their bisexuality stands out against an otherwise more colorless sexual background. In these people, it is as if one were oriented by the constant presence of a partner within, making for a higher unity of one's own being, which, for that reason, can never become a fully realized one-sidedness. Only in this situation can bisexuality become fruitful.[1]

This conception of a fruitful psychic bisexuality challenges the conventional Platonic terms, which demand that a woman or a man become heterosexual in order to be whole. Salomé locates wholeness within each sex. Woman, as we have seen, is whole and self-

---

[1] *The Freud Journal of Lou Andreas-Salomé,* trans. Stanley Leavy (New York: Basic Books, 1964), p. 189, translation modified, hereafter cited in the text as *FJ.*

sufficient in and of herself by virtue of the interpenetration within her of the capacities for self-loss and self-assertion. Neither she nor the actual women and men who retain access to her are threatened with the sexual one-sidedness that Salomé called "the usual heterosexuality" in *Mein Dank an Freud*. For that very reason, they were also safe from the sense of lack that ensured their dependence on (social) objects and their conformity to social law. And yet, given the terms within which Salomé worked, they were necessarily still grounded in the assumption of an underlying sexual difference, at least at the level of appearances. I have focused in this book on Salomé's particular negotiations of the constraints on the intellectual woman in late nineteenth-century Germany. I would like to close with some of the possibilities and limits of Salomé's figurative "woman" and the convolutions by which Salomé dodged what she and her compatriots saw as a "typical femininity" and a purely imitative manliness.

Salomé had no insecurities about her readiness or ability to assume a place in Viennese psychoanalytic circles not only in Freud's, Tausk's, and Adler's lectures but also in the Wednesday evening discussions among analysts, in which few women ever participated. Nevertheless, Salomé, her biographers, and Freud's biographers all agree that she never spoke up in those meetings, despite the fact that she wrote extended commentary and rebuttal in her journal when she returned home. At the end of her stay in Vienna, Salomé prepared a statement for the regular members of the Wednesday evening discussion group, which found its way into her journal and her memoirs but which Salomé never actually read or spoke of to the men. In that statement, she expresses her gratitude to Freud and to the "brothers," explains why debate and contestation are part of the living development of psychoanalysis, and then closes by saying why she has not participated in those debates and contests. The pattern of conflict and cleavages, she notes,

will certainly continue to be a problem for some time to come, but it is the stamp of a progress motivated not only intellectually but also personally, and as long as it abides by the ideal of the honest community, then it is also a beautiful thing and a joy, at least in a woman's eyes, to see men opposing one another in struggle. And it is all the more my

duty today to perform the other task, to give thanks. Thanks for all these
evenings, even the tiresome ones, on account of the man who presided
at them and devoted his time to them. And thus the tasks of the sexes
in this world have been done separately and still in union. For men fight.
Women give thanks. (FJ 130)

It is tempting to see Salomé's decision not to give the speech to
the brothers as symptomatic of the difficulty she had managing this
(sexual) division between fighting and giving thanks. It is not difficult to imagine powerful reasons why her silence served her in
Vienna. It certainly enabled Freud to "make her his point of fixation," as he said more than once, and it allowed Salomé to occupy
the position, once again, of his idealization and, perhaps, his envy,
without being rendered passive. All these possibilities depended on
feminine "appearances" or, perhaps, on the absence of manliness.

The few women intellectuals in the late nineteenth century in
Germany were caught in the bind that allowed women to pursue
an intellectual life only by opening themselves up to suspicions of
what Judith Butler calls "gender trouble," in *Gender Trouble: Feminism
and the Subversion of Identity*. To take up intellectual pursuits was to
take up a masculine, thus castrating, position in the terms of one
language and to arouse the suspicion of deviance in another. In
biomedical discourse the woman who engaged in "masculine activities" was often subject to categorization as a "contrary sexual type,"
and in psychoanalytic terms she was considered either asexual or
homosexual by virtue of her masculinity complex. The attribution
to women of an unnatural "masculinity" or "frigidity" reinscribed
intellectuality as well as active sexual desire as man's province.

Salomé's woman, however, appears to include "masculine" activity within a more universal femininity, within the spirals of an
autotelic, unrepressed feminine unfolding. According to a number
of her contemporaries, Salomé herself represented the most ideal
combination of masculine analytical skills and femininity. In the
context of deeply conservative discursive productions of natural sexual difference, this woman opened up a space in which "woman"
could exceed the constraints of "typical femininity" without having
to imitate man.

Freud characterized Salomé as an exceptional woman who was

also what he called a pure feminine type. In response to the news of her death in 1937, he wrote: "Those who were closer to her had the strongest impression of the genuineness and harmony of her nature and could discover with astonishment that all feminine frailties, and perhaps most human frailties, were foreign to her or had been conquered by her in the course of her life."[2] Apparently Salomé was a pure feminine type by virtue of having transcended typical feminine frailties, having been "reasonable" and "rational," without, however, becoming masculine in behavior or sexually virile, without becoming homosexual. Anna Freud seems to have perceived that her father's ideal for her was just such a convoluted negotiation of sexual difference. In a letter to Max Eitingon, Anna Freud expressed a desire to fit her father's desires—in terms Salomé herself might have used:

> I already know, Herr Doktor, why I always have a bad conscience when I am irrational. Because Papa always makes it clear that he would like to know me as much more rational and lucid than the girls and women he gets to know during his analytic hours, with all their moods, dissatisfactions and passionate idiosyncrasies. Thus I, too, would really like to be as he sees fit, first out of love for him, and second because I myself know that it is the only chance that one has to be somewhat useful and not a burden and a concern for others. (*AF* 156)

Elisabeth Young-Bruehl notes that Salomé was "an important synthetic possibility" for Anna Freud (*AF* 113). In this context, Salomé's own claim for femininity as the more human, by virtue of its integration of conflictual impulses, appears to be both resistant to and complicit with Freud's ideal. Both Anna Freud and Lou Andreas-Salomé, however, had to exceed typical femininity without appearing masculine in order to achieve that ideal.

Young-Bruehl stresses that Sigmund Freud was concerned about his daughter's "masculinity complex" and the dangers to her of her "departures from nature." These concerns are manifest in his responses to Anna Freud's work on beating fantasies, work that Young-Bruehl considers to have been a highly autobiographical

---

[2] Quoted in Elisabeth Young-Bruehl, *Anna Freud* (New York: Summit Books, 1988), p. 222, hereafter cited in the text as *AF*.

working-through of the issues that emerged in Sigmund Freud's analysis of his daughter. It is worth reviewing Young-Bruehl's treatment of both Sigmund and Anna Freud's work on those issues.

Anna Freud began work on her essay "Beating Fantasies and Daydreams" soon after the publication of her father's 1919 essay "A Child Is Being Beaten."[3] Freud had presented analyses of several cases of men and women who engaged in excessive daydreaming, which served as a mask for underlying masochistic beating fantasies in which individuals expressed their less acceptable and, hence, less representable incestuous desires for the father. Both Freuds were interested in the ways in which daydreams inhibited the daydreamer's ability to work and make decisions. In "Beating Fantasies and Daydreams," Anna Freud documents what Young-Bruehl identifies as Anna's own development from daydreams to the activity of writing stories, which Anna analyzes as a positive and hopeful "transformation of an autistic into a social activity," one that assumes and directs itself to a "prospective reader" (AF 106). Both Freuds were concerned with the female patients' assumption of a masculine role in the fantasies and daydreams and in their resolution.

Young-Bruehl emphasizes that Freud eventually derived female jealousy from a "masculinity complex," most emphatically in his 1925 essay "Some Psychical Consequences of the Anatomical Distinction between the Sexes."[4] She also suggests that Freud's 1925 paper may have grown out of his second analysis of his daughter. After the little girl has successfully transferred her love from her mother to her father, and "turned into a little woman," her attachment to her father could, according to Freud, "come to grief," and give way to "an identification with him and the girl may thus return to her masculinity complex and perhaps remain fixated in it" (AF 126). In "A Child Is Being Beaten," he had concluded that "when they [the daydreamers] turn away from their incestuous love for their father, with its genital significance, they easily abandon their feminine role" (AF 107). As Young-Bruehl suggests, it is significant

---

[3] Young-Bruehl quotes from Sigmund Freud, "A Child Is Being Beaten," *Standard Edition of the Complete Psychological Works of Sigmund Freud*, ed. James Strachey (London: Hogarth, 1953–74), 17:179–204.

[4] Young-Bruehl quotes from Sigmund Freud, "Some Psychical Consequences of the Anatomical Distinction between the Sexes," *Standard Edition*, 19:256.

that "Freud did not connect the female patients' assumption of a masculine role in the fantasies and daydreams with masculinized behavior or homosexuality." Instead, Freud argues that "the girl escapes from the demands of the erotic side of her life altogether. She turns herself in fantasy into a man, without herself becoming active in a masculine way, and is no longer anything but a spectator at the event which has the place of a sexual act" (*AF* 107). Freud imagines asceticism to be the most likely outcome for these women's, and perhaps for Anna Freud's, masculinity complexes, complexes associated elsewhere in his work with female homosexuality.

According to Young-Bruehl, Freud's prognosis of asceticism fit the facts of Anna Freud's development. Quite aside from the facts of Anna Freud's case, Young-Bruehl's treatment of Sigmund Freud's work on beating fantasies shows how limited the possible positions are for the heterosexual woman who identifies with the father. In each case, masculine behavior, including an active or virile sexuality, is eliminated, or at least masked, and femininity is recovered by way of ascetism or narcissism.

In 1929 Joan Riviere published "Womanliness as a Masquerade," a suggestive account of how an intellectual woman masks masculinity and improper appearances. Based on her work with several analysands and one intellectual woman in particular, Riviere suggests that "women who wish for masculinity may put on a mask of womanliness to avert anxiety and the retribution feared from men."[5] Womanliness masks the aggression and rivalry involved in women's wish to assume the place of the father by speaking in public. Riviere begins her essay with a testimony to the importance of Ernest Jones's work on female development. She reports that Jones had produced a scheme for two types of female development, heterosexual and homosexual, the latter further subdivided into two types. She then points to the problem with the schematic nature of his work in order to introduce her interest in a type of woman who is intermediate between heterosexuality and homosexuality.

Riviere offers her work with one of her analysands as an instance of a more typical phenomenon. "Not long ago," she says, "intel-

[5] Joan Riviere, "Womanliness as a Masquerade," *International Journal of Psycho-analysis* 10 (1929): 303–13.

lectual pursuits for women were associated almost exclusively with an overtly masculine type of woman, who in pronounced cases made no secret of her wish or claim to be a man. This has now changed. Of all the women engaged in professional work today, it would be hard to say whether the greater number are more feminine than masculine in their mode of life and character" (304). Yet even though her intellectual analysand "fulfills every criterion of complete female development," this feminine, heterosexual, intellectual woman experienced enormous anxiety after every public lecture and sought reassurance in the form of compliments and in sexual attentions from father figures in the audience. "The exhibition in public of her intellectual proficiency . . . signified an exhibition of herself in possession of the father's penis, having castrated him" (305). Because the woman speaker fears the father's revenge, she offers herself to him sexually, according to Riviere.

Having established this woman's history of masking her wishes for masculinity with womanliness, Riviere then anticipates questions about the difference between the woman who uses femininity as mask and the "real" woman. Riviere suggests that there is no difference, nor is there any absolute difference between homosexual and heterosexual women. She argues that heterosexual and homosexual women share frustration and rage over their castration and that heterosexuality and womanliness are, in part, a resolution of that rage. "Both heterosexual and homosexual women desire the father's penis and rebel against frustration [or castration]; but one of the differences between them lies in the difference in the degree of sadism and the power of dealing both with it, and with the anxiety it gives rise to in the two types of women" (313).

The origins of all these reactions lay in the child's response to the parents during the oral-biting sadistic phase, according to Riviere, who draws on the work of Melanie Klein. In consequence of disappointment or frustration in that phase, hatred and sadism emerge against both parents, as does "the fear that accompanies the hatred." Riviere emphasizes that the daughter fears her own hatred for the mother and her desire to surpass her even more than she fears the father. In her efforts to procure reassurance, or the figurative penis, from the fathers, the intellectual woman "becomes supreme," for she is protected not only from him but from the mother, who is excluded from the interaction altogether. In general, the analysand's relationships with other women worked, according to Riviere, only as long as the other women recognized her supremacy, recognized that "she had the penis," which she could then grant them in the form of generosity (307). Riviere also reports that when the analysis was well under way, and the analysand began to experience the rage and fear that underlay her heterosexual seductions, she temporarily lost her desire for her husband, as she was revealed, according to Riviere, to be "either castrated, or wishing to castrate" (307). Everything depends then on how that oscillation is resolved. At this point in the narrative, Riviere suggests that it is "striking that she had had no homosexual experiences" and reports that "this lack was compensated for by frequent homosexual dreams with intense orgasm" (307). In other words, her heterosexuality was not as stable as it may have appeared. In her concluding remarks, Riviere argues that "fully developed heterosexual womanhood is founded, as Helene Deutsch and Ernest Jones have stated, on the oral-sucking stage. The sole gratification of a primary order in it is that of receiving the (nipple, milk) penis, semen, child from the father. For the rest it depends upon reaction-formations" (313). Riviere's account appears to destabilize the border between heterosexuality and homosexuality, on one level, only to reinstate it in her effort to define an intermediate type of woman who "wishes for masculinity" but is not homosexual:

> The acceptance of "castration," the humility, the admiration of men, come partly from the over-estimation of the object on the oral-sucking plane; but chiefly from the renunciation of sadistic castration wishes deriving from the later oral-biting level. "I must not take, I must not even ask; it must be *given* me." The capacity for self-sacrifice, devotion, self-abnegation expresses efforts to restore and make good, whether to mother or to father figures, what has been taken from them. It is also what Rado has called a "narcissistic insurance" of the highest value! (313)

Riviere's work could be read as a diagnosis of a social and discursive problem, rather than an individual psychological one. In this context, Salomé's narcissistic woman operates not only to circumvent the constraints on intellectual women but also, necessarily, to mask the rage, frustration, and demands that Salomé and her compatriots saw as the signature of overt feminist struggle. Buttressed by the material privileges that allowed for such a mask, Salomé's deployment of affirmative femininity proved to be " 'narcissistic insurance' of the highest order"; it was insurance of her freedom to work among male intellectuals, and it was also insurance against her occupation of their (institutional) positions of authority. It necessarily also served as a constraint on any more radical critiques of sexual difference.

In her reading of Riviere's text, Judith Butler exposes some of the limits to Riviere's potential subversions of sexual difference. As Butler shows, Riviere interprets womanly masquerades as disguises for rage and aggression; she does not entertain the possibility that they are disavowals of potential homosexuality. She argues that Riviere reproduces Freud's and anticipates Lacan's insistence on desexualizing women who "sustain a masculine identification." Such refusals by Freud, Riviere, or Salomé, for that matter, fly in the face of the usual psychoanalytic collapse of gender identification with sexual orientation, according to Butler:

> The woman who "wishes for masculinity" is homosexual only in terms of sustaining a masculine identification, but not in terms of a sexual orientation or desire. . . . [Riviere] formulates a "defense" [against female homosexuality] that designates as asexual a class of female homosexuals understood as the masquerading type. . . . As in Lacan, the lesbian is here signified as an asexual position, as indeed, a position that refuses sexuality. . . . In any case, Riviere would have us consider that such women sustain masculine identifications not to occupy a position in a sexual exchange, but, rather, to pursue a rivalry that has no sexual object or, at least, that has none that she will name.[6]

What Riviere would have us believe runs counter to the usual fit of masculinity and femininity with (heterosexual) sexual orientation, to the ways in which psychoanalysis normalizes, as it glues together, masculine and feminine subject positions with an assumed heterosexual orientation. For Riviere, as for her masquerading women, says Butler, "femininity becomes a mask that dominates/resolves a

[6] Judith Butler, *Gender Trouble: Feminism and the Subversion of Identity* (New York: Routledge, 1990).

masculine identification, for a masculine identification would, within the presumed heterosexual matrix of desire, produce a desire for a female object, the Phallus" (53). Butler suggests that "the donning of femininity as mask may reveal a refusal of a female homosexuality and, at the same time, the hyperbolic incorporation of that female Other who is refused—an odd form of preserving and protecting that love within the circle of the melancholic and negative narcissism that results from the psychic inculcation of compulsory heterosexuality" (53). This possibility answers the Freudian and Lacanian suggestion that female homosexuality emerges out of the girl's disappointed love of the father, out of his refusal of that love, a suggestion that assumes female homosexuality to be the consequence of a repression of a more primary heterosexuality. Butler's reading exposes another possibility, one she finds in the repressions of psychoanalytic thought, the possibility that female heterosexuality might just as well be seen as the repression of a primary homosexuality. Butler suggests that it "may be less her own masculine identity than the masculine heterosexual desire that is its signature that [Riviere] seeks both to deny and enact by becoming the object she forbids herself to love" (53). As Butler explains, this "is the predicament produced by a matrix that accounts for all desire for women by subjects of whatever sex or gender as originating in a masculine, heterosexual position" (53).

Butler is not interested in positing a prior female homosexuality as woman's essence. She is interested in exposing the degree to which assumptions of a natural and necessary heterosexuality organize both Freud's and Lacan's work. Ultimately, Butler advocates moving from a heterosexual matrix that naturalizes libido as masculine and sexuality as heterosexual, to what she calls "a discursive account of the cultural production of gender" (53). Such a move was hardly available to Lou Andreas-Salomé.

It is not my purpose here to show that a repressed or invisible homosexuality necessarily underlay Salomé's construction of femininity and her production of herself as its purest type. I simply want to point again to a discursive production of femininity, which, for all its affirmation, had to avoid masculine appearances and "mannish behavior" and to disavow feminism as the manifestation of just such "distortions." The lure and dread of the "masculine" woman worked, and works now even within oppositional discourses on sexuality, to exclude positions other than man and woman and the heterosexuality that requires and reproduces them.

Index

49; and woman, 84, 94, 164–65. *See also* God: loss and death of representation, 24, 26, 113, 178; and sexual difference, 156–57, 169–70. *See also* self-representation. *See also under* woman
repression, 46, 173, 197, 239; and anal eroticism, 211–12, 214; masculine, 158–59; and narcissism, 204, 206–7, 220, 222; "repressive hypothesis," 13–15; return of the repressed, 4, 137; types of, 228. *See also* unconscious: positive vs. repressive
reproduction: and biological determinism, 15, 150, 152, 154. *See also* motherhood
ressentiment, 5, 22, 53, 120, 131, 170, 185, 222–23
Reuter, Gabriele, 170
Reventlow, Franziska von, 188
Rilke, Rainer Maria, 33, 120; Salomé's analysis and interpretation of, 6, 40–46, 94, 226; Salomé's relationship to, 1, 9–12, 40–47, 58, 60, 63
Riviere, Joan: "Womanliness as Masquerade," 235–39
Roustang, François, 194, 223
Russett, Cynthia Eagle, 15
Russia: Salomé's relationship to, 16–19, 38–39, 44–47, 70, 72, 120; social change of 1860s and 1870s, 4, 16–18, 38; stereotypes of, 46–47, 60, 72, 182
Russians: influence on Salomé, 17–19, 131; Salomé's idealization of, 10, 46–47, 182

sacrificial order, 28, 46, 121. *See also* man: as sacrificial and renunciatory
sadism: oral-biting phase, 236–37
Salomé (daughter of Herod), 19, 21, 140
Salomé, Eugene (brother), 73
Salomé, Gustav von (father), 1, 8, 10, 38–40
Salomé, Lou Andreas-: biographical writings on, 20–22, 24, 38, 54, 59, 63, 73–75, 86, 93, 123, 178, 191, 231; birth of, 2, 8, 28; childhood, 2, 4, 8, 10, 16–18, 29, 38–39, 53, 60; critics of, 20–22, 25, 38, 41, 52, 63, 87, 98, 139, 143–44, 167–69, 175–76, 178, 194–95; education of, 8–10, 34, 38, 40, 65; marriage of, 9, 36, 40, 53, 56–58, 61,

89, 118–19, 139, 147; relationship with family, 38–39, 61, 75, 88; sexuality of, 41, 56–59, 63, 167, 230; sexual relations of, 27, 58–59, 89, 191, 197 ——, writings of, 19, 23, 46, 59, 133, 144, 186, 188, 192–93, 195, 201; "'Anal' und 'Sexual'," 211–13; aphorisms, 84–85; "Aus der Geschichte Gottes," 92; correspondence with Anna Freud, 199–202; correspondence with Sigmund Freud, 191–92, 195–99, 206–8, 224–26; diaries and journals, 10–11, 19, 24, 26, 52, 79–82, 87, 109–10, 119, 197; "Der Egoismus in der Religion," 32; "Eine Ausschweifung," 189–90; essay on "woman," 83–84; "Fenitschka," 176–89; *Freud Journal*, 19, 26, 93, 197, 205, 209–10, 214–15, 217, 221, 223, 228–32; *Friedrich Nietzsche in seinen Werken*, 9, 19, 46, 89, 93–111, 192; "Gedanken über das Liebesproblem," 185–86; *Henrik Ibsens Frauengestalten nach seinen sechs Familiendramen*, 19, 23, 46, 117–40, 148, 164–65, 215; "Jesus der Jude," 32–33, 40, 92; "Ketzereien gegen die moderne Frau," 169–71; *Lebensrückblick: Grundriß einiger Lebenserinnerungen*, 7, 10, 24–30, 33–60, 62n, 63, 119, 146–48, 157, 176, 191; *Mein Dank an Freud*, 27, 195, 206–7, 210–11, 223–24, 227–28, 231; "Der Mensch als Weib," 73, 87, 111, 147–69, 189; "Narzißmus als Doppelrichtung," 201, 218; "Prayer to Life," 51–52, 95; *Rainer Maria Rilke*, 10, 19, 93; review of *Mißbrauchte Frauenkraft*, 171–75; *Ruth*, 35; "Von frühem Gottesdienst," 207; "Was daraus folgt, dass es nicht die Frau gewesen ist, die den Vater totgeschlagen hat," 216, 218–23; "Zum Typus Weib," 221
Salomé, Louise (mother), 10, 38–40, 64–65, 72–73
Schlüpmann, Heide, 145–46
Schnitzler, Arthur, 9, 191
Schopenhauer, Arthur, 66, 100, 102, 105–6, 109
science: and truth, 109, 167–69. *See also* biology. *See also under* psychoanalysis
scientific discourse, 195; Salomé's use of, 149–50, 152–53; on women, 141,

Library of Congress Cataloging-in-Publication Data
Martin, Biddy, 1951-
   Woman and modernity : the (life)styles of Lou Andreas-Salomé /
Biddy Martin.
     p. cm. — (Reading women writing)
   Includes bibliographical references and index.
   ISBN 0-8014-2591-3 (cloth : alk. paper). — ISBN 0-8014-9907-0
(paper : alk. paper)
     1. Andreas-Salomé, Lou. 1861–1937.   2. Authors. German—20th
century—Biography.   3. Women in literature.   4. Feminism and
literature.   5. Psychoanalysis and feminism.   6. Feminism.
I. Title.   II. Series.
PT2601.N4Z714   1991
838'.809—dc20
[B]   90-55718